Information Lives In DIY Music

Information Lives In DIY Music

Kirsty Fife

Litwin Books
Sacramento, CA

Copyright 2025

Published in 2025 by Litwin Books.

Litwin Books
PO Box 188784
Sacramento, CA 95818

http://litwinbooks.com/

This book is printed on acid-free paper.

Publisher's Cataloging in Publication
    Names: Fife, Kirsty.
    Title: Information lives in diy music / Kirsty Fife.
    Description: Sacramento, CA : Litwin Books, 2025. | Includes bibliographical references and
        index.
    Identifiers: LCCN 2024941127 | ISBN 9781634001458 (acid-free paper)
    Subjects: LCSH: Popular music – Historiography. | Music in museums. | Audio-visual archives –
        information services. | Music – Information resources. | Musicians – Information services.
    Classification: LCC ML3470.F54 2025 | DDC 780.74--dc23
    LC record available at https://lccn.loc.gov/2024941127

Contents

1	**Introduction**
31	**Activist Archivist Research**
65	**Resisting the Canon**
101	**For(a)ging Histories**
	Information Praxis in UK DIY Music Communities
147	**Presence, Absence and Deletion**
	Digital Information in UK DIY Music
177	**Unstable Alternatives**
213	**Archiving in/between**
	Exploring Relationships Between UK DIY Music Communities and Archives
249	**Conclusion**
259	**Bibliography**

Introduction

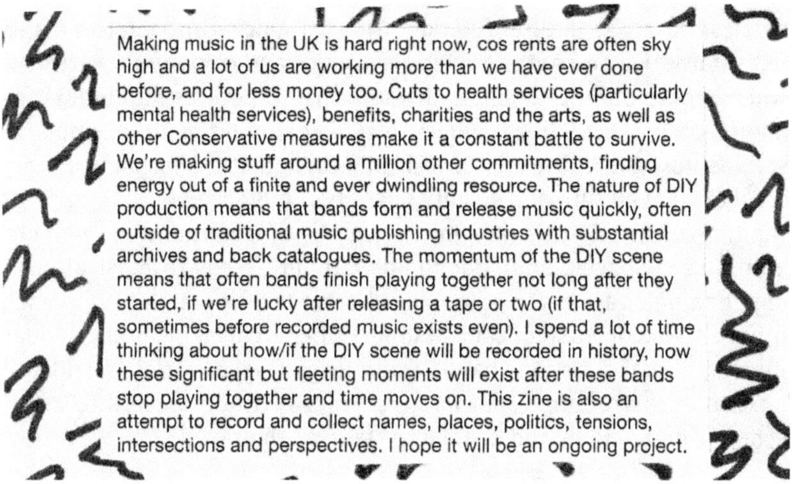

Making music in the UK is hard right now, cos rents are often sky high and a lot of us are working more than we have ever done before, and for less money too. Cuts to health services (particularly mental health services), benefits, charities and the arts, as well as other Conservative measures make it a constant battle to survive. We're making stuff around a million other commitments, finding energy out of a finite and ever dwindling resource. The nature of DIY production means that bands form and release music quickly, often outside of traditional music publishing industries with substantial archives and back catalogues. The momentum of the DIY scene means that often bands finish playing together not long after they started, if we're lucky after releasing a tape or two (if that, sometimes before recorded music exists even). I spend a lot of time thinking about how/if the DIY scene will be recorded in history, how these significant but fleeting moments will exist after these bands stop playing together and time moves on. This zine is also an attempt to record and collect names, places, politics, tensions, intersections and perspectives. I hope it will be an ongoing project.

Figure 1 Excerpt from introduction to Move Under Yr Own Power: Interviews with Women and Queers Making DIY Music. (Fife, 2016, p. 3)

The quote that begins this book is taken from Move Under Yr Own Power: Interviews with Women and Queers Making DIY Music, a zine[1] project I began in 2016 after several years of involvement in UK-based DIY music networks. In 2013 I started going to gigs in a small basement venue in East London–Power Lunches—and found myself regularly watching bands making noise in front of a small audience of queers, weirdos and punks. Around the same time, I formed my first band in many years. For me, forming one band led to playing queer and feminist gigs and meeting other DIY musicians. I played gigs, got to know

1 Zines are self-published booklets or magazines which are edited, compiled, and circulated within community networks by individuals or groups. (Eichhorn, 2001; Chidgey, 2006; Duncombe, 2008; Wooten, 2012; Lymn, 2014)

other bands, forged friendships and formed new bands. Via social networks, my bands played in other cities, with networks of organisers and other bands supporting each other by providing sofas to sleep on, meals and equipment.

Media articles from the 2010s describe the development of autonomous music spaces across the UK including DIY Space for London, Glasgow Autonomous Space, Partisan, and CHUNK (Clarke, 2015; Welsh, 2015; Amin, 2017; Phillips and Mokoena, 2018). The re-emergence of DIY cultural ideals during this period is situated as a form of resistance to austerity and the production of music through capitalist and elitist music industry structures (Clarke, 2015). DIY music communities establish alternative and autonomous economies and community networks which aim to operate outside of traditional structures and industries (Mōri, 2009, p. 485). In reference to zine communities, Duncombe describes how DIY culture is "a radically democratic and participatory ideal of what culture and society might be… ought to be" (2017, p. 5). At the time of writing this zine, I was awed by those around me who created music, spaces, and community without access to musical training, funding or access to resources. Working co-operatively with each other and making use of central tenets of anarchism including solidarity and mutual aid, many hands could forge fragile, sociable, and supportive infrastructures that nurtured those without access to music schools, equipment, and a stage to claim as their own.

In the current socioeconomic climate, it is important to note that doing it yourself is also a necessity as much as it is a political stance. Jones proposes a combination of these circumstances, the dominance of digital platforms and individualistic neoliberal rhetoric mean that DIY is in fact now the "mainstream" (2021, p. 2). As he writes, this is "a socio-economic consequence of changes in the music industries, as well as in the ICT… industries" (Jones, 2021, p. 3). Martin-Iverson proposes that even with explicitly anti-capitalist politics, alternative music scenes can align with neoliberal ideals because of the value afforded to autonomy and independence in both contexts (2012, p. 384). Although there is emphasis on radical forms of independence in DIY music, the conditions of subcultural work can nonetheless reproduce "a neoliberal form of labour flexibility and insecurity" and "self-exploitation" (Martin-Iverson, 2012, pp. 393–394). This is connected to the conditions of work in broader creative industries by other authors (Mōri, 2009, p. 485). The interrelation between those working in DIY traditions because of political, entrepreneurial or pragmatic motivations is a source of constant tension that often surfaces or tests the unspoken boundaries of these practices.

In the seven years since I published the first issue of Move Under Yr Own Power, sudden changes have affected the community initially represented. Many of the music spaces discussed in the zine are now closed and/or have been rapidly redeveloped into more financially viable businesses. Wider music industry reports have highlighted issues which have caused grassroots music venues to repeatedly close (The Mayor of London's Music Venues Taskforce, 2015). The remaining spaces were further threatened and/or closed during the Covid-19 pandemic due to a lack of long-term state support. In the two years between this zine and the next issue, half of the 30 bands interviewed had disbanded. Many of us had relocated due to rising rent costs, and our creative projects were unsustainable at a distance. Further bands had split up due to personal conflicts and what began as a warm and nurturing network rapidly dispersed geographically, socially and creatively. Digital content was lost when hard drives malfunctioned and social media platforms closed, culled storage or determined content inappropriate. These spaces and projects left little trace behind, and time to recover and hold onto what did exist was non-existent. This combination of factors means that as much as I associate my involvement in UK DIY music spaces with feelings of transformation, empowerment and excitement, I also associate them with feelings of anxiety, grief, loss and heartbreak.

In such rapidly changing circumstances, networks, spaces and projects emerge and dissipate before afforded value by cultural and heritage institutions. Objects representing subcultural life are ephemeral and small in number due to lack of financial or material resource, and little individual capacity to document (Downes, 2010; Withers, 2015). Previous generations of subcultural communities can be located in a scant number of paper-based materials such as newsletters, minutes and fliers, zines and a limited amount of recorded music, which can enable a recreation of the rough outlines of a particular era of DIY culture. However, in the 21st century these "traditional" traces dwindle in number due to the use of social media platforms for cultural organising and a move to entirely born-digital forms of record creation.

The relationship between DIY music communities and social media platforms is ambivalent (Pelly, 2018; Jones, 2021). There are already examples of ways in which reliance on social media platforms can lead to the erasure of records of this practice–for example, in 2014 music collective LaDIYfest Sheffield reported the deletion of their Facebook account containing information from four years' activity (LaDIYfest Sheffield, 2014). In 2019 Myspace Music reported the loss of 50 million songs uploaded to the platform between 2003 and 2015 due to an error that occurred during platform migration (DeVille, 2019). These experiences of loss and deletion are heightened in the current political climate in which memory constructed and documented by radical and marginalised groups on online social platforms remains "vulnerable to sudden and massive takedowns or closures" (De Kosnik, 2016, p. 14).

There has historically been an absence of representation of DIY music communities in museum and archive collections. Recent years have demonstrated an increase in the exhibition of popular music—however, as I will explore further later in this book, these exhibitions often rely upon canonical elements of these cultures. This is evident in recent attention to 1990s riot grrrl, 1980s hardcore and 1970s punk in exhibitions, history writing and archival collections. Acts, organisers or individuals who achieve some measure of commercial success and spaces which survive against the odds are over-represented in institutions, while the less mythologised fade away. These foci also indicate a nostalgic and retrospective approach to the representation of DIY music, rather than making use of collecting to prevent loss of evidence of current music communities or developing meaningful relationships which transcend the donation of collections or exhibition of objects.

Nonetheless, returning to my original zine I am reminded that we often want to remember and continue to value these experiences and take action to do so. For me, the small print run felt like an intervention in ongoing losses, an individual labour that was within my capacity and contributed to the persistence of memory through the sharing of personal stories about being involved. I had no control over whether museums would meaningfully represent our histories, but I could take action to document what I felt was important. In undertaking this work, I was not alone or unique—my project is joined by other zines, podcasts, blogs, photography and film projects, and social media accounts. These sources enable the persistence of our cultural legacies and affirm that what we did meant something to us. This collective memory practice demonstrates a mutual understanding that what we do is ephemeral, temporary and easily lost or destroyed, unless we ourselves intervene to collect, keep, and document. These actions also have a different temporality than that of traditional heritage structures (as described above)—archiving, documenting and collecting are activities which happen alongside and as part of the process of DIY cultural production.

Between 2018 and 2022, I undertook a PhD study at University College London, which explored methods for documenting and archiving UK DIY music spaces. This prolonged period of research provided an opportunity to engage in critical conversations about the meaning behind the practices discussed in the preceding section. I undertook this project as someone located inside DIY cultural communities and friendship networks, someone who has been archived (through donating materials, participating in oral history projects and community-led initiatives), someone who has archived (as an information and heritage sector worker), and someone who has observed the impact of archives and histories on my peers. The research undertaken in this period forms the backbone of this book.

Study Details

This volume aims to examine the production of cultural heritage about current or recently actively UK DIY music communities, through the following research questions:

- How are DIY music communities currently documented and remembered?
- How are external factors in the current political, technological and socioeconomic climate affecting documentary and archival activity in current UK DIY music spaces?
- How do DIY cultural politics intersect with processes of record creation, archiving and history writing?

The scope of this study is defined by two factors: firstly, a geographic emphasis on individuals who are or have recently been active in UK-based DIY music spaces. This project has a broader scope than many other studies of DIY music communities, which are typically bounded within one or two cities (Chrysagis, 2014; Griffin, 2015; Flood, 2016; Jones, 2018). This scope is influenced by the idea of "translocality", in which regional music scenes are in regular contact with one another via communication networks and the exchange of material objects or resources (Bennett and Peterson, 2004; Kruse, 2010; Guerra, 2020). In reference to riot grrrl communities, Leonard proposes that "sub-cultures should not be considered unified groups tied to a locality, creed or style but as dynamic, diverse, geographically mobile networks" (1998, p. 102), which speaks to my understanding of the current UK DIY music scene. "UK DIY" is also used colloquially to describe the national scene by journalists and community members (Dale, 2014), which means the geographic focus is also understandable within the community context.

Secondly, a temporal scope centres individuals either currently active within these communities, or who were active within the generation preceding my own (who were organising in the 2000s). This emphasis incorporates generations who have made use of emerging social media platforms in cultural organising and whose records are changed through digital transformation more broadly. By focusing on the records of current generations, the study engages with archives and histories from prior to the deposit of collections or the formal writing/publishing of a history. In this sense I am particularly influenced by Stuart Hall's description of the archive as an "on-going, never-completed project" which is dialogic and reflexive (2001, p. 89), informed by and evolving with the negotiation of many different voices. As a result, less emphasis is given to arguing the case for the representation of music communities in heritage settings (which has been the emphasis of previous scholarship preceding the popular cultural turn in heritage). Instead I focus on the impact of historicisation and archiving and the specific challenges current generations face when they try to create and keep records of their activities.

The study's scope is not limited by musical genre (e.g. punk; indie; alt-pop etc). As the interlude following this chapter will explore in more detail, DIY music communities are more consistently linked by shared politics and values than musical genre (Chrysagis, 2019; Pearce and Lohman, 2019). In live settings, this is demonstrated through line ups that contain performers from different music genres, or the blending of line ups to include music, poetry, dance and spoken word. Therefore, although certain genres dominate in the context of this study this was not used as criteria.

Global Developments

Having now outlined the personal and local foundations of this project and determined the scope of this book, I will now move on to outline external factors which have shaped the direction of the research. This research is informed by two main global developments which affect UK DIY music communities: the emergence and growth of popular music heritage, specifically initiatives led by national and regional cultural and heritage institutions; and the extended period of instability and insecurity that has been dubbed the "permacrisis". Specifically, the book is situated at the tense intersection of these two phenomenon, at which point museums and cultural institutions are able to profit from subcultural histories whilst grassroots spaces close and communities are simultaneously displaced, sometimes due to gentrification enabled by (in addition to other factors) cultural redevelopments led by authorities. These factors jeopardise the futures of these initiatives, and therefore the future histories of DIY music. The following sections briefly outline the emergence of these developments, summarising key scholarship and projects before concluding with a discussion of relevance to the context of this book.

The Emergence and Growth of Popular Music Heritage

In the last decade, there has been an upsurge in interest in popular music from large heritage institutions, which is evident through the recent curation of exhibitions of subcultural legacies. These include Punks (Museum of London, 2016-2017), London Calling: 40 Years of The Clash (Museum of London, 2019); Black Sabbath–50 Years (Birmingham Museum and Art Gallery, 2019); and Punk, 1976-1978 (British Library, 2016). Robinson's review of Punk London at the British Library situates the exhibition as one of the most popular free exhibitions in the organisation's history (2018, p. 311), confirmation of the audience appeal of popular music exhibitions.

Funding bodies including the National Lottery Heritage Fund have financially supported projects to repair, restore and archive spaces of historic music performance including Bristol Beacon (2018), Band on the Wall (2007) and Wilton's Music Hall (2012). The financial investment in these projects and others is an acknowledgement of "the crucial contributions that... [live music] makes to both the UK's economy and its social fabric" (Behr, Brennan and Cloonan, 2014, p. 1).

In the same period, popular music heritage has developed as an interdisciplinary and global area of research, which examines the turn towards popular culture in heritage institutions and in community-led initiatives. For example, Leonard describes the potential benefits of exhibitions of popular music in museums:

> museums are actively seeking to develop new audiences and... this activity is in part motivated by cultural policy agendas and government targets for museums aimed at facilitating greater social inclusion. The increasing interest that museums have shown in popular

music has been set against this picture of sectoral change to consider how music displays can be understood as ways to attract new or under represented audiences. (Leonard, 2010, p. 175)

For example, Black Sabbath: 50 Years at Birmingham Museum and Art Gallery successfully drew working class audiences into the museum space through intertwining narratives of class and metal music community (Baker et al., 2020, pp. 82–83). Exhibitions can have positive outcomes for both museums and music communities by increasing visitor figures, diversifying user profiles and contributing to the rebuilding of community networks.

Popular music heritage is also used heavily in cultural tourism. For instance, the heritage value of The Beatles raises income for Liverpool's tourism economy and influenced a significant amount of the city's programming as European Capital of Culture in 2008 (Cohen, 2013). Roberts writes that "the idea of music as cultural heritage is one that the UK tourism industry is keen to exploit" (Roberts, 2014, p. 266). It is in the overlap between heritage, development, tourism and economy that tensions between music communities and institutions can be found (Lashua, 2011; Ross, 2017; Knifton, 2018; Strong, 2018). Knifton refers to the

> homogenisation or ... "flattening out" of popular music into heritage "experiences"–a sanding down of music's many rough edges to package it for a global, wealthy, tourist (and predominantly Western) audience. (2018, p. 144)

The production of music heritage for tourism is underpinned by financial motivations, and often requires the smoothing out of controversial narratives in music histories. These activities become uneasily aligned with nationalism, tradition and wealth (Hall, 1999, pp. 3–4), arguably the antithesis of the politics of many subcultures.

Resistance to heritage and tourist industries from music subcultures has been expressed in several high profile cases, including the public burning of punk artefacts by the son of Malcolm McLaren, Joe Corré, in 2016 (Press Association, 2016). Strong links these destructive acts to historical parallels in (guitar-led) popular music which "reinforce the association between rock and rebellion" (Strong, 2018, p. 180). These actions indicate a collective unease over the use of music subcultures in industries aligned with capitalism, nationalism, and cultural or socioeconomic power (Graham, 2002). This tension is not exclusive to music heritage, and is articulated in other literature relating to the regeneration or authorisation of local heritage (Graham, 2002; De Cesari and Dimova, 2019). De Cesari and Dimova refer to "the heritagisation-and-gentrification nexus" and ask scholars to more deeply consider "the consequences that it has for different actors involved in the process" (2019, p. 868).

An alternative to institutional heritage projects can be found in the many grassroots community-led music heritage initiatives that have been established globally. The concepts of self-authorised and unauthorised music heritage (Roberts and Cohen, 2014) frame a cluster of scholarship exploring online, DIY and/or fan-led community music archives (Baker, 2015b; Collins, 2015; Collins and Carter, 2015; Collins and Long, 2015; Withers, 2015; Baker, 2016; Strong and Whiting, 2018; Baker, 2019). Sarah Baker uses the term "DIY institutions" to refer to

> a group of popular music archives, museums and halls of fame that were founded by enthusiasts, run largely by volunteers and which exist outside the frame of authorised projects of national collecting and display. (Baker, 2016, p. 173)

Community-led popular music heritage projects are often epistemologically distinct from institutional projects due to the affective and often personal motivations underpinning this work. As Baker and Huber write,

> these DIY institutions are not solely about the creation of storerooms "for the future", but are equally as important for the memory practices of "the present"; by this we mean that those involved in the DIY enterprise are engaged in the process of materialising their own experience and expertise through the collection, declaring and naming its importance; another way of saying this is that they are enacting memory. (Baker and Huber, 2015, p. 122)

The term DIY resists the categorisation of community-based archival practitioners as "amateur". Leonard also problematises the use of "amateur" to refer to grassroots and community-led heritage practice, writing that

> while these individuals do not have formal archival or museum training, I wish to avoid naming their activities as amateur, as they might present their work in very professional ways and often bring

> other skills and knowledge that contribute to how music is understood and produced as heritage. (2015, p. 19)

Similarly, in reference to archiving zines Brager and Sailor acknowledge the multiple roles that one person may occupy in managing zine collections–it is possible to be a zine creator, information worker and/or academic simultaneously. By allowing subcultural producers to archive and create their own histories, these DIY institutions "acknowledge that we are the experts of our own lives"(Brager and Sailor, 2010, p. 3).

Music fandom research has identified informal practices of preservation, sharing and organisation that have always existed in music cultures (Bennett and Rogers, 2016; Strong and Whiting, 2018; Thalmann, Wilmering and Sandler, 2018). Thalmann et al write that traces of live music

> survive as artefacts and memorabilia such as recordings, photographs, program booklets, posters, clothing, autographs, or newspaper articles. Many of these artefacts are eagerly collected by music fans, organised in shadow boxes, aggregated in scrapbooks, written about in fanzines, exchanged and copied among peers, and passed on through generations. (2018, p. 1)

These materials are situated as "memory traces" of popular music by Bennett and Rogers who describe ticket stubs as "a convenient and efficient means of cataloguing and displaying/recalling memory" (Bennett and Rogers, 2016, p. 38). Other authors situate record collectors, bootleg makers, reissue labels and underground tape collections as informal heritage practitioners (Kwame Harrison, 2006; Berg, 2018; Carlson, 2018; Maalsen and McLean, 2018). The emphasis on fan labour in heritage is explored in relation to other areas of popular culture (De Kosnik, 2016; De Kosnik et al., 2020; Keidl, 2021), who emphasise fan curating as "a form of work that creates cultural and economic value for different agents" (Keidl, 2021, p. 407).

Although it is easy to assume that the alternative organisational structures and practices of DIY music heritage projects also produce more diverse archival collections, scholars have nonetheless criticised the production of subcultural histories by former community members for reproducing absences of women, people of colour and queer people or nostalgic narratives (Strong, 2011; Nguyen, 2012b; Downes, Breeze and Griffin, 2013; Downes, 2014; Nguyen, 2015; Strong and Rush, 2018; Brunow, 2019; Davila, 2019; Stewart, 2019). Osa Atoe writes that "racism is incorporated into punk narratives and punk history through omission" (Atoe cited in Stinson, 2012, pp. 267–268). Zuberi calls for a "committed research and critical interrogation of race in the study of music and sound" (Zuberi, 2018, p. 37). In order to accurately produce histories of music in society, it is crucial that heritage projects and historians acknowledge conflict and hold music communities and subcultures accountable for the reproduction of "whiteness as the centre of meaning" (Zuberi, 2018) in mainstream and alternative music heritage.

Music Communities in (Perma)Crisis

Numerous terms have been coined to refer to the collision of multiple overlapping crises that characterises recent history. These include the concepts of poly- and perma-crisis, which are both used to conceptualise the relations between multiple simultaneous crises–for instance, encompassing the covid-19 pandemic, climate change, racial injustice, Brexit, the cost-of-living crisis, the Ukraine-Russia conflict and other periods of political unrest.

The word polycrisis, originally coined by Edgar Morin (Morin and Kern, 1999), has subsequently been interpreted as by Swilling as "a nested set of globally interactive socio-economic, ecological and cultural–institutional crises that defy reduction to a single cause"(Swilling, 2013, p. 98). Henig and Knight propose that the polycrisis involves scrutinising society "through a lens of... knotted eventedness" (2023). This enables exploration of the ways in which simultaneous crises are experienced–for instance through a ripple effect in which the impact of one crisis is heightened indirectly due to co-occurrence of a separate crisis development.

The term "permacrisis", although originally coined by Stephen Cohen in 1972 (Montgomery, 1985, p. 242), has rapidly gained traction in the 21st century following global crises such as COVID-19. Deviatnikova proposes that

> the word permacrisis typifies the present time as continuous and uninterrupted stressful period with undulating focal points: pandemic, inflation, political turmoil, climate change, global conflicts, etc. (2023, p. 366)

Permacrisis is differentiated from the polycrisis by two characteristics: firstly the term refers to an ongoing and perpetually endless climate of insecurity and instability; and through the term's emphasis on "the state of the speaker or the situation as a whole" (Deviatnikova, 2023, p. 369). As Turnbull writes, permacrisis denotes "a static and permanently difficult situation" (Turnbull, 2022)–this means that, unlike previous philosophical interpretations of crises, the permacrisis does not resolve in social transformation of any kind.

Despite being named as Collins Dictionary's word of the year in 2022 (Turnbull, 2022), permacrisis has had limited exploration within culture, music or heritage research. Emphasis within existing research about the permacrisis has focused on policy implications (Zuleeg, Emmanouilidis and Borges de Castro, 2021; Vanhercke, Sabato and Spasova, 2023) or on the evolution of the term and its use (Deviatnikova, 2023; Henig and Knight, 2023). However, with a few exceptions (e.g., Janik and Vella, 2022), there is a peculiar absence of scholarship considering how cultural communities–especially music communities–are navigating this period, despite the catastrophic impact of recent global crises on cultural industries. As O'Sullivan writes in reference to DIY music in Ireland, "for musicians young and old, experienced and starting out, the situation has never been more precarious or uncertain" (O'Sullivan, 2022, p. 7).

The connection between music communities and broader concepts of crisis, however, is a fruitful area of focus. Theorists and historians have situated the emergence of many subcultures within contexts of social crisis (Haenfler, 2006; Hebdige, 2013; Shuker, 2016). Subcultural communities have also been linked to cultural crises–for example the relationship between emo subcultures and a cultural crisis of masculinity (de Boise, 2014, p. 230). Scholars also explore examples of local crises disrupt and transform music scenes–for example, Nogic and Riley explore the impact of the stabbing of two teenagers outside an independent music venue in Pennsylvania on a music venue and local subculture (2007). Broader crises–whether regional, national, global in scale–continue to transform the nature of involvement in music communities, how music is created, and who has access to creative and cultural production. These studies highlight the importance of examining the production of music–and therefore also music heritage–in a specific and situated context.

This unexamined intersection of music heritage and the permacrisis is worth exploring, precisely because insecurity–whether forcibly engendered through the external environment or chosen as a lifestyle–is

Figure 2 Spaces, capitalism, disruption (original illustration)

(ironically) one of the few stable characteristics of involvement in music communities. Tsioulakis describes how musicians are "always struggling and yet always creating; always working and playing; always in crisis" (Tsioulakis, 2020, p. 164). Analyses of the popular music industry–whether examined at a regional, national or global level–have consistently positioned it (and other creative and cultural industries) as in crisis or at the very minimum, in "transition" (Burnett, 1993), due to external factors. In their exploration of regional music in Gippsland (Australia), Stromblad and Baker write that participation in DIY and independent music industries requires "cultural resourcefulness" due to lack of economic infrastructure (2023, p. 7). These factors include changing consumption practices (Forde, 2004), the emergence of new intermediary platforms (Prey, Esteve Del Valle and Zwerwer, 2022), the cost-of-living crisis (Greig, 2022), and the continuing impact of the COVID-19 pandemic (Messick, 2021; Fife, 2022; Khlystova, Kalyuzhnova and Belitski, 2022), amongst many other issues. In many ways, the concept of the permacrisis is a succinct summary of experience within music communities which extends far beyond the contemporary articulation of the term.

At the outset of this project, my intention was not to explore the intersection of the permacrisis environment and DIY music heritage. However, as the subsequent analysis will demonstrate, this constant climate of chaos and anxiety nonetheless bled into every area of my data collection, making the intersection of the two impossible to ignore. This experience became heightened as I, too, personally experienced substantial turbulence between 2018 and 2022. The emotional impact of this period of time made me conscious of the ways in which archiving and archives of DIY music could be shaped by perpetual experience of insecurity and crisis–in terms of their form and nature, who is able to archive, how and why archives are created, and factors which affect their potential for long-term preservation and use.

Theoretical Orientations

The preceding section outlined external global developments which informed the development of this research project, justifying the need for a full length study located at the intersection of DIY music heritage and the permacrisis climate that typifies lived experience within modern society. Having now explored why this book is an essential contribution to the field through its relation to existing research, this section explores the theoretical and disciplinary orientation of this project, focusing on the application of critical archival theory and the living archive to the study of DIY music heritage.

A Critical Approach to DIY Music Heritage

This book approaches archives and heritage as constructions of sorts, following the lead of subcultural theorists who have queried and highlighted omissions in the narratives of subcultural historiography and archiving (Nguyen, 2012b, 2012a, 2015; Downes, 2014), and critical archival theory, which is an emergent area of archival theory. Critical archival studies developed from the work of practitioners and researchers interrogating the relationship between archives and power, and the capacity of archives to bring about or prevent social justice (Harris, 2002; Schwartz and Cook, 2002; Duff et al., 2013; Gilliland and McKemmish, 2014). The framework also builds upon calls for a more active and reflexive approach to archival practice, which in turn challenges emphasis on neutrality and objectivity within the profession (Zinn, 1977).

Critical archival theory aims to build "a critical stance regarding the role of archives in the production of knowledge and different types of narratives, as well as identity construction" (Caswell, Punzalan and Sangwand, 2017, p. 3). The application of critical theory within a practice-led field enables scholars to acknowledge that "power permeates every aspect of the archival endeavour" (Caswell, Punzalan and Sangwand, 2017, p. 3) and to analyse how power is dispersed through institutions, processes, and the archival profession. Archives are shaped through archival work and processes which narrow the total available documentation of society (Cook, 2011, pp. 606–607). The positioning of archives as neutral, untouched lands by historians and cultural theorists minimises the subjective value judgements embedded in such processes, limiting the opportunity for a critical examination of archival work (Cook, 2011).

It is important to view DIY music heritage through this theoretical lens to achieve a deeper understanding of how power can be produced through the archiving and historicisation of communities. As Nguyen writes in relationship to riot grrrl historiography, "it may be that we more or less know this history by now, but how we relate it matters still" (2012b, p. 174). As I have argued elsewhere (Fife, 2024), although popular music heritage research to date has been located primarily in the humanities, this research has rarely engaged with critical archival theory and, to some extent, archival theory more broadly. Michelle Caswell has previously criticised humanities research about the archive for failing to engage with archival theory and with the practical work of archiving, writing that "humanities scholarship is suffering from a failure of interdisciplinarity when it comes to archives" (Caswell, 2016, p. 3). This means that existing work often fails to account for the role of both archival labour and the ideological influence of an archive organisation and archive workers in shaping narratives of popular music's past.

The location of this study within critical archival theory also shapes how key terms—e.g., archive, record, archiving, recordkeeping—are approached in this book. I approach these terms through "an expansive and generous view of what might be considered a record", acknowledging that community conceptualisations of these terms might not "always conform to disciplinary ideas about what records are and what types of roles they fulfil" (Douglas and Alisauskas, 2021, p. 14). The archive can be both a physical place and/or organisation, and/or a "floating signifier" which gives meaning to materials stored outside of formal archive spaces (Halberstam, 2005, p. 170). My interpretation of these terms is also informed by their questioning by postmodern archival theorists and the subsequent development of the concept of the "archival multiverse" in which there is a

> plurality of archival traditions with distinct epistemological, ontological, ideological, practices, even linguistic aspects at work within the contemporary professional archival and recordkeeping landscapes as well as within different communities that carry out record- and memory-keeping functions outside professional archival purview. (Gilliland, 2017, pp. 50–51)

In this framework, recordkeeping, record creation, history and archiving have been transformed into "a civic/political tool and, even, a means of production" (Gómez and Vallès, 2020, p. 2).

To summarise, critical archival studies therefore provides an opportunity to reorient this study from a new direction. This is done in two ways: firstly, by reframing discussion about DIY music heritage through a more critical lens, and secondly, by conceiving of archives, archiving and record keeping through broader and community-determined definitions. This study therefore approaches the archiving of DIY music ambivalently, as a process which has the potential to include and exclude, to have positive and negative impact, and which can reaffirm or challenge traditions within the archival profession. I do not argue the case for the value of DIY music heritage, as existing collecting within these spheres is already occurring. Instead, I focus on how heritage is produced, who can produce heritage, how discourse about DIY music communities shapes representation in archives and museums, and how meaning is attached to archival traces and practices within communities. This allows me to critique existing practice, surface alternative forms of archival praxis and elaborate on how existing practice could be transformed.

Information Lives in DIY Music

The title of this book—information lives—situates record keeping, archiving, records and archives within the broader landscape of information. For those unfamiliar with the field, archival studies is established as "a subfield of information studies that is concerned with records as persistent representations of human activity that travel across space and time" (Carbajal and Caswell, 2021, p. 1103). Although the initial focus of this research was to examine archival materials and practices, over time it became clear that archives and archiving were two elements in a constellation of activities which form an information infrastructure. The following analysis, therefore, does not clearly delineate between information and records, instead acknowledging that the assignment of "record-ness" or archival value is firstly subjective (what is one person's information is another's archival record) and secondly is in flux (meaning that documents become records, and that records are dynamic in nature). To examine archives without also considering documentation or information creates an incomplete picture. By exploring across these practices, I am also informed by McKinney's work on information activism in lesbian organising, which encompasses "a range of materials and processes constituting the collective, often unspectacular labour that sustains social movements" (McKinney, 2020, p. 2). McKinney's framing of information activism encompasses work across the fields of computing, communications, and archival practice.

Information lives

The second critical framing which is essential to explore at the outset of this volume is the notion of information as living. Life has proved to be a compelling metaphorical hook within information studies (Brothman, 2006). Notions of birth, growth, decay, death, decomposition, afterlife, and transformation frame practice and theory across time, space and worldviews. This study is informed by the concept of a "living archive", originally coined by Stuart Hall (2001). In "Constituting an Archive" Hall asserted that an archive should be "not an inert museum of dead works, but a "living archive", whose construction must be seen as an on-going, never completed project" (2001, p. 89). Hall's vision of the archive has subsequently informed scholarship about archives of music, performance, activism, and other topics (Vaughan, 2015; Joseph, 2018; Aasman, 2019; Almeida and Hoyer, 2019; Alto and McKemmish, 2020; Chidgey, 2020; Sabiescu, 2020).

The application of this idea across numerous spheres can make it hard to determine the central tenets of the theory. In the following exploration, I am informed by Joseph's unpacking of Hall's work in which he identifies three central principles of the theory:

- The archive as a "generative organ" enabling new growth (Joseph, 2018, p. 42).
- Capacity "to expand, or provide alternatives" (Joseph, 2018, p. 42), specifically alternatives to heritage traditions and their implicit whiteness.
- The involvement of subjects in the process of archiving, which normally objectifies them (Joseph, 2018, p. 43).

These principles will now be explored individually before I summarise my application of the concept.

The archive as generative

For Hall, the archive as an ongoing project invokes the opposite to the stasis implied at the end of the records lifecycle. In relation to activist memory, Chidgey describes how "the concept of the living archive challenges entrenched notions of the archive as a closed, retrospective, "dead" repository of historical knowledge" (2020, p. 226). Living archives can place emphasis on the important of "live-ness and presence" (Chidgey, 2020, p. 227), which can incorporate, for example, the collection of current materials (Kitch, 2018; Chidgey, 2020), building community and making space through archives (Almeida and Hoyer, 2019) or the activation of archives through re-use, citation and re-telling of histories via creative practice or within current activist struggles (Joseph, 2018; Alto and McKemmish, 2020; Sabiescu, 2020). The activation of archives is driven by emotional resonance (Joseph, 2018, p. 86) through which users, record creators and communities represented in records are connected to one another.

Archives as expanding

Living archives are expansive both in form and in underpinning politics. Archives can be expansive by taking new forms–for example through digitisation or creation through digital technologies (Vaughan, 2015) or by originating in non-traditional archival formats, for example performance (Vaughan, 2015), languages (Bow, Christie and Devlin, 2014), storytelling (Ramirez, 2005), social media content (Aasman, 2019), or textiles (Strohmayer and Meissner, 2020). In this sense, living archives push at the limits of the archive and records, highlighting the Western bias of dominant definitions of these terms within archival theory.

By virtue of their expansive nature, living archives also counter norms and traditions within society, archival education, theory and the profession. Almeida and Hoyer claim that the living archive" counters existing systems of power and oppression, including the power encoded in professionalism" (Almeida and Hoyer, 2019, p. 18). When produced from positions of marginalisation, documentation and archiving can be forms of intervention and social change (Appadurai, 2003).

Archival subjects

Living archives place emphasis on the impact of subjectivity on the formation and use of archives. All archives are created by specific individuals, whose shared cultural understanding constitutes the archive (Joseph, 2018). However, rather than positioning this as a limitation, Joseph argues that the living archives celebrate subjective choices–"both those that lead to material accretion and those that select which aspects of these accretions are to be activated and invoked anew" (2018, p. 84). Rather than acknowledging subjectivity, this approach actively frames subjectivity as a strength, which enables the proliferation of multiple, sometimes contested histories.

Almeida and Hoyer describe how living archives make space for bodily records, lived histories and the documentation of emotional impact (Almeida and Hoyer, 2019). This includes the emotional impact of being archived as an individual or member of a community. By prioritising subjectivity, living archives also aim to centre the subjects of records and the broader community represented within a record in decisions about the management of a collection (Almeida and Hoyer, 2019).

Application

I use the notion of living and life across the boundaries of information, archives and records within this project. The idea of information living within a specific context is an evocation of the way in which information infuses and pervades cultural activism, creating an infrastructure through which we find each other, build community, undertake creative work, and organise collectively. As McKinney writes in relation to historical lesbian networks, "information brings a public into existence by giving shape to networks, framing common interests, and acting as a shared resource for activists" (2015, p. 16). Information is generative (of community and new sources of information), expansive (in politics and form), and formed through subjectivity, relationality and emotional resonance.

The idea of life and livelihood also necessitates discussion about needs–to live we need sustenance of various types. The same can be said of information–which, in order to survive, requires periodic human intervention to (for example) migrate materials or to deposit materials when initiatives are closing. Without the care labour of community members and/or information workers, information can become temporarily or permanently inaccessible, effectively decaying into absences. As I explore in subsequent chapters, there is a perpetual tension between the life, livelihood and loss of information in this context. This tension is shaped by the external circumstances in which communities and spaces operate, and in which information is produced.

Overview of Book

The final section of this introduction provides a short overview of the content of the remaining chapters. Following the introduction, there is a prelude to the analysis which outlines a series of critical definitions of key terms in this project. The development of these terms through scholarship is presented in tandem with personal narrative/illustrations exploring my journey into DIY culture and the record keeping profession.

Chapter two–"activist archivist research"–uses personal narrative and methodological scholarship to explore the challenges of conducting activist research as an archivist. The chapter is structured using a series of tensions that are shared between this study's context and other forms of activist research. This chapter also explores the development of this project's methodology and my own positionality as a researcher.

Chapter three–"resisting the canon"–explores the relationship between DIY music communities and existing processes of historicisation, canonisation and archiving. This chapter sets the foundations for the rest of the analysis by identifying tensions between the values of DIY music communities and selective traditions. I argue that the reliance on hierarchical notions of value and importance contribute to the ongoing erasure of marginalised groups within histories and archives of DIY music. Finally, I identify the potential for histories and archives to have a positive impact on community members through a reframing of the archive as a space of representation, dialogue, accountability and learning.

Chapter four–"for(a)ging information"–pivots away from the heritage institution and into community-based forms of information work. The chapter identifies an infrastructure of information and archival work which underpins DIY music communities and enables the ongoing development of communities. This work is positioned as "archival praxis" due to shared motivations to transform futures through documenting, keeping materials and facilitating access to information and memory through various methods. In this context archival praxis is often happening outside of and sometimes actively resisting traditional heritage practices. This chapter posits that a capacious view of record keeping and the archive is needed to frame the diverse practices at work in many cultural communities.

Chapter five–"digital decay"–explores the relationship between DIY music communities, information and heritage, and digital platforms. Following research which identifies a relationship between DIY music communities and digital platforms (Jones, 2021), the chapter examines what impact reliance on digital platforms might have on the longevity of born digital heritage of UK DIY music communities. This chapter identifies opportunities, possibilities, challenges and threats in the relationship between UK DIY music communities and digital platforms and connects these struggles within a broader tension between digital corporations and social movements.

Chapter six–"unstable alternatives"–examines how socioeconomic circumstances affect the production and preservation of archives of UK DIY music. This chapter identifies intersecting forms of precarity which affect the networks, lives, spaces, and archival traces of community members, drawing attention to the impact of austerity, casualised forms of employment, the housing crisis and gentrification on individuals, communities, spaces, and archives. The focus on the socioeconomic climate in which archives are (or are not) constructed highlights how instability affects not only the immediate experience of individuals but a broader community capacity to remember and build archives.

Chapter seven–"archiving in/between"–focuses on the relationship between DIY music communities and heritage organisations. Existing perceptions of these relationships are identified and analysed, using the often-cited phrase "no future" to explore why punk communities as positioned as quintessentially anti-heritage. This perception is challenged using examples which indicate that queer and/or feminist DIY music communities are engaged with grassroots forms of archiving. Following this, the progression of community members into information work is examined. Utilising the concept of third space subjectivity (Licona, 2005), the blurring of boundaries between community member and information professional is identified. The chapter takes the position that when community members move into institutional posts, they can challenge the perceived dichotomy between organisation and community.

Finally, chapter eight's concluding summary revisits the arguments made in each chapter, returning to the original research questions to identify the key findings of the study. A reflective auto-theoretical narrative exploring the shifting circumstances encountered by music communities during the course of the study follows, before a series of potential future directions for research and practice are outlined.

Interlude: Definitions

Activist and community-led heritage researchers are often expected to spend an unnecessary amount of word count defining common concepts for perceived outsiders. As Faulkhead and Thorpe write, "too often in our writings we spend our time—and much of our word limit—explaining and redefining common concepts from our worldview" (2017, pp. 3–4). These concerns are shared by researchers located in similar research contexts to my own (Downes, 2010; Griffin, 2015) who describe how this labour of definition feels dull, unachievable and repetitive, and has curtails more meaningful "discussion of the complexities, contradictions and power dynamics of DIY cultures" (Downes,

Breeze and Griffin, 2013, pp. 117–118). Such expectations presume that these community contexts will be Other to the reader and the academy (thus positioned within majority identity categories), whilst often not requesting the same of those undertaking projects from more "traditional" backgrounds.

In reference to zines, Lymn proposes that "the lack of fixity in defining zines is productive; borders are continually reimagined between practitioners, researchers, consumers and collectors" (Lymn, 2014, p. 84). The fluidity of DIY culture parallels that of "community heritage", which similarly preoccupies scholars. Of the latter Gilliland and Flinn write that

> It may be that the diversity, fluidity and lack of fixity which makes the community archive sector so dynamic and vibrant, also means that attempts at providing useable yet inclusive definitions are destined to be unsatisfactory and more importantly misunderstand the point of such activity. (2013, p. 2)

A concrete definition of DIY is an undesirable goal of research, which focuses researchers on well-trodden paths rather than critical analysis of underexplored areas. Therefore, this book does not provide detailed interrogation of the definition of key terms in this study. Instead, I contribute short, theoretically-informed descriptions which situate my own understanding of these terms in relation to scholarship and the ongoing evolution of their meanings.

DIY

"DIY" is an acronym for "do it yourself" which describes an ethos of cultural production that is "symbolically and ideologically distinct" from traditional creative industries (Guerra, 2020, p. 58). Instead of locating DIY music within specific genres, researchers emphasise how shared practices (Lymn, 2014) values (Chrysagis, 2019) and/or ethics (Kotrady, 2016) can be more effectively used to cluster together communities under this umbrella term.

Shared practices and technologies are used to identify developments in the history of DIY culture (Lymn, 2014). Historical practices including home improvement, radical pamphlets, Victorian scrapbooking, science fiction fan-made magazines (Spencer, 2008, p. 113) and the Situationist International movement (Guerra, 2020, p. 58) are often suggested as preceding influences that informed the development of DIY cultures in the 20th century. These precursors to the formalisation of DIY culture can also be clearly connected to the development and democratisation of technology. Although these practices often result in the production of products, less emphasis is placed on this with DIY cultural communities than the underpinning process and relationships generated through collaborative efforts (Sicca, Auriemma and Napolitano, 2022). This decentres the cultural object, otherwise positioned as a commodity in traditional cultural industry settings. DIY culture also overlaps with a number of other terms, including maker culture and communities, hackspaces and fabrication laboratories (or "Fab Labs") (Richards, 2016). Rather than viewing these terms as distinct, it is more helpful to the boundaries between these communities as indistinct, often messy, fluid, and ever evolving.

The DIY ethos is connected to music subcultures including skiffle (Bragg, 2017), post-war folk (Dale, 2012), punk and subsequent developments (e.g. hardcore, riot grrrl, post-punk) (Spencer, 2008, p. 268), indie (Dale, 2009), hip-hop and rap (Reitsamer and Prokop, 2018), electronic music (Richards, 2016; Taylor, 2023), noise (Fitzpatrick and Thompson, 2015), and grime (Fatsis, 2019). Although DIY is often associated with specific genres, recent evolutions of DIY music have transcended genre and traditionally bounded subcultures. In relation to his analysis of American DIY music scenes, Verbuč states that

> This particular DIY culture is an outgrowth of late 1970s British and US punk culture, which later expanded into more transnational and heterogeneous scenes that today also encompass aspects of indie rock, experimental music and certain singer-songwriters. (Verbuč, 2023, p. 7)

The historical development of DIY culture should not be viewed as a linear journey with a clear origin point—instead it is more logical to view the development of DIY culture as forming through traditions of cultural resistance across spheres, which gather momentum and increased collectivism during significant periods of political upheaval.

Instead of seeking to define DIY through practice or genre, theorists have suggested that shared values may help in the definition of DIY culture (Chrysagis, 2019). Values of action and participation (Martin-Iverson, 2012, p. 386), cultural resistance (McKay, 1998; Downes, 2010; Duncombe, 2017; Chrysagis, 2019, p. 752; Jones, 2021), amateurism or anti-professionalism (Kwame Harrison, 2006; de Farias, 2022; Sicca, Auriemma and

Napolitano, 2022), independence (Sicca, Auriemma and Napolitano, 2022), and reciprocity and mutual support (Taylor, 2011; Chrysagis, 2019; Verbuč, 2023) are commonly identified in critical evaluations of DIY culture. When employed in practice, these values demonstrate a shared understanding that cultural production is a form of power (Jones, 2021, pp. 63–64), and a collective desire to build an alternative world (Guerra, 2020, p. 64). These values are not always present in DIY cultural communities but form a useful and informal framework of overlapping ideals within which we can situate communities and projects.

It is important to note that commitment to these values does not mean that in practice alternatives are successful. An initial illustration of this is the practical implementation of anti-capitalist ideals within DIY cultures, which often involves "the coexistence of both alternative (reciprocal) and dominant (capitalist) [economic] systems" within DIY music communities (Verbuč, 2023, p. 6). Reciprocal relations (involving, for example, volunteering at community spaces, cooking and providing spaces for touring bands to sleep, collective gardening in houses) aim to completely take the place of traditional economic structures (2023)–however, as Verbuč identifies, scenes are "laterally supported by the larger capitalist framework, exemplified by their utilisation of consumer goods" (2023, p. 17). Verbuč proposes that these oppositional "poles of reciprocal vs capitalist economy… are not so much in opposition as they are in dialogue with each other" (2023, p. 19).

A second tension which emerges in relation to the practical implementation of DIY cultural values relates to the dynamics of amateur, semi-professional, and professional cultural production. DIY music communities have historically placed emphasis on supporting "novice, untrained, or otherwise amateur musicians starting bands, playing shows, releasing albums, and touring outside of professional music channels" (Woods, 2020). However, some musicians engage with DIY as "a pragmatic strategy that enables them to acquire skill, shows, and social connections in the beginning stages of their musical careers" (Verbuč, 2023, p. 16). Jones highlights how DIY music communities emulate the "organisational forms of the popular music industries" (Jones, 2021, p. 61), despite being ostensibly focused around the development of alternative and more equitable structures.

A final example of a clash between espoused values and practice relates to the aim of inclusion in DIY cultural communities. Despite outward emphasis on world-making and diversification of music-making, power and hierarchies can continue to surface in subcultural spaces (e.g. punk communities dominated by white people and/or men) and can go unacknowledged by community members. Thornton's concept of "subcultural capital", which "confers status on its owner in the eyes of the relevant beholder" (1995, p. 27), remains relevant here. Thornton describes subcultural capital as having a "masculine bias" (1995, p. 161), which indicates that the accumulation of capital contributes to the reproduction of inequalities in subcultural spaces.

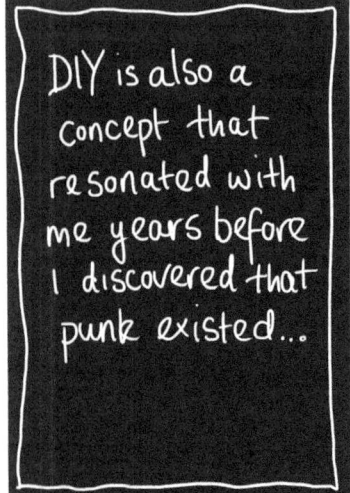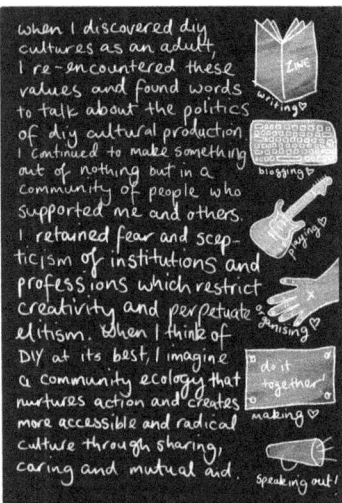

Figure 3   DIY (original illustration)

Archive/record/recordkeeping

The above terms are used with regularity throughout this analysis and can seem at odds with the context of this study due to the association of such terms with organisations and bureaucracy. Archives have been positioned by theorists as spaces of power, which service social elites and colonial regimes (Hall, 1999; Harris, 2002; Mbembe, 2002; Schwartz and Cook, 2002; McKemmish, 2005; Flinn, 2007; Flinn, Stevens and Shepherd, 2009; Cotera, 2015; Ishmael, 2018). The term record also has definitions rooted in institutions—BS ISO 15489-1-2016 defines a record as "evidence of business activity and information assets" (British Standards Institution, 2016, p. 4), which emphasises organisational use and value.

The archivist also holds power and influence (Cook and Schwartz, 2002; Harris, 2002; Lee, 2017; Wright, 2019). Archives can be constructed and shaped through archival work and processes—for example, collecting, appraisal, description and access all contribute to narrowing the total available documentation of society (Cook, 2011, pp. 606–607). The positioning of archives as a neutral, untouched land by historians and cultural theorists erases archival labour and the subjective value judgements embedded in such processes (Cook, 2011), and as such minimises the opportunity for a critical examination of archival work. Therefore, wherever recordkeeping is undertaken (e.g., in an institution or in a community setting) this work remains a political task.

The characteristics and roles of records, archives, and recordkeeping have been questioned over recent decades (McKemmish, 1996, 2005; Cook and Schwartz, 2002; Williams, 2013; Ketelaar, 2017; Yeo, 2018). In archival theory, this interrogation began in a postmodern shift in thinking which critically unpicked previously accepted definitions and practices in recordkeeping and seeks to broaden what is associated with these terms. This postmodern view of archives and recordkeeping is described as an "archival multiverse" in which there is a

> plurality of archival traditions with distinct epistemological, ontological, ideological, practices, even linguistic aspects at work within the contemporary professional archival and recordkeeping landscapes as well as within different communities that carry out record- and memory-keeping functions outside professional archival purview. (Gilliland, 2017, pp. 50–51)

Heritage, too, is described by Smith as "not so much as a 'thing', but as a cultural and social process, which engages with acts of remembering that work to create ways to understand and engage with the present" (Smith, 2006, p. 2). Theorists in this cluster engage with these terms as social constructions formed in specific cultural, community and socio-economic contexts.

The archival turn in the humanities, community and activist spaces within recent decades is evidence of an alternative engagement with these terms (Flinn, 2007; Flinn, Stevens and Shepherd, 2009; Bly and Wooten, 2012; Eichhorn, 2013; Erde, 2014; Cotera, 2015; Carter, 2017; Ishmael, 2018; Joseph, 2018; Solis, 2018; Chidgey, 2020; McKinney, 2020). This turn is also informed by rapid developments in digital technology (Gómez and Vallès, 2020, p. 2). It is in this collective body of work that I situate this project.

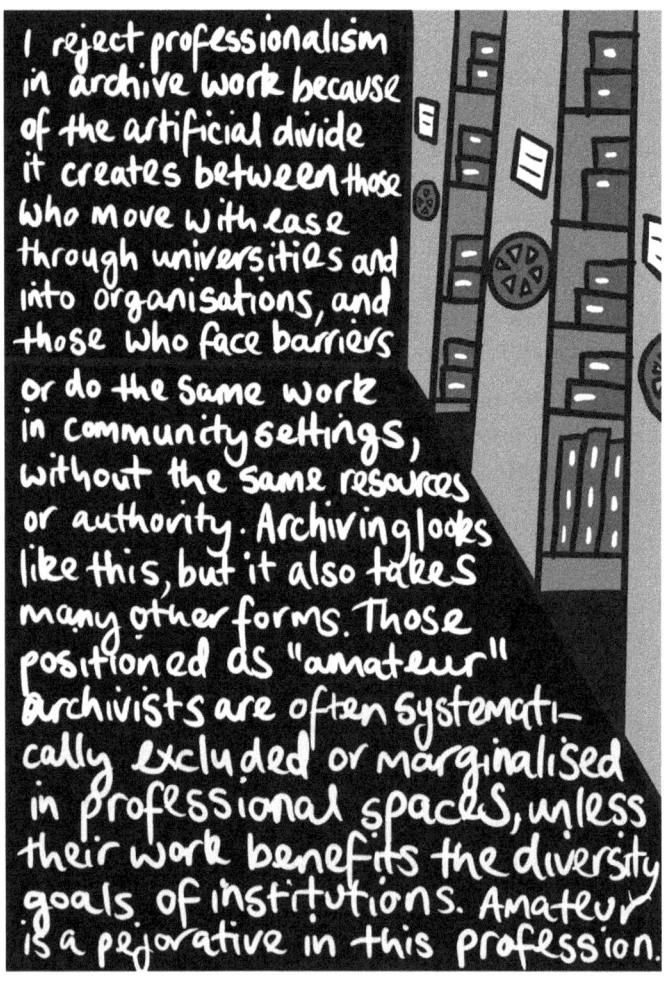

> Outside of professional spaces, amateur feels less like a loaded term. In DIY music, it can create a feeling of possibility. When we reject the standards that govern music making in the music industry, we are making space for new forms of creative community. I spend a lot of time thinking about the space and community we could create if we also reject the role of "experts" and "professionals" in archives and archiving.

Figure 4 The first of many divides (original illustration)

Activist Archivist Research

Previous research about DIY cultures has called for "useful" and "relevant" research methodologies (Brager and Sailor, 2010; Downes, 2010; Furness, 2012; Chidgey, 2013; Downes, Breeze and Griffin, 2013; Griffin, 2015; Jones, 2018). The perceived uselessness of academic research within DIY music communities is a tension which preoccupies community members instigating research projects. Of UK riot grrrl communities, Downes asks "what does this/our community gain from becoming visible in an academic context?" (2010, p. 67). Irrespective of cultural context, researchers working within grassroots cultural and activist communities share feelings of tension and conflict experienced when attempting activism within academic research structures.

I publish a sustained and transparent examination of my research process within this chapter because I am aware of the impact of these tensions on community-located or insider researchers. I begin with a succinct summary of the way in which research was conducted during this project, before moving into an exploration of a series of four tensions which emerged in this project. To put this less formally, I'll start by explaining *what* I did, before exploring how I *felt*. The thematic hooks are explored through dialogue between my own experiences and methodological scholarship. By sharing my experience–and emphasising points of tension between values and research processes–I seek to leave a trace and an account of lessons learnt for others navigating projects from similar positions.

Academic authors commonly provide accounts of research practice in publications, justifying decisions in research design for readers. For me, giving space to the *process* of research in this book is also an opportunity to discuss how the critical values of DIY cultural politics can shape research practice. Activism is grounded in critical thought and self-reflection (Choudry, 2015, p. 1). Downes et al similarly propose that academic research can be a "logical outcome of the critical thinking skills acquired in a life embedded in radical pedagogies and alternative knowledge production" (2013, p. 103). Like Lymn, I believe that research projects can ask important methodological questions about how DIY cultural practices can inform the process and progress of research (Lymn, 2014, p. 13). The transparent discussion of an activist undertaking research serves to challenge a dualism between activism and research through identifying how activist praxis can shape research practice. Tensions therefore are not explored to emphasise divides, but instead to elaborate on the experience of *navigating* spaces and contexts, even at points when those contexts seem to be in direct conflict with one another.

Methods Summary

Research data was gathered through multiple qualitative methods: autoethnography, interviewing, and workshops. The combination of different methods is particularly common in queer and feminist research contexts (Halberstam, 2005; Eichhorn, 2013; Lymn, 2014). Halberstam proposed that

> A queer methodology is [...] a scavenger methodology that uses different methods to collect and production information. (2005, p. 13)

In Halberstam's context, these methods may be a combination of "methods that are often cast as being at odds with each other", disregarding "academic compulsion toward disciplinary coherence" (2005, p. 13). Lymn also makes use of the idea of "scavenging" to describe building a body of sources that equally values more formal data sources (interviews; academic texts) and unconventional sources (gossip, zines, and objects of DIY culture) (2014, p. 13). Eichhorn describes her methods as "dirty" and "disloyal" due to an inability to conform to one methodological framework (2013, pp. 17–18). In Eichhorn's case, this enabled the archive to be understood through both cultural theory and the reflections of information professionals, transcending the boundary between theory and practice (2013, p. 18).

The patchwork of my own methodology is informed by my own academic history, in which I have studied and taught across disciplines (photography; gender studies; information studies; music). From these disciplines I bring different skills and frameworks—primary source analysis from Cultural Studies, autoethnography and interviewing from Gender Studies, and archival practice from Information Studies.

It is also influenced by my history of DIY cultural production, from which I bring experience of cultural organising, music and zine making and politics about accessible knowledge production. Finally, it is informed by a career in the information sector doing the work of archiving, from which I contribute knowledge of organisational contexts, standards, processes, and workflows.

This unruly mix of research methods also speaks to my desire to resist the production of binaries through this work. Waite writes that

> binary logic is precisely the kind of logic that dictates we must either write narrative or scholarship; we must be men or women, scholars or poets. (2015, p. 52)

Rather than disentangle the various roles I occupied in this project (archive worker; community peer; musician; researcher), I sought to write each of these roles into my analysis. In doing so, the project interweaves the self, a community, and a model of cultural production into research.

This section outlines how these methods were employed across the project. Although I briefly introduce the methods chosen, I do not expend much energy justifying their choice or systematically evaluating their application in relevant fields as I did in my original thesis. Instead, I describe what was done before allowing more space to explore the tensions that emerged through taking this course of action, in the following section.

Autoethnography

Autoethnography refers to a cluster of qualitative research methods centring around "the use of personal experience to examine and/or critique cultural experience" (Holman Jones, Adams and Ellis, 2013, p. 22). Autoethnography has several strands, each of which has ideological differences–for example, evocative autoethnography (Ellis, 1999), analytic autoethnography (Anderson, 2006), and critical autoethnography (Boylorn and Orbe, 2016). The method has been used to examine subcultural identity (Williams and Jauhari bin Zaini, 2016). Researchers have situated autoethnography as a punk research method (Attfield, 2011), a queer method (Adams and Holman Jones, 2008), and a "millennial methodology" (Griffin and Griffin, 2019). DIY practices including zines and blogging share motivations with autoethnographic research (Boylorn, 2013; Gabai, 2016), particularly the utilisation of personal narratives as history (Chidgey, 2006; Ramdarshan Bold, 2017).

I situate myself as a critical autoethnographer. In an examination of critical autoethnography, Holman-Jones identifies three central tenets of the method—a combination of theory and story, a material and ethical praxis, and commitment to process and change (Holman Jones, Adams and Ellis, 2016, p. 229). I place emphasis on the interplay of theory and practice, purposefully avoiding reproducing the "analytical, observational *view from above* featured in the language of theory" (Holman Jones, Adams and Ellis, 2016, p. 234). Finally, I transparently document the *process* of research throughout my analysis.

During this research I undertook several periods of autoethnographic analysis. I began by reviewing outputs of prior DIY cultural projects— or my personal cultural artefacts (Chang, 2008, p. 80). Such exercises can be used to surface alternative understandings of histories and challenge rehearsed narratives (Dampier, 2008, p. 368). This was sometimes instigated by themes emerging in my analysis which prompted me to revisit my own work, and sometimes acted as the starting point for the development of ideas.

Secondly, I am visible within this text as a narrator. In relation to analytic autoethnography, Anderson describes how the researcher should be positioned as

> a highly visible social actor within the written text. The researcher's own feelings and experiences are incorporated into the story and considered as vital data for understanding the social world being observed. (2006, p. 384)

When analysing data, I considered my own experiences as another source, drawing connections between what was shared and what I felt using memos. The emotive dynamics of this project are surfaced by the regular interjection of zine pages throughout the thesis (see later in this chapter). Similar methods have been employed by researchers working on projects about zines (Lymn, 2014).

In writing up my analysis chapters, I integrated these elements—the voices of myself, participants, and cultural artefacts piece together with theory. Butz and Best propose that

> autoethnographies are necessarily trans-cultural communications, articulated in relation to self and a wider social field that includes an audience of "others". (2009, p. 1660)

Although I resist oft-stated critiques of autoethnography, I was wary of representing *only* my voice through using this as my sole method. In a cultural context which values diversity in voice and experience, centering an analysis around the experiences of one individual felt inadequate. Therefore, autoethnography was used with other methods. These methods are explored in the following sections.

Interviewing

Interviewing is a well-established method within social research (Morris, 2015). As Pickard writes, interviews are often used to collect "descriptive, in-depth data that is specific to the individual and when the nature of the data is too complicated to be asked and answered easily" (2017, p. 172). Compared with other more structured data collection methods (for example, surveys), interviews enable participants more freedom in terms of linguistic expression as well as allowing interviewers to ask follow up questions to clarify meanings as needed (Pickard, 2017, p. 172). In this project context, interviews were chosen to collect data because they provided the opportunity to have in-depth conversations at a relatively intimate scale. Due to my immersion in the community, I was not concerned about needing to develop rapport with participants.

I chose to use a semi-structured interview guide because of the flexible and dialogic nature of this approach (Brinkmann, 2018, p. 579). This structure was more helpful in some interview settings than in others—for example, with friends the structure added unnecessary formality and prohibited meaningful data collection rather than enabling it. In these settings, it made more sense to begin with several structured questions and then follow the direction of interviewees, prompting them back to the topic if necessary. However, with acquaintances I made more use of the structure of the interview guide to direct our discussion. Interviews were conducted in a location chosen by participants, either in person or via video call.

Interviews were recorded and subsequently transcribed prior to data analysis. The anonymisation of research data (e.g., interview transcripts) has been identified as an ethical issue in DIY cultural research (Downes, Breeze and Griffin, 2013). Pseudonymising or anonymising data can provide protection for research participants. However, as Downes et al. write,

> the practice of imposing pseudonyms and removing identifiable information can undermine participant labour, power and agency... in

> research on DIY cultures the explicit naming of participants can become a moral and ethical obligation. (2013, p. 108)

In addition, anonymising interview data does not guarantee confidentiality for interview participants in small community settings. For example, Tolich distinguishes between external confidentiality, or "traditional confidentiality where the researcher acknowledges they know what the person said but promises not to identify them in the final report" (2004, p. 101), and internal confidentiality which is "the ability for research subjects involved in the study to identify each other in the final publication of the research" (2004, p. 101). The latter is often unacknowledged in ethical codes of practice, however, can cause rupture in communities and harm to individuals.

I opted to leave the decision about naming in the hands of my participants. Participants could elect to be anonymous, referred to by a pseudonym, referred to by first name alone, or named in full. In practice, most participants opted to be referred to by their first or full name. When discussing these options, participants reflected that community peers would be able to identify them from their responses. This indicated that anonymising offered little in the way of protection in this specific context. However, taking this flexible approach to naming did create the space for transparent discussion about each option. This was a clear benefit and established a continuing dialogue about participation in the research that extended beyond first meetings.

I identified participants through a purposeful sampling strategy. As data collection began, I also employed snowball sampling by following recommendations for participants that were suggested by others (Tracy, 2013, pp. 135–136). Because I was aware of the limitations of snowball sampling, particularly the capacity to reproduce certain demographics (Tracy, 2013, pp. 135–136), I began by approaching an initial sample located in different scenes within DIY music communities (e.g., hardcore; riot grrrl; pop punk). As well as reaching out to immediate friends and peers, I was able to connect with people I had no pre-existing social connection with via recommendations from peers.

Participants were asked about their identity characteristics at the start of an interview. Workshop participants contributed anonymously, and I did not collect identity information for these groups. Interview participants described their identity characteristics as follows:

- Gender: Cis men (5), cis women (9), trans woman (1) non-binary (2), uncertain (2)
- Sexuality: Heterosexual (6), lesbian (2), queer (7), bisexual (2), dyke (1), uncertain (1)
- Race: white (10), mixed race (3), Black (2); South Asian (2)
- Locations at the time of interview: London (8), New York (1), Bristol (1), Margate (1), Sheffield (1), Leeds (4), Surrey (1).

In some cases, participants described themselves using multiple identifiers (e.g., identifying as lesbian and queer). In these cases, I have included them in multiple categories rather than choose one. This sample of participants is representative of the DIY music communities in which I have close involvement—this is particularly evident when looking at the dominance of women and queer people (which mirrors my own friendship circles). The fluidity of queer DIY music community members can be used to situate those who provided uncertain responses to these questions, demonstrating an ongoing reflexive, and evolving approach to gender and sexuality within these communities, in which identity is not fixed or pre-determined by how individuals are assigned at birth. In relation to trans identity within DIY music, Pearce and Lohman describe this process as a process of simultaneous construction and deconstruction of identity which builds community based on "shared experience of exclusion and oppositionality" (2019, pp. 102-103) whilst maintaining an ambivalence towards the rigid identity categories.

The geographic foci of these interviews (Leeds and London) also represent the localities and scenes in which I have had active involvement. Plans to visit other cities (e.g., Glasgow, Bristol and Cardiff) for interviews were curtailed by the onset of the COVID-19 pandemic in 2020, as were opportunities to run more workshops in festivals held in other cities. Most interviews were conducted in urban settings, with a small minority located in small towns. This is reflective of geographic concentrations—however further studies could develop through surveying communities based in more rural settings.

I ceased interview data collection in May 2020 after evaluating the data I had collected to date. At this point the impact of the COVID-19 pandemic was unclear, and many potential participants were facing loss of some sort (employment, income, family illness, childcare issues). My initial coding exercises also indicated that I had reached data saturation in interviews. Initial themes that emerged in the early stage of data collection had retained their prevalence through the rest of the interviews (Guest, Bunce and Johnson, 2006, p. 73). The data I had collected was also rich—many interviews exceeded the original suggested length (45-60 minutes) and contained a lot of relevant material. As a result, and cautious of not acquiring too much data to manage and unnecessarily burdening participants, I decided to cease data collection at this point.

Workshops

The final method employed at the start of this project were creative discussion-led workshops. Downes et al. argue that insider or participant research can "reveal the limits of conventional data collection methods" (2013, p. 116), instead calling for researchers to find "new ways to co-construct data in the everyday activities of what DIY cultures already do" (2013, p. 117). This might include using creative methods to collect data, implementing practises already familiar to those in communities (for example, zine-making, music-making, or skills sharing). These activities naturally enable collaborative knowledge production and result in outputs that are useful to participants, In contrast to the outputs of traditional qualitative data collection tools (e.g., interview transcripts, field notes). Although this doesn't resolve the "unequal rewards" (Downes, 2010, p. 68) afforded by participation in academic research (which—it is important to underscore—provide economic and cultural capital to me), the results of these data collection activities can also produce knowledge that is available and meaningful within DIY cultural communities.

As cultural and creative practice is key within DIY music networks, I was keen to explore facilitating creative workshops within routine DIY cultural spaces or during events. In 2019 I began to run pilot workshops to try out different approaches and activities, with the aim of further expanding these into different spaces during 2020 and 2021. However, my ability to further develop this aspect of data collection was affected substantially by COVID-19 pandemic and the subsequent closure of many grassroots spaces for the majority of 2020 and 2021. During this period, other researchers employing creative methods developed online alternatives to in-person workshops (e.g., Ptolomey and Nelson, 2022). However, as my approach was informed by the desire to do research within the everyday physical spaces of DIY culture, this did not seem appropriate. In addition, the years of 2020 and 2021 were emotionally challenging for both my peers and I, and it did not seem appropriate to undertake data collection during this turmoil. Although I therefore only facilitated two pilot workshops, I will briefly give an account of these as I do make use of the resulting data at several points in subsequent chapters.

The first workshop was facilitated at North West Zine Fest (a self-publishing fair based in Manchester) in 2019. This workshop was called "Document it Yourself: Developing a DIY Archiving Manifesto". The workshop was attended by 20 people (maximum capacity), each of whom had booked in advance via the festival's programme, therefore the sample was a convenience sample pooled from people interested in the project. This demonstrated an interest in the topic from the festival attendees. At the outset of the workshop, all participants were provided with consent forms and participant information sheets to ensure they understood the project details. The 60-minute workshop then involved discussion and mind-mapping activities exploring the contents of DIY cultural archives and ethical issues relating to their management. The data gathered from this workshop included a transcript of the (recorded) discussion and the results of the mind mapping exercise, both of which were imported into Nvivo for analysis.

The second workshop was facilitated at Bent Fest (a queer punk festival hosted in London) in 2019. The workshop was described as a "history making/archiving" workshop, and consisted of two parts: firstly, a discussion about how DIY music is documented and archived as well as the issues which prevent better record keeping within these cultures; and secondly, a timeline mapping activity in which participants added memories relating to DIY music spaces to a physical timeline. As I will explore in more detail in chapter seven—where I give a more detailed account of the workshop–this method was informed by the use of timeline mapping activities in various activist and music community settings (Cooper, 2012; Lashua, 2015). The initial workshop was attended by 11 people, each of which were provided with information sheets and consent forms. The subsequent timeline activity was engaged with by a broader pool of festival attendees. I recorded and transcribed the workshop discussion, and transcribed the timeline, both of which were subsequently imported into Nvivo for the analysis phase.

Data analysis

Data analysis followed an inductive approach, which is described by Guest et al. as "a descriptive and exploratory orientation" to this work

(2012, p. 7). The principal method of analysis used was thematic analysis. My data analysis can be divided into several stages: pre-coding, description-focused coding, developing categories through clustering, identifying themes from categories, and finally drawing conclusions from the data. Before I began this analysis process, I had undertaken informal "pre-coding" work—by bolding, highlighting or underlining sections of data that I found particularly interesting, and adding small analytical or reflexive comments to transcripts. An initial bank of codes was generated through pattern coding after around half of my data collection was completed. These codes and categories were revisited and refined over the following twelve months. The final selection of categories is shown below in table 1:

Research Question	Question Number	Category
How, if at all, are DIY music spaces currently documented and remembered?	1	Archival processes
	1	Documentary practices
How are external factors in the current political and socio-economic climate affecting record keeping in current UK DIY music spaces?	2	Issues
	2	Feelings
How do DIY cultural politics intersect with processes of record creation, archiving and history writing?	3	Motivations (for practices)
	3	Definitions
	3	Organisations
	3	Networks
	3	Politics
	3	Archival concepts

I made use of code frequency tables to determine how frequently codes and categories surfaced in data. Evaluating the data through code frequency tables was one way to find meaning in my data. This helped me to understand the dominance of practices, issues, or motivations within DIY music communities, as well as the weight given to themes within interviews. I also evaluated using my own knowledge and history, which provided me with additional insight.

Tensions in DIY cultural research

Having now outlined how I conducted research, collected data, and analysed data, I move onto exploration of the experience of undertaking this research—or how doing this work *felt*. This section focuses on four tensions which were felt throughout the project: position and power; distance; voice; and wellbeing. These tensions are the subject of a prolonged analysis because my experiences are shared by others—others researching DIY culture as participant-researchers or insider researchers, others conducting research within their own leisure settings, and others conducting insider community-based research. Scholars from each of these positions have highlighted the competing ethical frameworks and challenges that researchers need to navigate, as well as the consequences of these tensions on their wellbeing (Downes, 2010; Downes, Breeze and Griffin, 2013; Griffin, 2015; Jones, 2018; Hannell, 2020). For example, insider researchers may experience conflict between notions of privacy as determined by research norms and legal rights, and alternative community-led expectations of privacy (for instance, in online community settings) (Hannell, 2020, p. 66).

However, university research ethics committees predominantly focus on procedural aspects of research and whether recruitment documentation conforms to expected academic practice (Carpenter, 2018, p. 36). This evaluation is based on compliance to academic practice rather than accountability to a community. Therefore, DIY cultural researchers often need to take sole responsibility for the labour of navigating and responding to ethical conundrums in their community. Although I was lucky to have access to peers with similar experiences, not everyone has this available. Therefore, this section documents several key tensions, focusing on both emotional impact and strategies for navigation.

Tension 1: position and power

The context in which we are located as a researcher has a "complex and multilayered" impact on research practice (Freshwater et al., 2010,

p. 499), as well as the general "social conditions under which "data" and data analysis are produced" (Buscatto, 2016, p. 160). I approached this project multiply located as a community peer, archivist and researcher. The simultaneous accountabilities of each of these roles informs research design, archival practice and the argument I put forward. It was impossible to therefore disentangle my own history from the focus of this research. However (and as I explore further in chapter seven), being multiply located in this way created many points of tension throughout the project. The negotiation of these tensions is the subject of the following analysis.

Before continuing this exploration, I will elaborate on my individual position. I am white, British, non-binary, disabled, working class, highly educated and queer. The intersections of my class, sexuality and disability have often made me feel othered in DIY cultures dominated by straight, white, middle class and able-bodied men and led me to pursue involvement in communities led by people from minoritised backgrounds. However, because of my whiteness and British background, I have also been able to participate in white-led cultures without experiencing othering because of my race or ethnicity. Disclosures of experiences of racism in DIY music spaces including Wharf Chambers (Anonymous, 2018 via Wharf Abuse and Racism; Wharf Chambers Coop and Club Collective, 2018) and zine writing by people of colour-led collectives including Decolonise Fest (2017) provide first person testimony about the way in which racism and white supremacy manifests within DIY cultures, often alongside perceived anti-racist political stances. As a person with a non-visible disability, I am also physically able to participate in the majority of DIY music spaces without any additional accessibility needs. My ability to participate in these cultures is thus framed via experiences of both power, privilege and marginalisation in different measures and at different points, both of which inform my ability to organise, remain and participate in DIY music spaces. This is an illustration of how I, and others, can "simultaneously inhabit a position of privilege in some regards, whilst not in others" (Griffin and Griffin, 2019, p. 18).

Insider-outsider

A researcher's position can be further explored through the role of "insider" or "outsider". I immediately positioned myself as an "insider" researcher, which refers to a researcher "sharing the characteristic, role, or experience under study with the participants" (Dwyer and Buckle, 2009, p. 55). Referring to insider research, Merriam et al. write "the more one is like the participants... the more it is assumed that access will be granted, meanings shared, and validity of findings assured" (2001, p. 406). Problems otherwise encountered, for example access to gatekeepers or developing rapport with research participants, are less of an issue. In Merton's exploration of insider and outsider knowledge in sociology, he describes how insider researchers sharing identity characteristics with participants may reach a deeper level of meaning than outsider researchers due to their pre-existing understanding of culture and identity (1972, p. 13). However, insider researchers may struggle to critically engage with information due to their close proximity to research context (Drake and Heath, 2008, p. 129).

In my context, it was important to understand the different spaces in which I could be situated as an insider–for instance, in addition to DIY culture I was an insider within the information profession and university. Similar experiences have been articulated in scholarship–for example, Evans et al. utilise the term "double insider" to consider the implications of being located as both a community member and a researcher (2012, p. 1056). I am located as a community member, academic and archivist, and in each of these spaces I have accountabilities. This straddling of multiples spheres can be as alienating as it is including:

> The researcher may be valued by both communities for his or her bridging capacity and insight, but is also often called upon to negotiate or mediate the expectations, tensions, and differences between academic and community partners. At times, this might mean experiencing being an 'outsider'... or even a 'double outsider'. (Evans et al., 2012, p. 1056)

Cresswell and Spandler similarly refer to experiences of "lived contradictions" which are experienced by activism-aligned academics (2013, p. 139). Rather than belonging in both spaces, often insider or activist academics can instead feel as if they are outside both structures.

Although initially helpful to explore during the development of my project, the division between being an insider or outsider researcher was not an adequate framing for understanding the multiple roles I occupied in this project. At first glance, I was certainly an insider researcher–however, by virtue of accessing funding to research the communities I participated in during my leisure time, I gained a level of privilege and new accountabilities that distanced me from the position of my peers. Immediately, it felt as if the ground we stood on–which previously felt like level footing–was becoming uneven terrain.

Although my work life before and during my PhD required me to navigate precarious employment in higher education and heritage, my scholarship provided me with temporary access to a reliable income and funded research time. I was also aware that producing knowledge is a way to exercise power (Sawicki, 1991, p. 22). By being named as the author of this research, I have acquired cultural capital and, subsequently, economic capital through appointment to a permanent position in a higher education institution.

The language of insider/outsider research provided no means for me to articulate and navigate the shifting power dynamics which I observed at work. Whilst I could locate myself as an insider, the stasis this role implies was inadequate for considering how power dynamics could shift within a research project. Instead, my understanding of position and power was informed by theorists who approach insider/outsider research in a pluralistic manner, in which the two positions are viewed as part of a continuum (Mercer, 2007, p. 7). Instead of viewing these roles as dualisms, Merton calls for insider and outsider dynamics to be interrogated instead via consideration of their status within social structures (1972, p. 22). For example, insider positioning in one context can still produce other inequalities—dynamics of privilege, employment, payment, and intersectional identity can cause discrepancies even between two "insiders".

To navigate the complexity of insider research, Merriam et al. call for researchers to consider their positionality, power, and representation throughout the entire research process (2001, p. 413). In this project, I approached all research interactions through radically empathy-informed practice. Radical empathy advocates for a combination of relational research practice and routine self-examination (Arroyo-Ramírez et al., 2021). The concept has been applied to archival practice by critical archival theorists (Caswell and Cifor, 2016), who argue that archivists (and, in my case, archivist-researchers) are not "liberal autonomous individuals" but instead are bound "in a web of relationships" across the divisions of user, archivist, record subject, record creator and broader community (2016, pp. 41–42). As Arroyo-Ramírez et al. argue, radical empathy is also "bound by its insistence on uprooting structural harms… [and] making intentional shifts and actions with the aim of transforming our systems" (2021, p. 3). In practice, I sought to make research decisions with a sense of emotional responsibility to my participants, to acknowledge and address power discrepancies, and to embed subjectivity in my analysis (as is explored in the following section).

To provide an example of this in practice, I regularly had to make ethical decisions about information that was disclosed to me by research participants with whom I had pre-existing friendships. In their examination of ethics in DIY cultural research, Downes, Breeze and Griffin describe how researchers need to develop "skill to negotiate what participants tell you as a friend and what they tell you as a researcher" (2013, p. 109). The act of researching with friends also requires willingness to navigate both the emotional nature of friendships and the need to generate original research. Taylor also uses the term "ethical friend" to refer to a model of research practice which centres both academic and intimate accountability (2011). I regularly had to decipher information passed onto me as a researcher from information passed to me as a friend and peer. To give an example, at the start of my project I had regular conversations with friends about the project at gigs. During this time, I was given private information relating to individuals working at archive services in the UK. This information related to the personal politics and actions of the individuals in question and affected the decisions I made with regards to where materials collected during this project would be deposited. However, the same information was not disclosed during a one-on-one interview with the same friends at a later point in the project. When instances such as the above situation occurred, I reflected on them in the private space of my research journal—however, it would be unethical for me to discuss the same instances in my analysis.

For insider researchers with unclear boundaries between research and personal life, it is important to develop dynamic and dialogic ways of gaining consent (Downes, Breeze and Griffin, 2013, p. 111). Clark and Walker call for ""virtuous" investigators [who]... explore embedding ethics in every step of study development, implementation, analysis, and dissemination" (2011, p. 1496). Cresswell and Spandler similarly conceive of the "engaged academic", who is both insider and outsider and carries with them the (often contradictory) concerns and goals of both activist communities and academic institutions (2013). Researchers need to go beyond the limits of institutional ethics procedures, to identify, write about and resolve issues using their own community knowledge. Radical empathy can therefore underpin decision-making which is necessarily informed by care and emotional responsibility towards those represented in research.

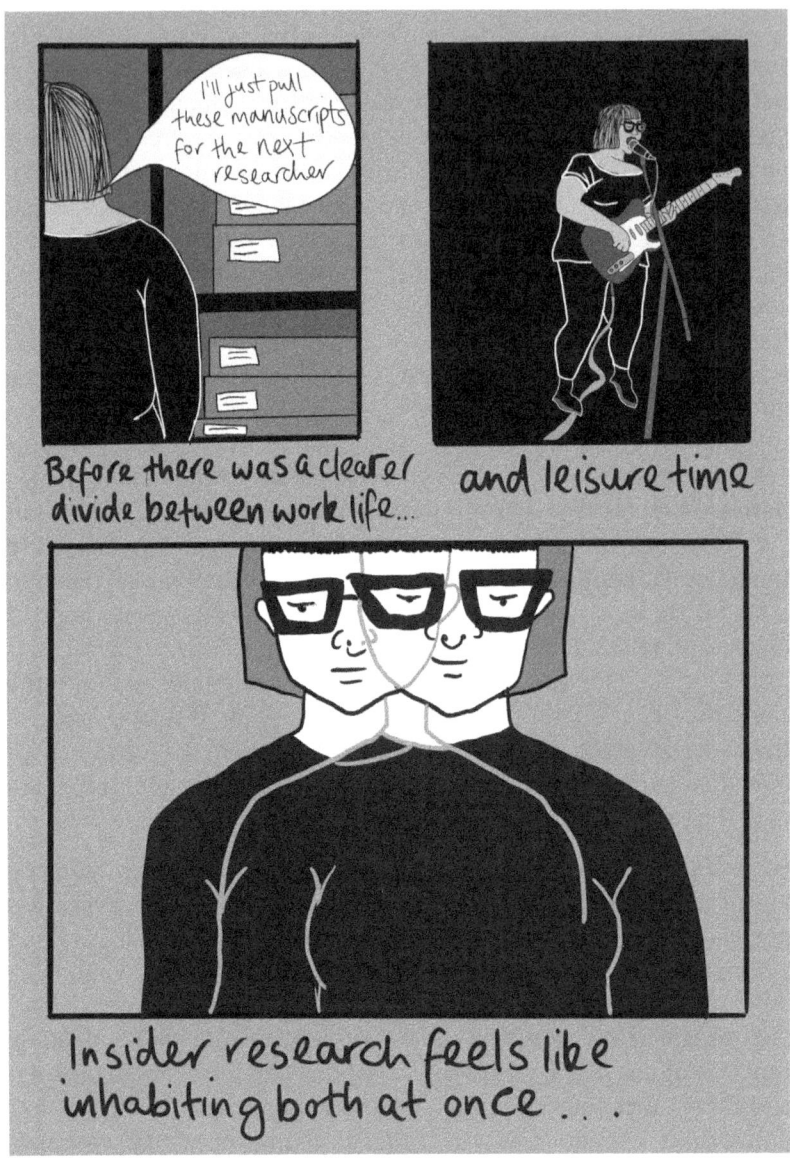

Figure 1 Insider research (original illustration)

Tension 2: distance

The preceding section identified my insider position in this project, whilst also questioning dynamics which commonly remain unaddressed in scholarship exploring the insider position in research. Although my relationship to the insider role is complicated, I nonetheless inhabited the multiple spheres (DIY music spaces and networks; the information sector; academia) of this project as a peer. With prior knowledge and background shaping my research, I immediately felt at odds with my training both as an archivist and as a researcher, in which contexts neutrality and objectivity were positioned as important professional values. Archival practitioners are trained "to divorce our identities and act impartial and unfeeling" (Arroyo-Ramírez et al., 2021, p. 2) to be perceived as professional. In turn, researchers have historically been expected to forge "objective distance" (Pearce, 2020, p. 814) between themselves and their research topic, even when researching a community in which they are already a member. As Detamore writes, this is commonly an "institutional expectation" of researchers (2010, p. 181).

At an early stage of research I was uncomfortable when contemplating how I could create distance in my project. This discomfort was informed by the questioning of neutrality across both academic research and archival practice. Many qualitative researchers now acknowledge that "the writing of a qualitative text cannot be separated from the author" (Creswell, 2014, p. 215). This shift is located within subjectivist approaches to philosophies of knowledge production, within which knowledge is always "value laden" (Levers, 2013, p. 3). As Denzin and Lincoln write, knowledge is

> always filtered through the lenses of language, gender, social class, race, and ethnicity. There are no objective observations, only observations socially situated in the worlds of—and between—the observer and the observed. (2011, p. 16)

Research analyses are shaped by decisions made by researchers about which quotes to include, the analytical narrative and who is represented (Hoskins, 2015, p. 398). As Costantino writes, knowledge is also "constructed between inquirer and participant through the inquiry process itself" (2008, p. 117).

As a consequence of these significant philosophical shifts, qualitative researchers

> can eschew the questionable metanarrative of scientific objectivity and still have plenty to say as situated speakers, subjectivities engaged in knowing/telling about the world as they perceive it. (Richardson and Adams St. Pierre, 2018, p. 1413)

The direction of my research was influenced by the arguments of critical feminist scholars, who position "illusory scholarly objectivity" (Schuchter, 2019, p. 335) as antithetical to ethical practice, instead asserting the need for "a relational mode of being in the archive that refuses to erase the researcher… and instead wants to acknowledge the lived experience on and off the paper" (Schuchter, 2019, p. 335).

Traditions of archival training and practice have also historically relied upon building professional values of objectivity and neutrality (Caswell, 2020). However, this guise of professional neutrality has been described as "fake" (Zinn, 1977, p. 20), or as a "semantic marker" (Ramirez, 2015, p. 352) for whiteness which serve to reinforce privilege and white supremacy within the archival profession. As Zinn writes,

> The scholar may swear to his neutrality on the job, but whether he be physicist, historian, or archivist, his work will tend, in this theory, to maintain the existing social order by perpetuating its values, by legitimizing its priorities, by justifying its wars, perpetuating its prejudices, contributing to its xenophobia, and apologizing for its class order. (Zinn, 1977, p. 18)

Theorists in this field have instead highlighted the subjective nature of many archival processes, including description (Charlton, 2017), appraisal (Caswell, 2019), and digitisation (Ferris and Allard, 2016).

At the conclusion of the preceding section, I began to explore how radical empathy informed decisions made in interactions throughout the research project, focusing on positionality and relationality. The emphasis on subjectivity within radical empathy and feminist standpoint appraisal theory (Caswell, 2019) provided a starting point for me to begin the reorientation of my research practice. As I have explored already, there are established theoretical foundations on which research can be conducted in a way which emphasises relationality and acknowledges the impact of lived experience on knowledge produced in a project.

However, these models of practice can focus on mitigation of subjectivity within research, which implies that the impact of subjectivity is necessarily negative. I wanted to explore what it meant to reject this assumption and to actively embrace the radical potentials of subjectivity rather than mitigate its consequences. Joseph, too, argues that when researchers do not "explicit relation of their feelings, sensations and emotions in response" (2018, p. 206) to a topic, the natural "'affective proximity'" (Clary-Lemon cited in Joseph, 2018, p. 206) of such research "makes a significant contribution to the knowledge which is produced by the research process" (2018, p. 206). In this project, I embraced subjectivity by attending to position and relations (as explored in the previous section), and engaging with emotions as a form of data and knowledge production—which I will go on to explore now.

In her exploration of liberatory memory work, Caswell argues that "we need to value emotion as a way of knowing" (2020, p. 154), giving the example of the experience of "gut reactions" in response to routine archival processes which do not "'feel right'" (2020, p. 154). The metaphor of the gut is something that I have also routinely engaged with in prior creative practice—for example, in *From The Gut* I wrote that "writing from the gut is writing from the hard places... it is a commitment to ongoing digestion of things that have happened" (Fife, 2021b, pp. 13–14). As the following chapter will outline, emotional responses to the experience of being archived are important because of their capacity to pinpoint inequalities in archival processes. As Caswell asserts, radical empathy "is a way of thinking through feelings in relation to structures" (2020, p. 164).

Popular music heritage is also fundamentally affective, embodied, and subjective in dynamic. These qualities are highlighted by popular music heritage researchers across musical genres (Baker, 2015a, 2015a; Long et al., 2017; Joseph, 2018). As Joseph writes, as a result musical memory involves understanding how musical spaces are "remembered as feeling for different people at a range of points in time" (2018, p. 204). He argues in favour of engaging with "the affective potentials" of music archives (Joseph, 2018, p. 86), highlighting how musical practices (including sampling and dubbing) can be used to transmit numerous versions of a memory or record (Joseph, 2018, p. 19). Therefore, the active engagement with emotion and subjectivity I employ is also appropriate for an investigation into the topic at hand.

I engaged with emotion in two different ways—firstly, by responding to the experience of research through zine making, and secondly by coding interview data for emotive language. I integrate a selection of the resulting zine pages in this book, informed by Lymn's use of zines within their thesis (2014). As they write, the zines may at times disrupt the flow, or bring the intimate or personal to the forefront, or even bore you, or distract you from the topic at hand. These 'zine interruptions' demonstrate how zines are sites of eruptions and disturbances, and continue to reinforce the position that zines are best defined through practices, including reading. (p. 21)

I have often struggled with when and how to emphasise my own emotional responses within my academic writing. The embedding of zine pages throughout enables me to interrupt the narrative of my analysis with evocative and emotional responses, maintaining a constant tension between critical analysis and my own subjectivity in the project. This also resists what Goodlay and Moore describe as "the tendency to position first person and reflexive pieces as addendum to more 'scholarly' pieces of work" (2000, p. 873). In this project, emotions interweave through the entire narrative rather than at expected points (the beginning of chapters; at the start of the book etc).

To engage with the emotions my participants expressed, I experimented with coding interview data for emotive language. This was done by creating a coding category for emotions. This exercise generated a representation of the emotional landscape associated with sources, processes, and activities. Examples of codes include excitement, joy, grief, anxiety, fear, anger, tiredness, and satisfaction. These were integrated into my analysis in chapters—for example, chapter three explores examples of anger expressed in response to institutional archival practice. Chapter five explores feelings of anxiety in response to insecurity of digital information. Chapter six examines the articulation of grief after the closing of spaces or conclusion of projects. By purposefully exploring my data for emotion, My research demonstrates how emotion can be used to shape future models of archival practice. We can learn from and change behaviours based on how we, and those around us, feel.

Activist Archivist Research

I'll look at emotional associations through the example of my old iPod. I used this in the 2010s to listen to music, then eventually I caved and got a Spotify account. I found it in a drawer in 2021 and set it to charge again.

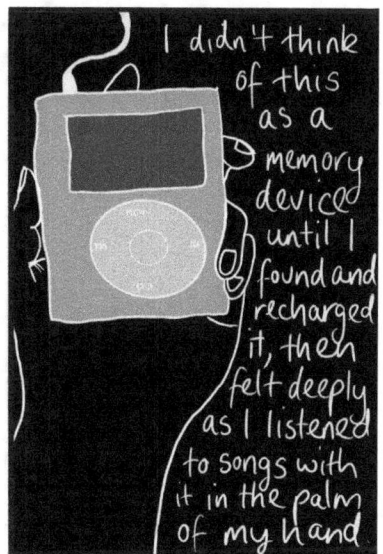

I didn't think of this as a memory device until I found and recharged it, then felt deeply as I listened to songs with it in the palm of my hand

I hadn't updated the songs on there since about 2013. The experience of looking at the display and listening to the playlists took me back to rediscovering playing music and getting involved in the DIY scene. It was weird to feel this after rebooting what was always just a mundane and everyday object at the time.

This set of memories isn't apparent in the object, which just looks like any other iPod.

Figure 2: Old iPod (original illustration)

Tension 3: voice

Voice is a logical tension following on from the idea of distance in academic research. Having decided that it was important to foreground subjectivity within my research, I then needed to consider how I surfaced within the subsequent outputs of the project–specifically considering what voice (or voices) I spoke through. For example, should I separate my written voices into sections of personal experience narrative writing and analytical writing, as is common in autoethnography (Butz and Besio, 2009, p. 1665)? What form should personal narrative take? At what points should I address the research process? Which of my multiple roles (archivist, activist, academic) was I writing from, and who was I writing for?

Early on in my project, I was concerned with the potential for what Toy-Cronin describes as a key ethical issue in insider research–"role conflict" (2018, p. 457). The concept of role conflict places the roles of activist and academic in opposition to one another–a relationship which I would come to question over the duration of my research. This led me to the work of academic activists who query the construction of dichotomies between these roles. For example, Choudry argues that the assumption that it is necessary (or even possible) to separate research and activism produces binary thinking that separates, fragments, and compartmentalises activities into categories of "research" and "organising", and actors into "researchers" and "organisers". (2015, p. 128)

In *Discipline and Punish*, Foucault describes how disciplinary power is exercised through classification based on differences (1991, p. 192). Dividing practices create "dualising mechanisms" and norms which enable domination and marginalise the non-normative (Foucault, 1991, p. 193). In her analysis of zines and third space subjectivity, Licona describes how dualisms and binaries are "demarcations that have divided and defined in the context of identity formation" (2013, p. 6). As Licona writes, this configuration of identity

> Disallows the visibility of lived experience (as both produced and productive) and those third spaces that exceed and are excluded from identity binaries. (2013, p. 6)

Licona describes third space subjectivity as "the lived conditions of crossing borders and existing in the realm of both/and together" (2013, p. 11). Individuals can occupy third space as a *location* and can also undertake third space *practice*, which undoes dominant rhetoric and creates new forms of knowledge.

Licona's ideas inform research about community-led, queer and activist archives and histories (Eichhorn, 2010, 2013; Lee, 2015, 2017, 2020; Honma, 2016; Moore, 2017, 2020; Ramírez, 2019). This concept is used to explore the potential of third space archiving, in which lived experience and community co-location can transform the dynamics of archival work. For example, in exploring their work with the Arizona Queer Archive, Lee states that

> In the in-between space between what archival education taught me and what I knew from working in and with communities, I found how I could be an archivist with integrity and enact archival praxis. (p. 27)

The interweaving of archival, theoretical and personal narratives within the voice of research is also employed by critical archival studies scholars. This includes Brilmyer's research about disability and archives (Brilmyer, 2020b, 2020a), Douglas' exploration of grief and recordkeeping (Douglas, Alisauskas and Mordell, 2019; Douglas and Alisauskas, 2021), and Caswell's work on liberatory archives (Caswell, 2016, 2019, 2021).

Influenced by this work, I resist the separation of self into activist, researcher and archivist, and instead speak from the position of being multiply located. In practicality, this means that I do not separate "voices" in this book—for instance by employing sections of personal narrative writing or by clearly demarcating the personal from the analytical voice through formatting choices. I acknowledge that the multiple accountabilities of each role can create tensions that are sometimes unresolvable. This is a central tenet of Licona's third space practice, which often occurs in contexts "where contestations, ambiguities, and contradictions abound" (2013, p. 9). Rather than attempt to separate voices and artificially resolve these tensions, instead these are central points of investigation and "generative spaces" (Licona, 2013, p. 82) in my analysis.

The second division challenged in this book is between creative and analytical theorising, or cultural production and knowledge production. Here I am informed by Choudry's work on the intellectual life of social movements, in which he describes forms of "incremental, below-the-radar learning and knowledge production [which occur] in the course of organising and action" (2015, p. 9). In DIY cultural spaces, theorising occurs informally in discussion and collaboration, as well in the production of sources (for example, zines, music, podcasts), and the forward momentum of spaces is informed by this theorising and strategising.

This book interjects zine pages throughout the analysis. This choice is informed by scholars who interweave artistic and analytical theorising in texts, through practices including creative writing, photography and zine making (Kuhn, 2002, 2010; Lymn, 2014; Lee, 2020). Kuhn argues that this form of analysis can "tread a line between cultural criticism and cultural production" (2002, p. 3). As an example, in the body of their thesis about zine archives, Lymn reproduces eight zines. The zines do not have a unified purpose—some respond to the subject matter or key themes in the narrative, and others are zines which were created during the project (2014, p. 19). The zines integrated in Lymn's thesis sometimes respond explicitly to the research, and at other points represent the researcher's own emotional journey through the project.

The zine pages I reproduce are not visualisations of data collected during the project or literal illustrations of key moments, but creative responses which document points of resonance within the project. In her analysis of video games and queer identity Ruberg describes resonances as

Activist Archivist Research

resonance can refer to evoking an emotional response or connection

in sound resonance refers to vibrations which amplify and intensify sound.

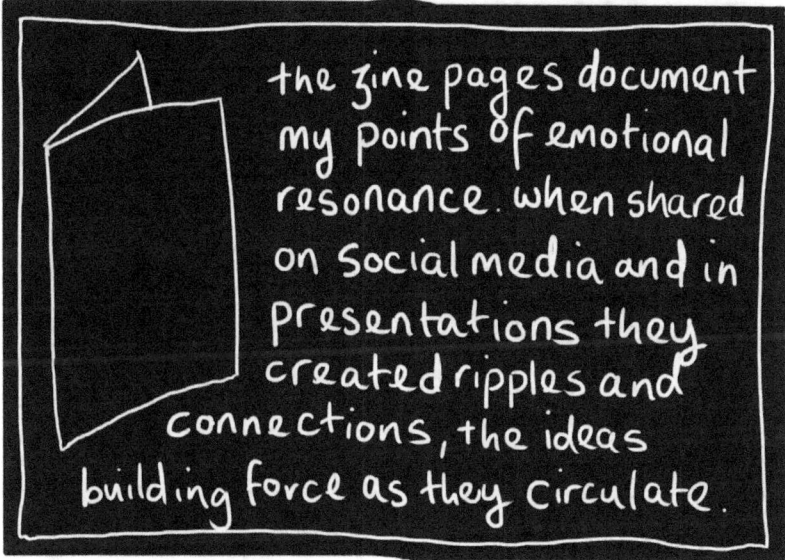

the zine pages document my points of emotional resonance. when shared on social media and in presentations they created ripples and connections, the ideas building force as they circulate.

Figure 3 Resonances (original illustration)

points of relationality, moments when the structures and messages of video games echo and are echoed by the structures of queer thinking. (2019, p. 20)

In an exploration of listening to archive recordings of queer performers, Hale Wood refers to "audible waves that reverberate and resonate between subject and listener" (2021, p. 114), creating "queer sonic intimacies" between the a listener and a recording of a performance (2021, p. 112). Resonance infers connection, relations, and dynamics forged through ongoing practices of transmission and consumption. The zine pages reproduced here document points of resonance encountered during the process of research when collecting and analysing data, reviewing literature and constructing my analysis. They surface intimate connections and dynamics which would otherwise not be documented in my analysis. These pages were also shared to communicate the research (e.g. on social media or during presentations about the project), in turn generating further points of emotional resonance and dialogue with others, effectively intensifying or amplifying the findings of the project.

The zine pages also foreground the process of research. In the context of critical animal studies, Stephen Griffin describes how "comics have been used to literally and symbolically emphasise the "messy" parts of a research process that are usually deliberately hidden" (2014, p. 125). Zines are commonly used to share information and skills within DIY cultural networks (Chidgey, 2014; Abtan, 2016). In the context of research, zines can be used to emphasise lived experience of the research process, specifically the more challenging points in projects. The documentation of these moments benefits not only the researcher by enabling them to process experiences, but a wider community of research in a particular context through transparent sharing of the results.

This section has explored my strategies for navigating tensions around voice during this project. I anticipated conflicts relating to reconciling the various roles I occupied and explored approaches to separating roles through writing in different voices. However, the separation of voices to reflect roles (activist/archivist/researcher) or practices (cultural/knowledge production) felt inauthentic and created problematic dichotomies. This created a separation of voices which did not correspond to the lived experience of simultaneous responsibilities and positions, in which it is often not possible to create the same separation. The reflexive narrative approach to writing employed in this book therefore serves to embody the lived experience of co-location in community and professional contexts and challenge the production of binaries between research and activism, and cultural and knowledge production.

Tension 4: wellbeing

The final tension I would like to address relating to conducting research within my own community relates to the impact of this on the self. This is an under-examined area of methodological scholarship and is pertinent to the development of radical empathy as a framework for practice and research.

There can be emotional tolls on researchers conducting research within their work or leisure settings. Because of regular access to their research context, researchers may struggle to draw boundaries between life, work and research (Mercer, 2007, p. 6), and their opinions may influence participants (Mercer, 2007, p. 8). When remaining in a setting after the conclusion of research, researchers may have ongoing relationships with those criticised in analyses, which can affect their wellbeing after the conclusion of research projects.

These issues are often experienced when insider researchers come from backgrounds marginalised within the academy. Pearce argues that marginalised researchers "can face specific and severe challenges that put them at a disadvantage with respect to their less marginalised peers" (2020, p. 808). Pearce situates "challenges associated with structures of oppression" as "a methodological problem" (2020, p. 808). Iphofen and Tolich refer to a researcher's aim to "do no harm" to participants, calling for risks to be identified and minimised during the development of a project (Iphofen and Tolich, 2018, p. 8). However, as Pearce identifies, ethical considerations should also consider the potential of harm to researchers, especially those researching within their own communities and marginalised researchers (2020).

It is often not possible to predict the emotions that can surface during research into your own communities. If succinctly summarising my emotional journey during this project, I would describe the experience as an emotional rollercoaster in which I experienced both extreme highs and extreme lows. After receiving confirmation of a successful funding application, starting this project felt like an immense privilege—it provided time and space, neither of which I had access to in my prior cultural activity. Being deeply immersed in and critically engaged with this topic has felt incredibly rewarding at points and enabled me to reconnect with the radical potentials of archiving after becoming professionally disillusioned.

However, despite these periods of joy, research has fundamentally changed my relationship to DIY music—a consequence I was never fully prepared for when beginning my project. By virtue of committing to research the topic for 3-4 years, it quickly became clear that, even if I wanted to, I couldn't take a break from my level of involvement in the community. This became challenging at specific points: for example, during periods I felt burnt out and exhausted due to overcommitment to specific projects. During these moments, I would usually take a break from cultural organising—however, due to the time constraints of the project I often felt unable to do so. Half of the project duration was also affected by the COVID-19 pandemic, during which the community in question was radically disturbed through the closure of spaces (some temporarily, others permanently), financial turmoil, experiences of loss, and changes to lifestyles, and caring and work arrangements. In this period, DIY music was no one's priority—but it felt like it had to be mine, if I was to finish my PhD. In both of these examples, the obligation to remain involved and active within a community felt like a weight on my shoulders, at points when it should have been more important for me to have recovery time. This fundamentally changed how I related to working in these settings, and I have yet to resolve these dynamics and return to my original joyous and empowering engagement with DIY music.

My experience is not unique—for example, during a reflection about undertaking research within a local DIY music community, Griffin writes:

> Doing research on a topic so personal to me has, and continues to have, an impact on my relationship with and feelings towards the group, scene(s), community/communities and movement that I studied. Before I started the project, I was unprepared for the emotional turmoil that could result from doing research on such a personal topic. (2015, p. 105)

Griffin describes experiencing anxiety when encountering ethical issues and when making decisions about how individuals were represented (2015, p. 105), which also resonates with my experience. Similar experiences are highlighted by other DIY cultural scholars (Downes, 2010; Downes, Breeze and Griffin, 2013; Cooper, 2023). These negative experiences are exacerbated by disparities between institutional and community ethics, the navigation of which can provide labour-intensive and challenging for researchers.

When equipped with knowledge about the potential for emotional turmoil or anxiety, it is possible to develop skills, strategies, and support networks in anticipation of unease, upset or burn out. Pearce proposes that a methodology for marginalised researchers should include

ethical responsibility towards the self, and a supportive community of scholarship. These are intended to support the survival of scholars who are themselves marginalised, especially if they are also studying marginalised communities. (2020, p. 809)

I first became aware of the need to develop support strategies during my first year of study, in which I encountered the aforementioned publications. This made me aware of the potential emotional impact of working within my own community, but also highlighted that there was limited research to learn from in this area. I found that reflective accounts of emotional disturbance in research were predominantly found in PhD theses, and (occasionally) within journal articles.

Critical writing about the lived experience of insider research can equip a wider research community with knowledge and skills to navigate these dilemmas. Although some of the intimate details of a researcher's experience are not appropriate to share with wider audiences, the publication of reflective accounts of research journeys from this perspective is a valuable addition to methods literature. I chose to document and publish my own PhD journey through a personal zine series (*Adventures in Academia*). The zines combined reflective writing with illustrations, comics, and resources I found useful during my research. The zine project became an important way to openly talk about these negative affective dimensions. The zine was a suitable medium for this work (as opposed to, for example, publishing an academic account) due to its short form, responsive and intimate nature. This meant that I could publish a more informal account and do so without the usual publishing timeframe of academic publishing.

I was also reminded of the need to care for myself within an early panel review for my project, when an internal examiner prompted me to explain what self-care strategies I would employ in the project. This question was unconventional in academic reviews, which conventionally focus on procedural aspects of a research plan. However, it prompted me to consider my own wellbeing within the overall management of the project. The subsequent conversation continued to resonate with me throughout the rest of the research. Conversation and dialogue remained an important source of support for me as I moved through the project. I was lucky to have close friendships with people who had experienced similar challenges during research. I also participated in a weekly writing group with peers undertaking community-based research projects. As well as helping with writing progress, the small and intimate space of this regular meeting created room for informal discussions about issues we faced in our research.

Finally, I had to acknowledge that as my leisure activities also became spaces of research, I needed to have other leisure activities that were outside of these communities. This contributed to me stepping back from some of my community responsibilities during the project, which in turn meant that I was less "immersed" in my research. This could potentially negatively impact the quality of my research, but also crucially enabled me to maintain emotional wellbeing throughout my project. The image on the following page (reproduced from *Adventures in Academia* #1) illustrates some of the activities I engaged with in this time, including dog walking, gardening and crafting.

Figure 4 Toolkit for DIY cultural researchers (Fife, 2019)

Conclusion

This chapter had two aims: firstly, to transparently account for how the research in this project was conducted; and secondly, to provide a critically reflective account of the experience of conducting insider research within DIY culture. I chose to document my experiences within this book because I experienced challenges whilst conducting research within my own community–a sentiment which is echoed in prior insider research within activist and music cultures (Downes, 2010; Downes, Breeze and Griffin, 2013; Griffin, 2015; Stephens-Griffin, 2015). To return to Pearce's reflections on undertaking trans health research as a marginalised researcher, these are methodological concerns (2020, p. 808) which require consideration throughout the research process, from project proposal to completion. Publishing experience ensures that there are sources of evidence for those without supportive peer networks.

By focusing on points of tension and conflict, this chapter has also highlighted the limitations of institutional research guidance, policies, and processes, including research ethics committees. These processes often prioritise the protection of institutions from litigation and adherence to contractual obligations over the nuanced ethical decision making required in community-based research. The repeated questioning of research methods, practices and tools should be understood as an example of activist practice within academia—through challenging what is expected and adapting these tools, it is more possible to bridge the space between academia and activism.

Resisting the Canon

After decades in which pop culture has had a minimal presence in heritage institutions, subcultural communities and spaces have been the subject of exhibition and collecting initiatives facilitated by national and regional heritage organisations, as well as community-led archive projects. Examples of these include the British Pop Archive (John Rylands Library, University of Manchester); Punks (Museum of London, 2016-2017), London Calling: 40 Years of The Clash (Museum of London, 2019); Black Sabbath–50 Years (Birmingham Museum and Art Gallery, 2019); Manchester Digital Music Archive; and the Museum of Youth Culture. For Bennett and Janssen this increased interest is evidence of wider acknowledgement of the "sociohistorical significance [of popular music] in a post-1945 context" (2016, p. 2).

However, responses to national punk exhibitions have been ambivalent, with writers drawing attention to negative responses to several large-scale exhibitions. For example, Bulut (2016) describes the defacing of a British Library interpretation panel by Viv Albertine, who objected to the representation of punk as led by white men in Punk: 1976-1978 (British Library, 2016). Albertine changed every reference to Sex Pistols to The Slits and added "what about the women!!" to the panel (Bulut, 2016). The highly selective nature of such interpretative narratives often excludes the contributions of individuals from minoritised backgrounds (Strong, 2011). Queer and feminist art historians have also engaged with the "hauntings" of the spectral figures of queer feminist past, who persist beyond the ephemeral spaces of cultural organising and despite histories that centre white men (Cowan, McLeod and Rault, 2014; Mitchell and McKinney, 2019). These examples amongst many others set the precedent for histories and archives as battlegrounds and conflicts (Fraser, 1995; Sturken, 2008), on which the right to representation, presence, and persistence is only accessible to a few.

Using these issues as a starting point, this chapter explores how members of UK DIY music spaces and communities relate to processes of historicisation, canonisation and archiving. The first section of this chapter explores connections between heritage, archiving and canonisation. I explore how canons are formed, and the way in which heritage can rely upon selective traditions of collecting and narrow definitions of expertise to create archives. I then go on to problematise these processes, particularly canonisation for its reliance on practises of exclusion and hierarchical value to determine collective memory. Finally, I explore how these terms are understood and related to in a digital age, with particular emphasis on the ways digital networked technology enables the proliferation of individual cultural canons.

The second section explores canonisation in relation to music heritage, and specifically DIY music heritage. In this section I continue to problematise the forming of cultural canon through the selective tradition, articulating the reasons why the cultural output of UK DIY music communities should not be canonised in this way. In this section I argue for the valuing of canonical practices rather than objects, which can be understood as more inclusive of DIY cultural production than object-led heritage practice.

The third section of this chapter engages with the negative impact of processes of historicisation and canonisation on individuals within DIY music communities. Utilising examples of research, history writing, and interpretation undertaken within and outside of these communities, I explore how the historicisation of music communities and who undertakes this work often intersects with power and privilege and, as such, devalues the contributions of marginalised people and/or minimises or erases conflicts.

The fourth and fifth sections of this chapter seek alternatives to these methods. The fourth section explores the use of archives, histories and documentary projects to resist the erasure of the contributions of individuals to DIY music heritage. Utilising the concept of "representational belonging" (Caswell, Cifor and Ramirez, 2016), I propose that individuals marginalised by some of the actions explored in the third section are able to utilise archives and histories to amplify and reassert their presence within the cultural legacies of these communities. In the final section of this chapter, I explore the potential use of archives for accountability, learning and the complication of simple narratives of participation, empowerment, and collaboration. In this

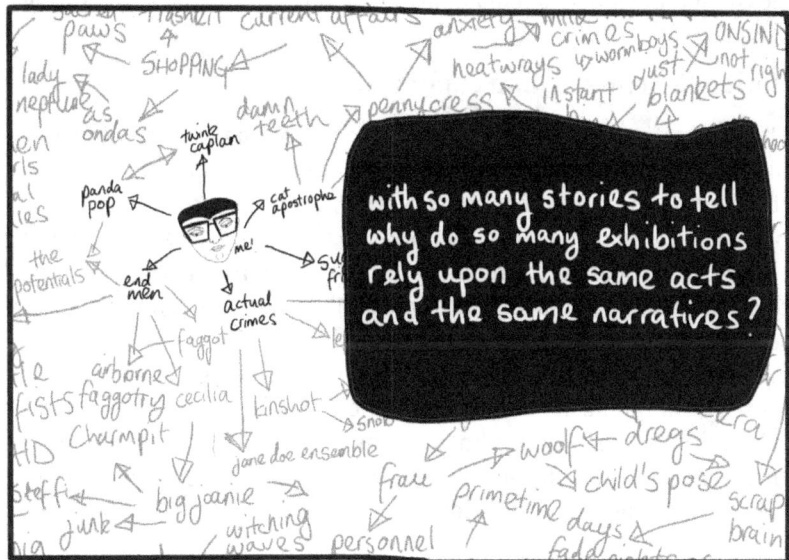

Figure 1 Punk heritage (original illustration)

section I emphasise that the archiving of the experiences of working and participating in UK DIY communities can be an activity which is of use both the current activisms and future activisms.

Hall asserted that an archive "should be, not an inert museum of dead works, but a 'living archive', whose construction must be seen as an on-going, never-completed project" (2001, p. 89). Histories of UK DIY music are living histories, based on work and cultural production undertaken by individuals who are sometimes still active–as such, processes of archiving and history writing need to be re-envisioned in a more dialogic model to minimise harm and allow community members to retain control over and connections to their own histories. Histories can be spaces for imagination, accountability, learning, connection, solidarity, and information sharing across generations. By utilising the creation of histories and archives of DIY music for these purposes and not shying away from representing complexity, trauma, conflict, and hardships, it is possible to enable the growth of current and future DIY music communities through dialogue and connection to past generations.

Heritage, archiving and canonisation

The production of canons concerns those working in cultural communities because canons ensure the persistence of cultural legacies via the continued circulation, preservation, and citation of cultural outputs. The canon is particularly apposite to explore in relation to punk cultures (or those aligned with a punk ethos), because of the negative responses to the canonisation of 1970s punk (Cogan, 2003). Cultural canons can exclude or minimise the contributions of marginalised individuals, and actively work against the values of participation and non-hierarchical cultural production that underpin DIY music. This section therefore explores how canons are established and preserved, then identifies the differences and connections between canonisation, and archiving as practices.

In "Canon and Archive" Assmann proposes that cultural memory is formed through the shortage of space, which mandates that only a selection of materials can be preserved. As she writes, the canon

> is built on a small number of normative and formative texts, places, persons, artefacts, and myths which are meant to be actively circulated and communicated in ever-new presentations and performances. (Assmann, 2008, p. 100)

De Kosnik similarly writes about a close relation between the canon and what is archived:

> What is canonical therefore is, de facto, what is "archived" by the culture and society; canonical works are preserved, both virtually (theoretically everyone knows them and remembers them) and literally (they are conserved in repositories and kept safe from material degradation, as much as possible). (2016, p. 65)

Objects which are canonised are assumed to be valuable through their preservation and repeated use. These selected objects are used to write histories and inform the production of culture, becoming difficult to unseat from positions of relevance.

Canons are formed through the "selective tradition" of culture (Williams, 2006, p. 38). As Williams writes, this process of selection determines an overall view of a period and, in doing so, rejects other "considerable areas of what was once a living culture" (2006, pp. 38–39). When selections are made, some people are remembered and others are forgotten, minimised (Assmann, 2008, p. 97). Hall similarly writes views the selective tradition as key to the formation of national heritage, in which

> nations construct identities by selectively binding their chosen high points and memorable achievements into an unfolding 'national story'. This story is what is called 'Tradition'. (1999, p. 5)

Selecting canonical materials is a practice which assigns importance and value to some materials, whilst also "foreshortens, silences, disavows, forgets and elides many episodes which — from another perspective — could be the start of a different narrative". (Hall, 1999, p. 5)

Assmann distinguishes the archive from the canon, referring to

> the actively circulated memory that keeps the past present as the canon and the passively stored memory that preserves the past as the archive. (2008, p. 98)

In Assmann's view the archive is also more diverse, due to it undergoing a less rigorous process of refinement and selection. The resulting materials are "a meta-memory, a second-order memory that preserves what has been forgotten" (2008, p. 106). The archive can also be activated for reuse by those who can interpret their contents. Assmann proposes that

> the knowledge that is stored in the archive is inert. It is stored and potentially available, but it is not interpreted. This would exceed the competence of the archivist. It is the task of others such as the academic researcher or the artist to examine the contents of the archive and to reclaim the information by framing it within a new context. (2008, p. 103)

Although I agree that the archive is a potentially more diverse body of materials than canons formed via the selective tradition, Assmann's vision of the archive undervalues the role of the archivist and forms of archival work through which cultural memory is shaped. The canon may symbolise a further step in this process, in which archives are refined or selected from by "experts", however the archivist also warrants scrutiny in analyses.

The status of archives and the process of appraisal is often overlooked by cultural theorists, with the archive instead positioned as a neutral, untouched land (Cook, 2011). Archival theorists, however, have drawn attention to the selective nature of archival practice (Harris, 2002; Mbembe, 2002; Stoler, 2002; Cook, 2011). For Mbembe, the archive is

> fundamentally a matter of discrimination and of selection, which, in the end, results in the granting of a privileged status to certain written documents, and the refusal of that same status to others, thereby judged 'unarchivable', The archive is, therefore, not a piece of data, but a status. (2002, p. 20)

Foucault's work on the relationship between archives and discourse also highlights how the archive is a space which authorises knowledge and produces truth. The archive is not

> that which collects the dust of statements that have become inert once more, and which may make possible the miracle of their resurrection; it is that which defines the mode of occurrence of the statement-thing; it is the system of its functioning. (1972, p. 146)

Through archival processes, archivists make decisions about what is kept, and what is disregarded. In a discussion of archival appraisal, Cook writes:

> archival appraisal decides, with finality, which records are to be destroyed, excluded from the archives and thus from all these subsequent archival processes and enhancements, thereby effectually removed from societal memory, from the archive. (2011, pp. 606–607)

The choices of archivists not only define the boundaries of the archive, but potential for recovery, transformation and connection through history (Sutherland, 2017, p. 7).

When processes are managed by state authorities or institutions, archiving and canonisation often align with the interests of their governing bodies (Hall, 1999; Mbembe, 2002; Cotera, 2015; Ishmael, 2018). This form of heritage canon is positioned as a colonising force (Stoler, 2002, p. 92). In reference to Chicana feminist histories Cotera writes that

> traditional archival methods often nourish an invisibilising feedback loop in which one's access to power determines one's presence in the archive, and one's presence in the archive shapes historical knowledge, which, in turn, informs the system of valuation that structures the priorities that govern collecting and preservation in institutions. Those farther away from the mechanisms of power—women, the working class, ethnic and sexual minorities—are rarely represented in institutional archives. Consequently, their lives and interventions are rarely the subject of historical meaning-making. (2015, p. 785)

The archive nurtures and affirms histories for the state, the academy and other powerful institutions. Cotera calls instead for scholars and communities to use the archive as

> a place for producing and exchanging new knowledges, and for transgressing the traditional boundaries between scholars, their audiences, and the communities they study. (2015, p. 788)

Stoler proposes that we should view archives not as sources, but as subjects for analysis (2002, p. 93)–through which we are able to deconstruct the production of historical narratives through archival processes, canonisation and history writing. If analysing materials in such a light, it is possible to highlight what is erased or neglected, and the socio-political assumptions embedded in canonical narratives.

As the above quotes suggest, the canon and the archive can be deconstructed and re-envisioned to nurture different histories. Scholars suggest that digital technologies can be used to transform the archive and the canon (Earhart, 2012, 2015; Cotera, 2015; De Kosnik, 2016). De Kosnik proposes that we need to redefine both terms for the digital age, writing that

> "Archive" is now an incredibly tenuous construct given the instability of digital data, and "canon" can be interpreted either as a

> concept that is infinitely multipliable… or as a concept that is fully aligned with repertoire, so that we can have canonical practices but not canonical objects. (De Kosnik, 2016, p. 71)

Using digital technologies, it is possible for individuals to

> "activate"… materials they wish, constructing their own personal canons based on the materials that they use. In other words, if repertoire is canon, then whatever a user finds in an archive and chooses to use is a canonical work, for that person. (De Kosnik, 2016, p. 66)

Individual cultural canons when users curate their own collections based on subjective understandings of value rather than a more "authorised" institutional expertise. Whilst this is potentially transgressive and challenges the authority of institutions, these alternative canons often do not gain the same level of social acceptance as institutionally formed canons, unless a creator possesses existing cultural capital.

Individual canon curation could be enabled through mass digitisation of cultural heritage and the OpenGLAM movement (Terras, 2015; Valeonti, Terras and Hudson-Smith, 2020). However, the selective nature of digitisation and rights restrictions can prohibit the accessibility of digitised resources. As Terras writes,

> even if an item is digitised that does not automatically make it more open, accessible or reusable: it has also to be delivered in a way that allows, encourages and promotes reuse, in an adequate format, in high-enough digital quality, and with an open and progressive attitude to what people, organisations and industries are allowed to do with that content once they have access to it, to provide the benefits digitisation is touted as being able to deliver. (2015, p. 737)

Not only do such schemes restrict reuse, but they are often created to enable commercial exploitation by institutions rather than support reuse by end users (Valeonti, Terras and Hudson-Smith, 2020). Authors have also acknowledged the ways in which the selective nature of digitisation enables the reproduction of the Western canon in a digital format rather than its dissolution (Hitchcock, 2013). The persistent representation of digitisation as positive and neutral is also queried by theorists exploring queer and colonial archives, who highlight the potential for digitised materials to cause harm (Caswell and Cifor, 2019; Fife, 2019c; Odumosu, 2020). Thus, while I acknowledge the potential for digitisation to enable the proliferation of individual cultural canons, it is also important to acknowledge the limitations to making content accessible and the inequalities that manifest within these processes.

Alongside the potential for canons to diversify through user-led curation, digital technologies can be used to build new canons which centre those previously erased through the selective tradition (Earhart, 2012, 2015). These are referred to as "digital recovery projects" by Earhart, which refers to "the use of a digital medium to bring a lost or non-canonical and difficult to locate work to a larger audience" (2012). These projects seek to reinsert marginalised authors within literary canons, whose work has (via processes of printing and re-printing) become inaccessible. Earhart describes how literary scholars have employed alternative models of canon building using online bibliographies and small-scale web libraries. It is easy to find shared motivations between the actions of the literary scholars in Earhart's research and those engaged in DIY cultural production. Earhart also draws comparisons between DIY self-publishing cultures and those engaged in digital recovery work (2015, pp. 69–70). Both employ technology, seek to amplify the voices of marginalised communities, and develop community through linking and networking (Earhart, 2015, pp. 70–71).

This section has explored the concept of the canon and how it relates to heritage and archiving. I began with the development of traditional canons, which have historically relied on unchallenged notions of expertise, authority and creative skill. Rather than disconnect canonisation from archival practice, I have described how archival processes play a role in canonisation. With the advent of digital technologies, the democratisation of curating and accessibility of online technologies enables individuals to create alternative canons motivated by individual notions of value. However, as I will explore in more detail in chapters five and six, archives can exist in precarious states on digital platforms. The following section explores how DIY music heritage relates to the cultural canon. Drawing on data from interviews as well as popular music heritage scholarship, I will explore how the community of this research relate to canonisation.

Canonisation and DIY music heritage

Questions relating to how DIY music communities were represented in archives and histories preoccupied those who participated in this research. In the following section, I explore how participants responded to the issues raised previously. By exploring the role of the canon in these conversations, I highlight fears, anxieties, and uncertainties about the process of historicisation. However, I also identify cases in which the informal creation of canons by community members had a positive impact by providing opportunities for connection and network-building.

In the broader context of popular music heritage, Baker describes how "national institutions tend to have selective collection practices which work to reinforce existing musical canons" (2016, p. 183). Leonard calls for curators to engage

> with everyday music practices and the wider plurality of histories. With careful curatorship and the assistance of their audiences museums can develop for the future a popular cultural heritage which is non-linear, risk taking and which presents a diversity of experience. (2010, p. 180)

The reliance on selecting individual cultural objects to represent music is insufficient in a cultural heritage context—for example, a guitar can be a representative object of an individual's music practice but is insufficient without documentation of processes underpinning the production of music. In reference to the musical output of the women's liberation movement, Withers refers to the importance of the informal documentation of learning through lo-fi recordings:

> We can hear the chatter of 'I missed that bit' in the corner of the recordings, followed by frustrated laughter as the women attempt again. These archives indicate and re-enact learning. Recordings of practices and demo tapes by any band can capture that similar sense of 'working things out'. (2014, p. 695)

This is of particular importance in the context of UK DIY music, which places value on learning and process within cultural production. This is viewed equally as important as the resulting output (e.g., a record).

Tayyab (participant) engaged with album releases as canonical in popular music, but inadequate as a complete representation:

> You have these albums that are the canonical archive of what an act has achieved, but there should be some other way to actually learn about these bands and their presences and who the band actually is

Similarly, the results of an early research workshop indicated that, whilst the outputs of cultural production were part of a DIY cultural archive, many other components (ephemera, oral history, technological processes, platforms, materials, merchandise, badges, software, letters, contextual information) were as important to community members. These materials were often maligned by collecting institutions, who sought out outputs.

The selective tradition of collecting often focuses on "breakthrough" acts without critically considering the resources, energy and financial backing required to transition from grassroots music scenes to professional success. Aaron (participant) jokingly described DIY music as "a really long history of doing... shit that goes nowhere". For others, participation in music was something undertaken around many other commitments—childcare, caring, wage labour, or other forms of activism. In reference to the musical output of the women's liberation movement, Withers describes how commitments and lack of resource often meant that bands were unable to record music, and as such left behind fewer traces:

> Having such recordings can facilitate 'canonisation', a crucial technology of recognition in popular music history, and of course, wider culture ... Yet many feminist music makers did not manage to do this with all of their work. (2014, p. 694)

Although this study is undertaken at a later point in time to Withers' research, making music around other commitments and without resources is a shared experience. For example, the role of chronic illness was raised by several participants. Colette describes the impact that illness has had on her band's creative practice over a long-term period:

> in my own band with Woolf two members of the band have had problems with illness over the years, we've not been prolific, banging albums out every year and that's like something that we've become really happy [with], that we're gonna still be doing this band when we're grannies and maybe we'll have five albums to be really, really proud of (Colette, 2020)

The above quote shows the individual significance that is afforded to a long-term creative collaboration (of over ten years)–however (and in parallel to Withers' analysis) the output of this form of collaboration differs from that which is historically accepted into a cultural canon.

Figure 2 Validation

Recognition of such creative work requires a less hierarchical, selective, and object-led approach to heritage.

Access to technology, money, support, and time control access to any cultural canons. Although the proliferation of (digital and analogue) home recording technologies and streaming platforms across the 20th and early 21st century has changed the landscape of who can record and release music (Bennett and Peterson, 2004, p. 6; Goold and Graham, 2019), home recordings still carry less value in cultural canons than professional recordings. Genres or methods of music making are also afforded differing levels of value depending on access to funding, alignment with cultural policy or industry support (Behr, Brennan and Cloonan, 2014, p. 205). In the following quote, Emma describes the difference between recording and releasing with label support and self-releasing without financial backing:

> [In] DIY, sometimes bands don't record or do record but it was such low budget, they're not very happy with it, or they spent a bit more money but they weren't then happy with the recording they got. There's so many bands as well that have been blistering live and sound a bit limp when they recorded. (Falconer, 2019)

The above quote assumes a desire to produce albums or full-length music releases. However, other participants in this research who participated in electronic music scenes did not see albums as necessary within those scenes. For example, Tayyab said:

> there's a lot of talk in electronic scenes over the past couple of decades—it's been a contentious issue, does a techno album work, can you really call that an album? Should that music exist in album format or does it need to not be constrained by that? And the ideas around albums are less static now because major artists will release a playlist rather than an album. (Amin, 2019)

The changing context of music consumption (particularly music streaming) also call into question the central position of material cultural objects (in this case, albums).

For some participants, documentary and archival activities they undertook were an act of resistance against processes of erasure within histories, archives and canons. For example, Ben reflected on his knowledge about the canonisation of 1970s punk:

> I always make that joke about BBC Four [documentaries like]… Punk Britannia, you have The Ramones or bands who were great bands but they're not the only bands and not the only people… my mum was a punk in Croydon in 1977 and she was the first person that talked to me about [how] it wasn't all men in this scene and it wasn't all white people in the scene (Perkins, 2019)

Ben's projects (podcasting, radio and zine making) were undertaken to increase the visibility of DIY music projects that were otherwise easily lost or neglected by mainstream documentaries:

> with the event listings zine which I've just started doing now… there's a piece of paper that shows these gigs existed or that these bands existed and that feels …. very important when you think about things like the internet and [how] we're all busy and the canon, who's in the canon, who's left out, it's why everyone makes their own histories

Ben is motivated to document the activities of UK DIY music communities to keep their memory present, even after the conclusion or closing of short-lived projects and spaces. This can be connected to motivations of many community-led heritage projects. In reference to archiving of the Heygate estate following the gentrification of Elephant and Castle, Carter refers to archiving as

> a conscious and political means of keeping the memory of the estate and the campaign alive…The archive becomes the 'battle of memory against forgetting,' a struggle to ensure that the Heygate is remembered in the historical record rather than becoming a 'blank sheet'. (2017, p. 32)

As in Carter's analysis, Ben's work serves as useful for both current and future UK DIY music communities by enabling people to find out about gigs and events and by seeking to prolong the cultural memory of communities, spaces, projects and activities.

Individuals and communities can also intentionally or unintentionally perpetuate canons, even if otherwise viewing their formation in a negative light. For example, Bryony reflected that

> sometimes we engage with an idea of the past that is highly highly fetishised, but only on the basis that it's not our past, like when I think about the entire culture industry that exists around the first wave of punk, like 77, 79, there is–that is a cultural fetish object but

Figure 3 Citational practices (original illustration)

> I don't think anyone who is my age or younger who's like really into that sees it as their culture that belongs to them. (Beynon, 2020)

Bryony suggested examples of this fetishisation including the adoption of aesthetics from historic punk cultures (particularly 1970s punk and 1980s hardcore) in fashion (e.g. leather jackets, patches), illustration and/or graphic design (for example fliers). This informal referencing of "significant" moments in punk history is an example of what Chidgey refers to as "citational practices" (2013, p. 663). Of this practice in zine networks, Chidgey writes that

> one can critically consider which forms of ritualised, frozen and continued memories… are being reactivated and circulated in these networks, and how these texts are being accessed and transmitted. (2013, p. 663)

The "frozen" memory seems like an apt description of the repetition of familiar and now historic punk and hardcore aesthetics. These persist even in the most nihilistic of punk cultures, which would otherwise malign the desire to preserve any traces of punk subcultures but can seem like what Bryony jokingly referred to as a "leather jacket historical re-enactment society". The adoption of these aesthetic codes signify involvement in a subculture, but also alignment with the ideologies of previous generations of music communities.

Canons can be formed through intentional collecting (in heritage organisations, for example, or through individual action), but in other cases an informal compilation of materials can become canonical through repeated citation, circulation or in absence of other traces (whether informally, as in the case of the leather jacket above, or in more formal spaces such as academia). For example, Cotera writes about the canonisation of the anthology *This Bridge Called My Back*, an early anthology written by women of colour. The book's persistent presence in feminist scholarship often marginalised the contributions of other contemporaries or earlier generations of activists:

> if you took that volume, as did so many feminists in the academy, to document the first contributions of women of colour to the theory and practice of feminism, you would have been committing (however unwittingly) an act of erasure. (Cotera, 2015, p. 781)

In Cotera's example, this assertion by the academy (incorrectly) implies that women of colour were late arrivals to feminist cultural activism. Therefore, it is not the original book that is problematic, but the way in which it is utilised or referenced in other contexts, especially within the academy or other institutions.

In several interviews, participants referred to their activities as similarly unintentionally canon forming. Ruth and Kirsty described the experience of putting together an online curated list of active UK riot grrrl on their band Not Right's website. The website

> had some really interesting effects, because we put up this big list... Now we've got a history of people making links to each other [...] all of this stuff is meant to be demystification and sharing and opening up and it did that. But also what it meant was we were the band who kept the UK Riot Grrrl page, which became a little bit awkward at a couple of points. (Pearce, 2019)

Kirsty referred to Not Right's website as enabling the band to make connections without geographical constraints:

> at that point, there wasn't really much of a scene around any of this sort of stuff. So to be more part of this and to find our scene... having the website helped. And I think that's also where having that collection of other bands that are cool and doing similar sorts of things was part of ... [the] archiving side of it. That obviously isn't quite the same thing as having just a list of gigs and our record so that a promoter can find it. (Lohman, 2020)

In the above example, information and representation is used to build and define queer feminist community by drawing connections between one DIY project and other politically-aligned cultural production. In this sense, the formation of canons of queer and feminist cultural activity is an empowering action and enables community building. However, there is also an uncertain balance between making these important connections and increasing the visibility of those doing similar work, and the potentialto unintentionally categorise projects in a way that created unnecessary boundaries between cultural activists.

As this section has indicated, the relationship between cultural canons and DIY music is complex and warrants more attention. Many individuals found the selective formation of canons by institutions to be elitist, hierarchical, and not relevant in the cultural context of UK DIY music, which values the practice of doing as much as (or even more than) the resulting outputs. The undervaluing of the process of making and creating is identified through academic research into many DIY endeavours, from home repairs to music and self-publishing (Watson and Shove, 2008; Withers, 2014). To return to De Kosnik's examination of canons in the digital age, in the context of this study it seems more logical to pursue the representation of "canonical practices" (2016, p. 73) rather than canonical objects.

In other contexts, the opportunity to compile and collect was articulated as affirming, and nurtured the development of DIY cultural networks. Groupings of likeminded performers and cultural producers were sometimes referred to as unintentionally canon forming–or had the potential to become canonical when repeatedly used or circulated as a resource by others. In these contexts, individual capacity to create and circulate canons enabled both new connections within current DIY music communities and the opportunity to leave behind evidence and traces for people seeking these connections in the future.

Conflict, erasure and invisibility in DIY historical narratives

The formation of canons necessitates exclusion by the elevation of some materials above others (Assmann, 2008; Cotera, 2015; De Kosnik, 2016). History writing, also, relies on decisions to amplify certain voices often at the expense of others (Turrini, 2013). Archive workers make decisions to afford historical significance to a relatively small proportion of records through appraisal (Harris, 2002; Mbembe, 2002; Stoler, 2002; Cook, 2011; Ishmael, 2018; Bastian and Flinn, 2020). It is, as such, impossible to think about archiving and historicisation without considering potential for erasure and invisibility. This section therefore discusses dimensions of erasure and invisibility which were explored by participants.

The connections between history, archives, power and significance is articulated in the following quote by Kirsty, who reflects about her own experience of conducting research:

> I got so few women saying yes, because they all said oh, well, I'm not important enough, I don't know anything. I don't want to talk. There's this really complicated way in which research and archives all work together to continue to work on this hierarchy of who is and isn't important and is and isn't part of these networks. (Lohman, 2020)

This chapter began with the recent interpretation of punk subcultures by institutions–however, these processes of erasure and (in)visibility also happen within communities due to internal conflicts, manifestations of white supremacy, misogyny and other oppressive behaviours across generations, and/or the undervaluing of individual cultural production. In this sense history and archival practices can reinforce existing hierarchies as often as they problematise others. It is easy to present archival and history making activities that happen within communities through an inherently positive lens in which individuals are empowered into creative practice and cultural activism. However, many of the participants in this research also expressed annoyance, anger and sadness at personal experiences of erasure which happened through history writing, research and archiving undertaken by other community members.

Several individuals involved in the study had experienced direct experiences of erasure from histories written by individuals with prior involvement in DIY music. In the following quote Nazmia describes feelings of anger felt in response to issues around lack of representation that manifested in a recent riot grrrl history:

> there's this person of colour that I worked with... the [riot grrrl music history book] had just come out. This person who was part of that scene and was at those early riot grrrl meetings was completely incensed because the way that [author's] history works is a very white history. And this person who saw themselves as being part of the scene... said that they had been reduced in the narrative to the loud person with big features. I haven't read all the books, I don't know. But if that's how you perceive, that you've been anonymised into this loud person with big features, that is a problem. (Jamal, 2019)

The writing of history can be a form of cultural domination in which specific individuals are centred and others appear forgotten. Assmann refers to processes of active and passive forgetting which occur during processes of canonisation and archiving. The author defines passive forgetting as follows:

> The passive form of cultural forgetting is related to non-intentional acts such as losing, hiding, dispersing, neglecting, abandoning, or leaving something behind. In these cases the objects are not materially destroyed; they fall out of the frames of attention, valuation, and use. (2008, pp. 97–98)

In the case of the above instance, a history of riot grrrl music implicitly centres whiteness by sidelining the involvement of a woman of colour.

The neglecting of the contributions of marginalised individuals thus contributes to gradual cultural forgetting of these histories, while the contributions of white women become canonised and reaffirmed in histories and archives.

Some interviewees expressed anger, fear, or annoyance that their representation within research and histories would be oversimplified or edited into entirely positive, nostalgic narratives. Specific incidents and encounters with other representations, historians, researchers, or archivists had left them feeling like they had no control over the interpretation of their activities. Leigh mentioned a specific interaction with a researcher with academic interest in their former organising collective, saying that

> [the interaction] made me really fucking angry…. it's that classic thing where you take an object and look at the object and you ignore its context, how it was made or anything like that… and also the difficulties and the weight that that object can hold for different people and not exploring that… I don't know what I talked to [academic] about, it might have been maybe one or two email questions that were very specific. But like, I think the quote that [academic] included was just the peppiest thing I think I've ever [said]… and it feels like, it feels like I haven't said that. Like, it feels like I haven't said that! Do you know what I mean? I guess there wasn't much space to really talk about the complexity of that, so I find that stuff really difficult… [and] that's what leaves very simplistic stories about DIY culture (Leigh, 2020)

In this example the representation of Leigh's involvement oversimplified what was a complicated history within DIY music, instead presenting a nostalgic ideal of community (Waterton and Smith, 2010) to which they felt little connection. In relation to processes of revision of Black cultural production, bell hooks describes nostalgia as "a kind of useless act" (1989, p. 17) that has little meaningful consequence for cultural communities. The lack of control over representation in research, histories and/or archives is an issue also discussed by cultural theorists. Hall describes a shift in the way in which heritage is viewed by communities, identifying "a radical awareness by the marginalised of the symbolic power involved in the activity of representation" (1999, pp. 7–8). The power of representation connects explicitly to the power of being archived (or archiving) as explored in earlier sections of this chapter.

The above examples can be understood as instances of "cultural injustice". Fraser defines the term as follows:

> It is rooted in social patterns of representation, interpretation, and communication. Examples include cultural domination (being subjected to patterns of interpretation and communication that are associated with another culture and are alien and/or hostile to one's own); nonrecognition (being rendered invisible via the authoritative representational, communicative, and interpretative practices of one's culture); and disrespect (being routinely maligned or disparaged in stereotypic public cultural representations and/or in everyday life interactions). (1995, p. 71)

Fraser's concept of cultural injustice is applied in the context of popular music heritage by Long et al., who develop the concept into cultural justice (Long et al., 2017, 2020). These authors connect cultural justice to community-led archival practice by utilising the term as

> a critical concept that seeks to capture the manifest and implicit impulses of democratised practices, apparent in the formation and content of archives. (2020, p. 63)

Whilst I agree with the capacity for histories to provide cultural justice, community histories can also cause or contribute to experiences of harm via exclusion, minimisation or misrepresentation. The way in which cultural injustice manifests in the historicisation of these spaces and communities, especially internally within communities, is underexplored in academic research about the intersections of music, cultural memory and heritage. In the context of critical feminism and archives, Cifor and Wood write that

> Community archives have tremendous potential when they are developed critically for and with communities in which they are engaged. However, these same community archives can easily and do frequently serve to produce and reproduce hierarchies and exclusions through their processes and interpretations of records and collections that reify damaging and unjust social structures. (2017, p. 21)

Community-led archival practice is commonly positioned in opposition to "traditional" archives, but in doing so arguably these activities are viewed through a positive and uncritical lens which does not consider the potential for these initiatives to also perpetuate harmful practices.

Conflict is common in the community context of UK DIY music, and indeed within broader communities centred around activism and/or cultural production. Abuse and harm perpetuated within music communities have received mainstream media coverage in recent years with disclosures of abuse reported on from mainstream music industries and DIY/punk communities (Flanagan, 2017; Anonymous, 2018; O'Connor, 2018; Bowcott and Snapes, 2019). Many participants in this study informally reflected on how their histories of involvement in DIY cultural communities had involved either direct experience of conflict, harm, harassment and/or abuse, and/or organising against such incidents. The manifestation of conflict and abuse within broader activist communities has been explored by academics and writers (Chen, Dulani and Lakshmi Piepzna-Samarasinha, 2016; Downes, Hanson and Hudson, 2016; Downes, 2017). Of left social movements, Downes writes that

> emphasis on the State as 'the powerful' can lead to a tendency to locate the source of oppression outside immediate circles. This can obscure inequalities (of race, class, gender, sexuality, immigration status, age and disability) and conceal silencing strategies at work from inside social justice movements and disciplinary communities. (2017, p. 35)

Social movements and grassroots cultural communities, often forming in response or opposition to other communities or oppressive forces, tend to represent themselves as "safe spaces". As Downes et al. write,

> a legacy of being marginalised and subjected to state repression and scrutiny has led radical activist communities to develop important self-protective strategies to establish trust and belonging. (2016, p. 1)

As such the manifestation of conflict, harm and/or abuse in these spaces can be a shock, and leave communities ruptured and individuals isolated and/or silenced.

The themes of conflict, abuse, and harm were explored in relation to the formation of histories and archives. Colette described how information about abusers is passed around (often verbally) within queer and/or feminist punk networks:

> there's something quite interesting within [the] queer and female punk scene, circles of sharing information about abusers and knowing that that information is quite delicate and that ... there's often certain lines of consent from survivors... it often can be like I don't want this to be like publicly known but I want like women and queer people in our friendship groups to know….

Cassie articulates the challenges of including these narratives in archives and histories:

> Especially in the DIY scene when so much of what we do is so personal, that people might be more reluctant to put down their experiences or ... especially when we're organising around an incident that's happened at a venue, like, someone's been sexually assaulted, our ability to archive that in a way that isn't like anonymous

There are significant ethical implications around preservation of and access to survivor narratives, which rely on embedding an ethics of care (Caswell and Cifor, 2016) or survivor-centred archival practice (Caswell, 2014c). In relation to riot grrrl histories and archives, Keenan and Darms also highlight the different between community and archive spaces:

> The relationship of these two "publics"—the public from whom these personal papers are drawn and the public who uses the collection—raises questions about access, privacy, and privilege, as well as the protected but complex nature of the safe space that Riot Grrrl sought to establish and that the archive mirrors. (2013, p. 57)

The change in context from the intimate information sharing within UK DIY music communities to unknown but potential archival users, researchers and/or historians is significant. I have previously identified safety and trust as similarly key in archiving of queer zine histories (Fife, 2019c), and other researchers have discussion this in relation to activist archives (Allard and Ferris, 2014; WIlliams and Drake, 2017; Fife, Flinn and Nyhan, 2023). Engaging with conflict and harm in archives and histories of UK DIY music communities requires more intimacy and care than is traditionally expected of archivist-donor relationships.

Representational belonging

The final two sections of this chapter examine how archives and histories can positively impact or transform the experiences of those active in UK DIY music communities. This section explores the significance of the presence of UK DIY music communities within archives and histories. Using Caswell, Cifor and Ramirez's concept of representational belonging (2016), I explore how the persistence of cultural and community legacies impacts positively on individuals through the generation of connections and feelings of belonging, identification, and visibility.

In relation to community building through queer punk fanzine networks in the 1990s, Fenster writes that

> The struggle over the formation and meaning of identity, then, is literally a politics of position, a fight to constitute a meaningful group and individual identity that enables self-definition and, if constructed at the group level, political efficacy in the ability to gain recognition, represent itself, and make demands for rights. This is particularly important for dominated groups whose cultural practices are marginalised (1993, p. 89)

Throughout this section I will argue that archival representation on the terms of individual community members can be an important part of amplifying and affirming the identity and cultural activisms. Individuals undertaking archive or history projects about their own activities identified this work as a form of resistance against experiences of erasure, misrepresentation, or invisibility.

For archival theorist Yeo, records are "persistent representations" (2018, p. 130). The concept of

> representations—and ideas about representation—can help us to comprehend the material and social world in which we live and to make sense of many aspects of human behaviour and experience. (Yeo, 2018, p. 130)

Understanding records through this lens of representation reflects the situated and constructed nature of any archival trace, and the concept of persistence is relevant to the motivations underpinning work and projects. For several participants in this study, individual documentary projects such as photography or zine making created persistent traces of communities and spaces. For example, Bill reflected about zine making when asked about whether any of their own work could be considered as a record:

> I think there's always an element of that because it's about documenting something that you don't see anywhere else, even if it's just for the now... you are sort of writing it into being and then it endures

Scholarship exploring activist archival work has highlighted the importance of archives in knowledge production and circulation. In reference to feminist archives, Eichhorn writes that the creation of archives has become integral to how knowledges are produced and legitimised and how feminist activists, artists, and scholars make their voices audible. (2013, p. 3)

The above practice amplifies the visibility of what is personally significant and valuable, especially when archives and historical research have historically excluded their contributions. The act of writing down can thus be understood as the creation of a persistent representation of an activity, which can then be utilised both by community members and within more formal institutions.

Referring to the experiences of children of colour unable to find representations of themselves in schoolbooks, Marian Wright Edelman famously asserted that "it's hard to be what you can't see". As she reflects

> When we think about what it is to be 'connected,' we think about memory. We think about history. We think about storytelling. All of these words that we hear— 'literacy,' 'inclusion,' 'diversity'—those are all words for connection . . . When I say to people 'why do we need to have diverse books?' it's not because necessarily everybody needs to see themselves reflected in every book, but because we need that sense of connection. (2015)

In 2016, I participated in an event which referenced Wright Edelman's words–You Can't Be What You Can't See: DIY Musicians Talk Identity, Gender and Performing–produced as part of First Timers by Bryony Beynon, which was later converted into a zine of the same name by a small group of the participants (Brown et al., 2016). In the zine Beynon writes of the significance of

> people discovering that they can access this power [of making music] all the time, even after years of punk life, years of being told ex or implicitly that no, not them. (2016, p. 3)

Wright Edelman's quote indicates the power of that implicit no–that you can't be in positions of power or in certain spaces because you never see those representations of people of colour doing those roles. The assertion that you can be the representation you want to see in the world is held close by many involved in UK DIY music communities, who were inspired to start making music and organising by seeing other marginalised people on stage.

In an archival context this notion also relates to the "symbolic annihilation" of marginalised groups from the archival record (Caswell, 2014b). Gosselar, in relation to archiving black student-led campus activism in university archives, writes that

> people of colour—and their mistreatment—are often erased or excluded from the mirrors that the white culture in power holds up to itself in the media, in memorials and in the archival record. (2018, p. 93)

Processes of symbolic annihilation in archival practice are also addressed in a number of other community heritage contexts including queer heritage (Brown, 2020; Taves Sheffield, 2020), fat activism (Pratt, 2018) and archives of state violence (Solis, 2018). The establishment of independent community archives can be a response to these exclusions (Caswell, Cifor and Ramirez, 2016, p. 57). Activism against invisibility and erasure in archives can also be undertaken within a specific community heritage context–for example, Brown explores volunteer efforts to transform the Canadian Lesbian and Gay Archives into a more intersectional and trans inclusive space (2020).

When asked about the value of archival work or archives for UK DIY music communities, participants in interviews reflected on the value of archives and history to provide representations and connections across generations. This was particularly the case for people of colour, women and queers, who had felt previously marginalised within DIY music communities. For instance, Cassie reflected that

> Archiving is a form of representation… Say in 30 years time, there's another brown queer kid who's like oh, there was once this brown queer woman in this band, how cool that would be? And hopefully, there'll be loads more by then, I won't be one of the only ones then. I'm not the only one. It's a form of role modelling in a way that I reckon, like, it is embarrassing to think of yourself as a role model sometimes, but you have to remember that I never saw a brown queer fat women in a punk band when I was younger. And it's like, well, okay, let's be that representation that you wanted, or you wanna see, and if we can archive that power in some way, wouldn't that be amazing? One for the history books. (Agbehenu, 2019)

For Cassie, archiving provided an opportunity for connection in the absence of opportunity to make these connections with those around her. As Caswell et. al. write, in this sense "connection to the past can be a survival strategy that enables people to counter feelings of erasure and isolation" (2017, p. 5). The representation of personal experiences in archives thus provides the potential for cross-generational dialogue and connection.

Belonging, representation and connection in history underpinned many of the interviews in this study. For Nazmia, the deposit of her own archive at Glasgow Women's Library enabled the representation of people of colour in histories of queer and feminist cultural organising of the early 2000s:

> I think for me, it is just this exercise in saying, I was there, we were there, and we weren't just visiting, we created a lot of the space. And I think that having spent a lot of time feeling like when I first came into kind of post-riot grrrl scene and Ladyfest, it really felt like, in London, because I was the only person of colour that was involved in that core group … that meant that I was leaving quite a lot of myself at the door in order to feel like I was part of queer space …. I felt like I was just being the exception that proved the rules of that space was white and middle class. And that just isn't true. (Jamal, 2019)

Nazmia's assertion that women and queer people of colour were not only present but central to the operation and flourishing of these communities indicates how representation is often not enough–instead the deposit of her archive enabled a nuanced and detailed representation of the involvement of herself and her peers within these communities. In reference to representation of QTIPOC individuals in film and media Ziyad states

> We say 'representation matters,' but we rarely ask: to whom? What kind of representation matters? Representation in front of which audiences matters? How does it matter? These are the critical questions left out when the catch-phrase [representation matters] is used without intention, questions that illuminate a necessary and more nuanced look at how we as Black people define ourselves in relation to the world viewing us. (2017)

In Nazmia's comments above, existing representations of people of colour were viewed as inadequate, and the deposit of materials enabled better and more complex representations of their involvement. As Caswell et al. write, this can be understood as the power to "'imagine otherwise'" through taking control over the representation of a community's own past, constructing narratives of current work and anticipating future liberation (2017, p. 6).

Individual and community action to create persistent traces and to utilise archives and histories as places of connection and representation is common in the broader context of community-led heritage (Flinn, 2007, 2010; Stevens, Flinn and Shepherd, 2010; Baker, 2016; Cantillon, Baker and Buttigieg, 2017; Caswell et al., 2017; Zavala et al., 2017; Bastian and Flinn, 2020; Brown, 2020; Popple, Prescott and Mutibwa, 2020a; Taves Sheffield, 2020). Caswell et al. coined the term "representational belonging" to refer to

> the ways in which community archives give those left out of mainstream repositories the power and authority to establish and enact their presence in archives in complex, meaningful, and substantive ways. (2016, p. 74)

Community archives can have a multi-faceted impact on the wellbeing of individuals and communities through the assertion of their presence in history, which in turn

> asserts identities in the present, allowing individuals "to suddenly see themselves existing" in ways they previously could not and did not. (Caswell, Cifor and Ramirez, 2016, p. 75)

For the above quoted individuals, archives, histories and documentary work served to assert their belonging, particularly in the face of direct experiences of marginalisation in both current DIY music communities and in histories and archives of these movements.

This section has explored how individuals within UK DIY music spaces have harnessed documentary, history, and archival tools to challenge erasures and produce more complex representations. Through the exploration of the impact of such work, I have demonstrated the "ontological shift from not being/not existing/not being documented to being/existing/being documented" (Caswell, Cifor and Ramirez, 2016, p. 70) and the affective significance of undertaking the documentation of one's own history. This significance is shared between the context of this study and many other community-led heritage endeavours, in which marginalised individuals and communities seek to tell and regain control over their own story.

Archival accountability and multiplicity

After exploring the ways in which archives can cause harm, this section asks if they can instead be used to engage directly with these issues. By exploring alternatives suggested by interviewees, I argue that by working differently to create them, archives can form sources of learning, accountability and solidarity across generations.

Many participants in this study were motivated by a desire to create alternatives to traditional canons or historical narratives. For example, Ben described

> how important it is for us to find unearthed scenes and people and [write] our own histories or like people's histories that don't fit the official version. (Perkins, 2019)

Ben's comments connect to the motivations of many community archivists or historians—who create or enable others to tell their own histories. In reference to web memorials, Hess refers to the "struggles over public memory... found between institutional and vernacular versions of contested national narratives" (2007, p. 815). In this context, it seemed often that what individuals wanted was less the opportunity to write a definitive history of UK DIY music, but the proliferation of resources to enable everyone to contribute a perspective.

DIY music communities are sprawling networks of connections, in which collective work of many hands make things happen without access to formal musical training, industry support, or other resources. Colette reflected about the way in which autonomous space DIY Space for London was created collectively:

> there's a bit of pride in like I created it myself about that, like, I think there's something that DIY space like four, five years later that ... people who walk in now like the walls and roof's already there, before we opened, we were like, you know, god imagine if we had a space like this (Colette, 2019)

The necessity of multiple hands in such projects means that there is no single story of UK DIY music to be told—what might be transformative for one individual can also be harmful for another. For example, Bryony reflected that

> it all for me really comes down to storytelling and I think resigning oneself to or becoming at peace with the fact that there is clearly no

> one single story to be told when it comes to any physical space that is created because everyone who goes into that space or is part of that space experiences it from a different standpoint. I think that all sort of histories around anything to do with it are slippery and that is okay. (Beynon, 2020)

Memories of events, spaces and communities can be complicated, and to represent these through an entirely positive gaze is insufficient. Cotera, writing about digital archiving of chicana feminism, discourages the desire to tidy up historical narratives, writing that

> to tame this rhizomatic archive—forcing it to conform to a singular interpretive frame that might smooth over its productive sprawl and its unruly contradictions— would be to diminish it in a way that would inevitably enact new erasures. (2015, pp. 787–788)

Hall calls for archives to be

> rich, varied and in a sense 'eclectic' enough to bear the weight of different contested interpretations and to allow them to battle out their differences in relation to the different texts and inter-texts which the archive itself makes available. (2001, p. 92)

Rather than seeking linear narratives of DIY music communities, we might instead see the "slippery" and subjective nature of individual histories as a strength–that multiplicity of experience enables dialogue through and across different archives.

In their examination of queer subcultural histories, Halberstam calls for subcultural historians and archivists to "look at the silences, the gaps, and the ruptures in the spaces of performance, and… use them to tell disorderly narratives" (2005, p. 187). The holding of positive and negative emotions together was desired by participants–for example, Leigh referred to the harmful impact of the breakdown of collectives and friendships which formed a crucial part of their own personal history of involvement within DIY music:

> What I learned through… moving around scenes that have older people and being drawn to older people is that actually you can do this for a really fucking long time, and you can actually do this better, and that was a massive lesson for me to learn because after [collective] broke down for me in like 2009 I just thought I would never do any of this stuff ever again. Like it was all just a fucking lie

Figure 4 Antisocial memory

and I hate everything and everyone… so I think that was really restorative and I think that's a big part of why we should remember these things in their horrible complexity. (Leigh, 2020)

Holding negative and positive experiences simultaneously can therefore enable recovery through archival or history-writing practices.

Building on the exploration of the "anti-social" in queer history by Halberstam (2008), Reading calls for the "conceptual recognition of an antisocial memory assemblage" (2020, p. 280). In her examination of digital memory work, Reading argues that histories emphasise the "social" elements of activism, which produce "valorised liberal fantasies of togetherness, of association, of positive remembering" (2020, p. 280). In an interview, Kirsty described how individuals have "massaged our own histories" (Lohman, 2020) into utopian visions of subcultural involvement, which we might situate within this approach. Instead of centring these dimensions of memory, Reading instead calls for the utilisation of "antisocial memory assemblages", which acknowledge that although there will be experiences of "momentary coming together", there are also dimensions which "destroy connections and alliances and eschew companionship" (2020, p. 279). For Reading, social and anti-social elements of activist memory should be utilised together to document movement "successes" along with the "hidden" and anti-social elements, which might include instances of abuse, gendered violence, or conflict in activism. The two held together resist the silencing or misrepresentation of specific experiences.

The inclusion of difficult experiences in histories and archives of UK DIY music also enables current and future generations to learn from history. Researchers have explored the ephemeral nature of queer, feminist and DIY activist histories (Downes, 2010; Dyer, 2012; Chidgey, 2013; Mitchell and McKinney, 2019). The subsequent loss of many of these histories (whether intentional or unintentional) causes a

> discontinuity of history that so often happens when material is ephemeral or marginal… So much information and thinking is lost, and then so much information has to be rediscovered again and again, wasting time and energy that could be used to move forward. (Dyer, 2012, p. 12)

This discontinuity was evident when participants referred to rifts in DIY music communities. Lack of progress were evident when participants discussed manifestations of white supremacy. Cassie describes reactions to those who address the whiteness of punk scenes:

> there are these one-off points where you trigger that conversation and or something really shifted. And everyone's like, oh, shit, we need to talk about racism in the scene and like, and then everyone kind of forgets about it... (Agbehenu, 2019)

The manifestation of white supremacy within activist movements has been explored by social movement scholars (Gorski, 2019), who propose that these instances shorten and curtail the involvement in people of colour within movements—which in turn could cause them to be written out of histories due to shorter terms of cultural activity. With the passage of time, some of these rifts also were positioned as "personal conflicts" rather than manifestations of oppressive behaviour relevant to the whole community. Of one such conflict Nazmia said "we're not going to cast that period of time as a spat between friends, because it wasn't! It was an actual problem". Engaging with instances of harm such as the above through history work allows us to utilise what Waterton and Smith refer to as

> a politically engaged and critical conceptualisation [of community and community heritage]; one that engages with social relationships in all their messiness, taking account of action, process, power and change. (2010, p. 5)

This form of engagement with community enables collective accountability through history.

To use another example in which archival information can be used for learning, I will refer to the common experience of what Halberstam refers to as ""subcultural fatigue"–namely, the phenomenon of burnout among subcultural producers" (2005, p. 157). Burn out is defined by Gorski as

> a chronic condition in which activism-related stress becomes so overwhelming it debilitates activists' abilities to perform their activism effectively or to remain engaged in activism. (2019, p. 668)

Burn out is common when individuals are juggling unpaid creative projects with many other commitments (unless accessing financial support or other resources from other sources) but is elaborated on in a limited amount of research (Downes, 2010). Social movement scholars have drawn attention to burn out in other activist contexts (Chen and Gorski, 2015; Gorski, 2019).

Burn out was commonly experienced by participants in this study. In the following quote Bryony describes the potential value of archiving of internal communications and conflicts for learning:

> the naked frustration or rage or sadness that people feel because they are really invested in this thing [a DIY space], that tends to be in the form of the stuff that is more ephemeral or lost… just thinking about, if someone took the full archive of all the things that are on the organising platform that DIY Space used, they would find, you know, off the top of my head, at least four I'm stepping down I can't handle this anymore resignation statements that were long, big explosive dramas and the idea of learning lessons from people when they feel that they have to do that, so that the wheel just doesn't keep turning with the same mistakes in terms of preventing burn out, [that is] where archives can be incredibly important. (Beynon, 2020)

Colette also referred to conversations between herself and other individuals who had been involved in DIY spaces elsewhere in the UK:

> it's funny talking to friends who've been involved in other projects, or older people who are like, oh that's always what happens and I think there's wonderful naivety in running a space or something that is the reason why you do it in the first place because if everyone tells you all the hard bits, you're not going to do it (Colette, 2019)

These quotes together illustrate the short lived and labour-intensive nature of UK DIY music spaces, often due to a combination of close-knit friendship groups, financial or legal status and reliance on volunteer labour.

We are often drawn to documenting the triumphs and successes of our cultural activisms–and in doing so presenting our histories through a nostalgic gaze. Cifor explores how the endless repurposing of narratives and imagery from 1980s AIDS activist groups (particularly ACT UP) can divert attention away from necessary present action (2017, p. 122). Nostalgic representations of activism ignore social realities, ongoing harm, oppression, and inequality in favour of looking backwards uncritically. This attachment to nostalgic narratives has also typified popular music heritage (Reynolds, 2012; Roberts and Cohen, 2014), which faces different threats (for example, the likelihood of closure of music venues due to gentrification). Cifor proposes that we do not seek to abandon these historical triumphs but instead contextualise past actions in relation to ongoing challenges (2017).

In a similar vein, many of the participants of this study indicated that history and archives were most useful to DIY music communities when they enabled growth through the opportunity to learn from previous mistakes or experiences. Sheffield, writing about the archiving of LGBTQ histories in community-led archives, proposes that community archives can

> become spaces where past, present and future intersect, and where making and connecting in the present is foregrounded. (2020, p. 15)

Shared experiences across generations offer the opportunity for individual and collective reflexivity, learning, accountability and transformation.

This final section has sought to identify alternative ways of using history-writing and archival practice to prevent further harm, be accountable and learn from previous community conflicts. I have proposed that DIY music communities and spaces can make use of archival processes to engender dialogue between current and previous generations, to document, recover from and be accountable in internal community conflicts, and to develop and strengthen new activisms. The archive, in this sense, can be a space of hope, collaboration, recovery and transformation.

Conclusion

This chapter has demonstrated the inherent complexity of historicising and archiving UK DIY music—and that these processes in themselves hold the potential to cause harm. Some responsibility for this harm rests on the selective tradition that underpins frameworks for history writing, curating and archiving in Western society. This in turn requires us to reconsider how archives are formed and histories are written, and to seek alternatives. However, it is also important to highlight the harm that happens when communities themselves reproduce uncritical and limited narratives of DIY music. Although community-led archival projects often have freedom from institutional practices and biases, power is nonetheless exercised in these spaces, contributing to invisibility or misrepresentation of individuals.

The question remains—can we do better? How can we prevent harm and make space in historical narratives for difficult narratives of these spaces and communities, as well as those which emphasise the transformative capability of DIY music? In concluding this section, I am reminded again of interview participant Leigh's reflection that these histories should be remembered in their "horrible complexity" (2020). Without these dimensions included in and engaged with in processes of archiving, we risk the reproduction of the processes critiqued in earlier sections of this chapter. Archival theorists have stressed the capacity of archives to restore, nurture and grow communities through recovery, care and accountability (Caswell, 2014c; Caswell and Cifor, 2016; Sutherland, 2017; Ishmael, 2018). I proposed that representing the complexities of UK DIY music enables the development of these communities into new generations.

This chapter has begun the work of articulating why archives and histories are meaningful in the context of UK DIY music. Ajamu X et al. situate archiving as "a way of achieving some sort of visibility" (2009, p. 280). Cultural theorists, archivists and historians alike highlight the importance of both the ongoing documentation and archiving of subcultural histories, and the right of communities "to be documented and heard on their own terms" (Long et al., 2020). This is particularly important in the context of cultural communities—where representation and visibility can enable the persistence of cultural legacies (and the erasure or gradually forgetting of others). Having established some of the issues that have manifested in historicisation, canonisation and archiving to date, I now move to the actions taken to ensure the persistence of these legacies beyond their short-lived life spans.

For(a)ging Histories
Information Praxis in UK DIY Music Communities

In the title of this chapter, I use the verb "for(a)ging", which references Cowan and Rault's article "Credit for Debt: Queer History-Making and Debt Culture". Referring to the 1997 film *Watermelon Woman*, the authors describe an attachment to the "recuperative and critical feminist and queer storytelling" (2014b, p. 295) explored in Cheryl Dunye's fictional documentary, in which Dunye (playing herself) seeks out information relating to an unnamed black, queer actress listed only as "the watermelon woman" in the credits of several 1930s films. Dunye's research, which is undertaken in libraries, archives and through oral history conversations with elders, is motivated by the desire to find other black queer people in film history. At the end of *Watermelon Woman*, the audience is shown the quote "sometimes you have to create your own history" (*The Watermelon Woman* [DVD], 1997). In the absence of more formal records, the imaginative figure of Fae Richards (or the watermelon woman) stands in for the absent or under-represented black queer lives throughout history. As Kumbier writes, "in order to manifest a history that is present in memory and structures of feeling and absent from the archival record, Dunye exceeds the limits of the archive" (2012, p. 90).

I am drawn to the verb for(a)ging as a combination of both forging (which I understand as creating something or making space) and foraging (the process of searching for something in liminal spaces). For(a)ging can be used as a descriptor for practices which underpin DIY music, and particularly the practices of the participants in this study, who combined a desire to find themselves and community in previous generations of DIY music communities with work to make visible their own work and communities to future generations. The motivations of these communities are shared with other communities and activist movements engaging with heritage. In relation to queer Latino histories, Ramirez writes that archiving can be

> a weapon of evidence against historical erasure and social analysis that fails to consider the experiences of individuals and communities on their own terms. (2005, p. 120)

For many engaged with community heritage, information and archives are valuable tools to ensure the persistence of cultural legacies, and to afford meaning to individual lives and community actions (Mbembe, 2002). As Halberstam writes in relation to queer subcultural heritage,

> the archive is not simply a repository; it is also a theory of cultural relevance, a construction of collective memory, and a complex record of queer activity. (2005, p. 170)

Feminist theorists also situate the archive as an important source of knowledge production (Eichhorn, 2013; McKinney, 2020). This is shared by researchers exploring archives of different activisms (Gordon et al., 2016; Sheffield, 2016; Carter, 2017).

This chapter argues that the experience of searching and locating (or failing to locate) peers in prior generations of DIY music (particularly riot grrrl and queercore), and/or creating traces of your own involvement is an ongoing and central part of involvement in UK DIY music spaces. In relation to performance, Schneider writes that "we understand ourselves relative to the remains we accumulate, the tracks we house, mark, and cite, the material traces we acknowledge" (2001, p. 100). Although the records of DIY music may be different, the desire to create and keep traces remains a central part of how histories are understood and formed in this context. The archive, as such, is not merely a static representation of what has passed, but an important source of information and strategy for the development of activist futures as well as an acknowledgement of activist pasts.

Unauthorised heritage and information praxis

As the preceding chapter explored, the formation of an archive is a source of tension within DIY music communities. This section engages with another tension which requires critical pause: whether any individual projects or actions were archival. I pause here because during interviews, participants rarely identified their work as consciously archival. Instead, often projects were seen as records after their original production. For instance, asked if the podcast she co-produced could be thought of as a record, Cassie reflected:

> I never really thought about in that way, but it is because we're recording a certain point in time, about certain experiences... it's recording a distinct moment in time that we'll never get back again (Agbehenu, 2019)

In the following quote, Ben describes his impressions of activities within UK DIY music communities as "accidentally" archival:

> we all have this kind of accidental thing, I think there's definitely people who ... are archiving, but I wonder if most people back in the day, like to compare to the 70s, 80s, if we're talking punk histories and stuff, also didn't actively archive it, but the way that that stuff is still there and then people are like oh right there's value to this kind of stuff and [are] uploading stuff... (Perkins, 2019)

Others referred to the drive to document as being aligned to their regular use of digital platforms to share information and build community. Social media platforms provide the opportunity to create representations of our everyday life (Humphreys, 2018), which in this context includes experience of participation in DIY music communities. These materials–taking a myriad of forms–document individual experiences, promote events and activities, and share information and resources within networks, therefore often serving an initial purpose which is not archival (until subsequently viewed differently by the creator or others).

There are academic frameworks for understanding popular music heritage which could help to explore the materials and practices in question. In particular, Roberts and Cohen's tripartite model of popular music heritage–authorised, self-authorised and unauthorised heritage–has had significant impact on the development of scholarship in this field. Authorised heritage refers to heritage which has been officially validated by a government body or large heritage organisation, for example by awarding a plaque ((BBC, 2017) or marking on an official register (Roberts and Cohen, 2014, p. 249). Self-authorised heritage refers to community-led, DIY and local music heritage projects in which the process of authorisation of heritage happens through the intentionality of the individual(s)—whether friends, family members, fans, etc... It is self-validating in so far as it is not subject to the official approval of a legitimising institution or panel of experts and peers. (Roberts and Cohen, 2014, p. 249)

Self-authorised projects might seem to emerge in contrast to authorised heritage–however, it can become authorised and legitimised via receiving funding from a national heritage body or being acquired by a larger heritage institution. This can make the initiative more sustainable or larger in scale in the long term As Roberts and Cohen write, "official and self-authorised discourses may, thus, be closely interrelated and reaffirm or contradict one another" (2014, p. 248). The concept of self-authorised heritage frames a large amount of scholarship exploring community-led popular music heritage (e.g., Baker, 2015b, 2016, 2019; Collins, 2015; Collins and Carter, 2015; Collins and Long, 2015; Long, 2015; Withers, 2015; Long et al., 2017; Guthrie and Carlson, 2018; Strong and Whiting, 2018; Cuk, 2021) which is often framed as "DIY" music heritage (Baker, 2016, 2019; Cantillon and Baker, 2018; Long et al., 2020; Cuk, 2021).

Whilst the concept of self-authorised heritage is easy to connect to the establishment of archives within communities, I find it harder to map onto the work being undertaken in the context of my own study, which is rarely explicitly named as archival or part of heritage structures. Instead, in this chapter I turn to unauthorised heritage or heritage-as-praxis as a way of understanding the work of those in this study. Heritage-as-praxis or unauthorised heritage is described as outside of the boundaries, definitions and rhetoric of heritage. As they write,

> Perhaps a distinction between 'little h' heritage and 'big H' Heritage is apposite here. 'Little h' heritage does not draw attention to itself; indeed, for the most part it gets by without even an awareness that it is heritage. Abstracted from practice—from spatio-temporal grounding in the everyday—heritage-as-praxis transmutes to heritage-as-object. (Roberts and Cohen, 2014, p. 257)

To expand on this, I'll use the example of a zine made by an individual about their experiences and history in a local music scene. A changing context–e.g. moving a zine from an autonomous space's "free books" shelf to shelves in an archive store–can change an item from heritage-as-praxis to heritage-as-object by affording it a different type of value. However, before this movement the zine could be considered as an example of unauthorised heritage–although the author might not name their intentions explicitly as heritage (and they might actively dislike this notion), they could still be motivated by a drive to preserve, document, share or reference the cultural memory of UK DIY music communities. Thus, even when disconnected from heritage as a concept or sector, they could still be doing the work of archiving.

This ambivalent relationship between community-led history, memory or information work and the concept of heritage is not unique in DIY music. Sheffield describes how those working in LGBTQ+ community heritage projects might not self-identify with the term "archivist" (2016). Zine maker and cultural activist Osa Atoe similarly talks back to being positioned as an archivist in an interview with Elizabeth Stinson (Atoe cited in Stinson, 2012, pp. 263–264). Aware of these instances, I am reluctant to describe anyone in this study as an "archivist" unless they feel connected to the role themselves, and instead use the concept of unauthorised heritage to explore work done primarily outside of formal archival spaces.

There has been limited exploration of what heritage-as-praxis looks like in scholarship about popular music heritage. Strong and Whiting describe the common practice of "post-gig" posters in music venues as one example (Strong and Whiting, 2018). This practice has not been explored as extensively by scholars because music venues are not viewed as archival spaces. However Strong and Whiting propose that these displays

> shape notions of musical place and space, and the scenes they are part of, while also creating a sense of the venues' embeddedness in the collective memory and history of the musical past. (2018, p. 152)

The emphasis on authorised and self-authorised heritage within popular music heritage research inevitably situates heritage at the interface of institutions and communities. At this position, many question whether heritage is a productive framework for memory-motivated work in music communities (Roberts and Cohen, 2014, p. 15). However, I orient my project from a different position and instead seek to surface the ways in which DIY music community members engage with their pasts, thus decentring the heritage institution in my analysis.

To explore unauthorised heritage in my data, I reviewed interview data to locate what people did with information about their involvement in DIY music–or information practices. I chose to focus on practices because I was aware of archival scholarship which emphasises the performative and ritualistic nature of archival work (Cook and Schwartz, 2002). Lymn describes archiving as a series of "repetitive actions" which preserve "particular orientations and understandings" (2014, p. 407). Cook and Schwartz describe how the rituals of archival work construct a professional identity and traditional archival spaces (2002, pp. 176–177).

In Foucault's work on power and knowledge (1972, 1991), in institutions these practices cement the relationship between knowledge and power, producing the historical narratives viewed as truth (1972, p. 146) dividing the archival from the non-archival and professional and amateur archival practices. However, when undertaken in tandem with critical reflection and as forms of resistance, I posit that these practices become forms of information praxis.

The concept of praxis has resonance across numerous contexts in which information is used to enable social transformation. Following Marxist interpretations of the world, critical archival theorists have explored the idea of "archival praxis" in community-led archive projects (Cotera, 2015; Caswell, Punzalan and Sangwand, 2017; Kelleher, 2017; Agostinho, 2019; Ghaddar and Caswell, 2019; Sutherland, 2019; Alto and McKemmish, 2020; Emswiler, 2020; Lee, 2020; Campbell, 2021). Ghaddar and Caswell summarise decolonial archival praxis as

> archival praxis [which] considers how archives emerge through multifaceted global processes and structures, and are embedded within larger discursive formations, in which multiple cultural sites, texts and contexts are active. (2019, p. 78)

For Lee, archival praxis involves a combination of deep reflection, imagination and changing of practices to amplify histories of non-dominant communities (2020, p. 30). Archival praxis might involve undertaking rituals which exceed the narrow definition of the archive—for example, Ishmael et al. situate intangible cultural festivals (e.g. Notting Hill Carnival) in opposition to white Western archival drive to "capture" (2020, p. 211). Archival praxis is used to refer to the critically-engaged collections management decisions (e.g. post-custodialism or repatriation) (Kelleher, 2017) or establishing an archive to counteract historical absences within institutional archives (Cowan, McLeod and Rault, 2014; Cotera, 2015). The concept of praxis can therefore be used to group together actions taken with the intention of transforming archives—either through the establishment or imagination of alternative forms of history making, or through decisions made to radically re-orient archival practice in organisations.

Information praxis is used to describe information and communication practices strategies employed across settings (Nathan, 2012; Cifor, Montoya and Ramirez, 2016; Lee and Ting, 2017; Dunbar et al., 2022; Naicker, 2022; Nguyen, 2022; O'Driscoll and Bawden, 2022; Roy et al., 2022).The notion of praxis in library and information studies frames a special issue of *Education for Information* edited by Dunbar et. al, which examines the application of critical race theory and praxis to library and information sector work (Dunbar et al., 2022). This issue examines interventions in white supremacy in library and information work including positive action in workforce development (Nguyen, 2022), evidence appraisal (Naicker, 2022), and collections development (O'Driscoll and Bawden, 2022; Roy et al., 2022). Although the scholarship in this field is heavily weighed towards professional information environments and the education of those in this sector, praxis is also used to refer to ways in which communities and movements strategically and critically employ information to enable transformation. For example, in their examination of information praxis in Hong Kong's umbrella movement, Lee and Ting describe how activists employ "communicative strategies... to seek, evaluate, produce, and disseminate information, as well as to mobilise participation in collective action" (2017, p. 108). Similarly to archival praxis, information practice is motivated by "working in service for the benefit of communities of resistance" (Dunbar et al., 2022, p. 279).

I use praxis as a focus when exploring authorised heritage so as to divert attention from sources (e.g., the example of a zine or posters in venues) to behaviours and actions. This shifts my analysis away from defining the scope of records of DIY music, and towards a greater understanding of what these behaviours mean, and how they contribute towards the construction of DIY cultural memory. This focus also highlights the role of work in the construction of archives which, as Hall writes, do not arise "out of thin air" (2001, p. 89) but are instead formed through labour of individuals (Sheffield, 2016). The radical political underpinning of praxis, in which action results in social transformation, also informs the way in which information, documentation and archiving are viewed as forms of "intervention" (Appadurai, 2003, p. 16).

My analysis surfaced a series of activities which I situate under the umbrella of information praxis: searching; creating; keeping/caring;

forming; sharing and referencing/use. In coding these actions, I was conscious to use the language used by participants to describe practices instead of relying upon professional descriptors (for example, keeping instead of preservation). This follows the tradition of in vivo coding which emphasises the spoken words of participants (Manning, 2017, p. 1). In this context, the decision to build this category through the language used by participants allowed me to identify work happening (often at small scale, by individuals or local collectives) without then situating those actions through language developed through institutional traditions.

It is possible to frame this series through frameworks already developed through recordkeeping theory—for example, Upward's records continuum model (1996, p. 19, 1997), which has been used to contextualise the use of records within some community settings (Newman, 2012; Caswell, 2014a; Karabinos, 2015). Although the identified actions can be framed through the dimensions of the records continuum model, criticisms of the model warrant attention. The records continuum model was developed within an organisational recordkeeping context and assumes that records will be created as by-products of activity (Piggott, 2012). The inaccessibility of the language used to describe the model is criticised by some theorists (Piggott, 2012, p. 180), and the language used also fails to capture the affective dimension of recordkeeping work. Taken together, these criticisms highlight how, as Piggott writes,

> The innumerable contexts of document and record creation and non-creation defined in truly culturally inclusive ways cannot be fully represented in a model not primarily intended to theoretically address them. (2012, p. 188)

Wehr identifies how resistance to control from professions and professionalism is central to DIY cultural ideology (2012, p. 2). It therefore feels inappropriate to attempt to frame this work through models created in these contexts. With these criticisms in mind, I developed an alternative model which could more successfully encapsulate information praxis in community settings, using the descriptions of actions articulated by participants.

The following diagram connects the identified activities in a circular process. Individual practices can be connected to each other within this process through a shared motivation to find and forge space for community memory. In relation to emergent archival activity on Australian community Facebook groups, Gibbons writes that

> There is a sense that something is being preserved by the intention and stories being told by the description and actions. The archival nature of the space is not about permanence or enduring qualities but more concerned with constructing a space for documenting and sharing identity and memory over time (however long that is). (2019)

Similarly, in this project's context the identified practices only occasionally overlap with work done in institutional settings, but nonetheless represent labour being done within communities which is motivated by the sharing of information, memory, and history. These practices, done at micro or larger scales, actively space within which DIY cultural memory can persist. The next sections of this chapter use interview data and primary source analysis to describe and critically explore each of the stages in more detail.

Figure 1 Diagram representing forms of praxis identified during data analysis

Figure 2 Information praxis (original illustration)

Searching (foraging)

I was an isolated queer teenager in the early 2000s, and as such I spent a lot of my time online trying to find and connect with others. At the time this was a source of embarrassment, due to the shady reputation of message boards, as well as the knowledge that I was doing this because I struggled to make friends locally. Many participants shared this experience. Following discussion of her journey into DIY music communities, Ruth reflected

> this point where you find a way in... it was weird because... and that's why such a long story felt important to me, it was almost like I was searching for something and I didn't know what it was. (Pearce, 2019)

Whilst many interviewed for this project discussed using internet-based technologies to find connections, earlier generations used Teletext, personal ads or letters pages in magazines and fanzines. In reference to 1990s queer punk fanzines, Fenster writes that letters published in zines

> express a sense of not belonging, of wanting to share musical and cultural tastes with others without being able to find those others in a local community. (1993, p. 79)

Letters sections can be understood as fostering an "emancipatory possibility... [or] a focal point for a dispersed community" (Fenster, 1993, pp. 79–80). Researchers exploring the textual communities that form through zine making identify similar motivations (Eichhorn, 2001; Sinor, 2003, p. 244). The experience of foraging for others is core to the development and operation of UK DIY music communities, especially sub-sections informed by shared minoritised identities.

The desire to find others was also undertaken through historical research. Participants described searching for activists of similar identity intersections from earlier generations. This was particularly important for the queer people of colour who participated in interviews for this research, who were unable to easily connect with others within communities. For example, Nazmia says of her own desire to connect with other QTIBIPOC activists:

> I spent a lot of time digging and finding out of print books and finding out about OWAAD, hunting down Pratibha Parmar's films, and then making Pratibha Parmar my friend, and reading about Sunil

Gupta and being like you are now going to be my friend, and you are now my elders that I have made... so I think, for me, knowing people who come from the generation above is really, really integral to the way that I live my life... I did a lot of work to find the five or six books that were written about the period of the 70s and 80s when queer brown and black activism was happening in this country in a way that included lesbians explicitly (Jamal, 2019)

For Nazmia, the act of foraging for community through history was a method of connection with elders and finding/making community across generations of cultural activism. Of searching for black, queer histories, Ajamu X, Campbell and Stevens write that

"Sifting" the past to recover "what isn't there but was" is not just a solitary reflective endeavour for individuals from disinherited groups, it can also be an act of collective rebellion (2009, p. 272)

The whiteness of punk subcultures has been explored by researchers (Duncombe and Tremblay, 2011; Nguyen, 2012b, 2015; Hanson, 2017), and the potential for erasure of the stories of people of colour from histories and archives was explored in my previous chapter. For Nazmia, history became a space through which she was able to find queer activists of colour, in the absence of encountering others from similar backgrounds within contemporary music communities.

Bill also shared experiences of searching for archival traces of queer and feminist music subcultures as part of previous postgraduate research.

I remember I did a Master's dissertation about riot grrrl and I at that time found it so difficult to get hold of any of the zines. And I mean, maybe that's just because at that time it was just prior to me being kind of connected to people who would probably know how to get hold of those things. But I just couldn't find any. I knew it existed, I'd read about things, but it didn't seem to exist anywhere in a sort of archive and that's partly why we thought at Ladyfest that we would archive things. (Savage, 2019)

This quote speaks to experiences articulated by queer feminist historians and researchers. McKinney and Mitchell write of their own searches for lesbian-feminist art:

This anecdote describes a familiar situation for lesbian-feminist art. If you missed it, it doesn't exist, either because these works are by women, or lesbians, or queers or because they are so unsustainable in their ambitious scales and modest institutional supports that they only seem to be in the world for brief moments. (2019, p. 10)

As Bill articulates, many within communities know of the existence of events, sources or activities in queer feminist cultural activism–however, they are not necessarily represented in archive or library collections (and those that are may not be catalogued at all, or may be less visible due to their content or internal biases), and thus require additional work to find.

One of the most common fears expressed was about the potential future loss, erasure or forgetting of the activities of current organising groups. Stephanie articulates how this anxiety has motivated a festival collective to more actively document their activities:

> I worry a lot about archiving, cos there's no way that Decolonise Fest is the first festival for people of colour in the UK, there's no way. So that means that someone else did something, and then it didn't get archived, it didn't get documented. And it's kind of scary to know that your history and your work can just get wiped out so quickly …. At Decolonise Fest what we really want is to make sure that we get our things sorted… because I think unless you archive it, people are gonna say it never happened, and I definitely want to make sure people know, in 10, 20 years' time that this definitely happened, and not only did it happen, it was popular!

Ruth also identified her band's (Not Right) motivation to make their own history accessible via a website as motivated by awareness of previous loss and recovery of queer, trans and feminist histories:

> I felt like histories were important and having a sense of where you came from, because the line from Bikini Kill to Not Right, it's not that straightforward… I was inspired by reading The F Word pieces. I realised there were all these fucking histories that were getting disappeared. And I felt that about trans stuff as well, all these histories got disappeared. So with the punk stuff, I felt similar. (Pearce, 2019)

Chidgey describes how "activist ephemera and accounts of feminist individuals, groups and actions continually run the risk of being lost from the historical record and public memory" (2013, p. 659). Stephanie and Ruth's respective reflections show awareness of the legacy of loss of activist histories, and the need to take action to assign historical value to activities in the moment rather than retrospectively.

Individual documentary projects (zines, podcasts, blogs, websites) were viewed as beacons of information that could provide those important connections. For example, Joe reflected:

> if you can reach someone that wants to be involved in it, or has some kind of yearning, or is isolated but has this kind of connection to punk… I don't think that punk needs to do particular outreach in terms of getting people into it, because not everyone has to be into punk… but I think it needs to be open to people to find (Briggs, 2019)

Ruth also said of her band Not Right's website,

> I think this stuff is still not necessarily easy to find. I still see people stumble into it, and I think one of the things I was trying to do is almost put out a beacon being like, we're here, because it was so important to me to find this, so it was almost like I want other people to feel that they can find this. (Pearce, 2019)

Documentary strategies such as zine writing, websites and the publication of photography serve multiple purposes: they act as a persistent trace of DIY music communities and a method of community-building through creating points of access to information. Comparisons can be drawn between this context and McKinney's exploration of information projects that developed through lesbian networks. These are described as "information activism", generated by "women who responded to their frustrated desire for information about lesbian history and lesbian life by generating that information themselves" (McKinney, 2020, p. 2). The capacity of such projects to create connections is particularly important to those who are searching for points of access to DIY cultures.

This section has identified shared experiences of searching for connection. The quotes in this section have indicated how history and archives can be used as a source of connection, especially for those feeling isolated or marginalised within current UK DIY music spaces. In turn, the work of individuals to create connections through documentation enables the passing on of cultural legacies of DIY creative practice even where no explicit connections are made. Having shared these experiences of searching for space (and particularly safer spaces), connection and representation, I now move on to explore the activities undertaken by these individuals to create this space.

Creating (forging)

Creating—a core aspect of participation in DIY culture—helps to demystify skills and knowledge, empower individuals and build connections which resist societal alienation (Wehr, 2012, p. 6). The creation of information sources is a valuable element of the information infrastructure of music communities—especially for communities which are otherwise invisible or misrepresented in media and rely upon these alternative sources (Campbell and Stitski, 2018, p. 245). These sources are sometimes also afforded value as archival records, either through the process of creation or through retrospective reflection. The following examples illustrate how participants created sources, and the underpinning motivations between these practices.

Participants used a diverse array of practices to create information sources, including photography, film making, artwork, scrapbooking, zine making, publishing, recording music releases and the production of ephemera (including merchandise, fliers, and posters).These examples often demonstrated a close connection between the use of technologies and histories, which aligns with previous research identifying intimate relationship between activists and new media technologies (Harding, 1998; Eichhorn, 2013; Caswell and Mallick, 2014; WIlliams and Drake, 2017; Sheffield, 2018).

When motivated by history, these activities can be positioned as memory practices—which Sturken defines as "an activity that engages with, produces, reproduces and invests meaning in memories, whether personal, cultural or collective" (2008, p. 74). Sturken positions memory as personal and fluid, highlighting the role of individuals in reproducing and constructing memory. "Technologies of memory" as central to the production of traces, which she views as "increasingly visual technologies" (2008, p. 75). Although the above cluster of documentary practices are a more expansive selection, photography and filmmaking were regularly cited in interviews. Alex reflected about the motivations behind this work:

> people are more and more interested in photography, even like film, recording... I think a couple of Bent Fests [peer] would have recorded it. I think people are very keen to because of the known absence of it and also just to have that feeling of like making something and like carrying a feeling onward. (Trapp, 2020)

The impulse to document histories to prevent potential loss is shared by community-led archive workers, who, as Caswell et al. write, are aware of "the urgent need to undertake this documentation before such stories are lost" (2016, p. 71). The connection between photography, archive and memory is explored in photographic studies in which scholars note the use of the photograph as souvenir and mediator for memory and oral history work (Cross and Peck, 2010; Kuhn, 2010). In this context, photography was an accessible technology which could be used to create a material (or digital) trace of otherwise intangible activities.

The previous reflection suggests that creating is also a way to invest meaning in an activity as it occurs, which is a sentiment that underpinned other examples. On the following page I include a screenshot taken from a YouTube video series titled "Build Progress" produced by DIY Space for London (Build Progress #5: 26th July to 4th August 2015, 2015). The series documents the conversion of a warehouse into a multi-purpose autonomous space through digital time lapse video. The focus of the video on the physical labour involved in the conversion of the space is unique in comparison with the contents of the space's archive (which focuses on the activities and events which went on after the opening). In reference to lesbian information technologies, McKinney describes the "unspectacular labour that sustains social movements" (p. 2). This labour often goes un- or under-documented in the histories and archives of cultural activities (Mitchell and McKinney, 2019) in comparison to performances and recorded outputs. However, in this video we watch the partitions of the space emerge through socialising, manual labour, collaboration, and the skills of many hands, which renders it as a visual manifestation of the organisational politics of the space.

Figure 3 Screenshot taken from build progress #5, video produced via DIY Space for London (DIY Space for London, 2015)

Of the choice to film the development of the space, Bryony reflects:

> In terms of archiving, there was this sense when we got keys to a building and kind of jumped into the sort of countdown mode of oh god, we've got this long rent free and we've got to turn this into something that is a workable space and be able to hold events and have a bar and thus make rent … Whether they were thinking consciously about archiving or not, I don't know, but we were very lucky to have people who were really interested in filming the transformation of the physical space, which means that there are these videos that were made and put out during the kind of build process. There are these three videos that are time lapse shots that I think are incredibly personally precious things because they are this jolting reminder of, yeah, wow we really did that. There's that kind of archiving happening in real time. (Beynon, 2020)

The video is a tangible representation of work done and the conclusion of the space's prior fundraising campaign. The choice to film this process is also assigning value to the space's existence from its outset. Sheffield refers to the concept of "archival optimism" which is defined as

> the notion that we engage collectively in archival work because we have a sense of confidence in a future that will recognise the shared heritage that we build. (Taves Sheffield, 2020, p. 5)

The action to film the space from the outset shows this sense of shared confidence that these actions will be of importance in the future.

Zines and writing were also commonly utilised to document DIY music communities. Some participants made zines to share information or document local scenes. Tayyab said:

> I'd been involved in like putting on community events through the Leeds Uni music library… We kicked off by, in time for the freshers fair we actually made a zine that was all about the Leeds music scene. And I guess there we were archiving specifically mainly just to market it to the people new to the city. (Amin, 2019)

The role of independent magazines in music communities is explored by Campbell and Stitski in relation to hip hop music communities, who describe how street magazines provided an informal grassroots infrastructure during a period in which the genre was misrepresented in

the background labour of cultural activism is undervalued and underdocumented in our histories.

like painting walls

replying to emails

or getting everyone in the same room

not another doodle poll!

Figure 4 Background labour (original illustration)

the mainstream media. The resulting sources share information, document the community for future generations, and promote culture within contemporary networks (2018, p. 244). Similar motivations are articulated in McKinney's examination of lesbian newsletter networks (McKinney, 2020) and Leonard's examination of the use of zines in riot grrrl networks (Leonard, 1997, p. 238).

Other participants expressed a clearer link between zine making and archiving. In his second photography zine *Screaming Fatal Truths II*, Joe Briggs writes that

> People associate the act of cataloguing something with stasis, but history is not just a dry plod of facts, or it shouldn't be. It's a process unfinished, a marker or warning for what could lie ahead. The act of documenting a scene is not an archiving or an embalming, but a re-affirmation of these things we share, these things that can be created. These places that these gigs happen and these people making this music, or taking it in. (2018, p. 3)

In this quote, the processes of history writing, archiving, and documenting are each represented. Archiving is a way of enforcing stasis or fixity to the archival record, whereas history could be a more fluid and evolving process. This aligns with the "life cycle" model of records management, which is "based on the fact that most records become less useful over time" (Demb, 2012, p. 41). In the above example, documenting is situated as a way to represent, affirm, and communicate possibility to others in the present and the future. Archiving through documenting is not an end to a process, but a continuing and "living" history. Here I return once again to Hall's concept of a "living" archive–living as

> present, on-going, continuing, unfinished, open-ended...This notion of 'living' is strongly counter-posed to the common meaning accorded to 'tradition', which is seen to function like the prison-house of the past. (2001, p. 89)

A zine is created, reprinted and circulated, moving amongst the communities it represents and those seeking connection.

Individuals maintained websites to promote projects and share information. Though these websites were often afforded less value than paper-based traces, some participants engaged with them as digital repositories. For example, Kirsty describes the motivations behind the establishment of her band Not Right's website:

> Early on with the Not Right website, that definitely was set up as a kind of archiving thing. As a band, I think we all like to keep things and have mementos… for a while I ended up not having them anymore, but I would write every set list and then we'd keep them and take photos of them, and we had gig listings with the photos of each setlist and any photos that anybody had taken at the gigs and given us permission to put on the website…. and I think posters for the night so that you can see who else was playing. (Lohman, 2020)

Bandmate Ruth also reflected on the value of the websites she created for Not Right and queer feminist organising collective Revolt:

> I think with Not Right, I never envisaged it ending but now the entire website is an archive. And there was a point when we stopped playing when I realised that was the case and like, I'm happy with that… Similarly with Revolt I'm really happy for this to just sit here and one day someone would be like riot grrrl Coventry, fuck, loads of shit happened, I should do something myself (Pearce, 2019).

Websites were often developed to share information and promote projects through acting as a digital presence. However, over time they were afforded value by individuals as archival spaces of sorts, which could be used to prompt memory for band members and as a source of information and connection for others. Again, here there are parallels between the relationship to cultural memory in both website-building and zine making—for example, Lymn describes the ways in which zines, as traces of practices and lives, also form an archival space (2014).

This section has explored the action of creating representations, which follows logically after periods spent searching for information. I have demonstrated how participants created sources as part of creative practice. These sources can also be motivated by the desire to share information, make connections, and/or document projects, spaces and communities that might otherwise go undocumented. The drive to create and document can be situated as an intervention in existing representation of DIY music communities within media and, later, history writing. This connects to the fear of erasure identified in the previous chapter.

Keeping and/or caring

This section explores actions to keep and/or care for records and information sources. I compare the notion of keeping and caring to the archival practice of preservation, following the lead of critical theorists who engage with new conceptualisations of preservation. There is a regular emphasis on the importance of storage and management in preservation, which implies that preservation is logistical rather than critical (Angell Brown, 2021). Lewis calls for preservation to be understood

> as being about keeping: keeping in the sense of holding and passing on, not in the sense of keeping things the same or keeping things forever. (2018, p. 66)

Similarly, Ishmael et al. describe how cultural participation in Notting Hill Carnival ensures

> that it continues to live on and inspire new generations. It is in this act of living and regeneration that its true preservation occurs. (2020, p. 211)

These point to preservation as beyond a simple "resting" process, instead taking a variety of forms both in and outside of formal repositories. In my analysis, keeping is a personally motivated action taken to enable future re-use.

In the following quote, Leigh describes the use of their filing cabinet to keep materials relating to organising collective Manifesta:

> I was in student housing but I always kept everything that we did... so like fliers and posters and stuff like that... [collective member] kept photos of us doing stuff like going out at night and pasting posters where we shouldn't have. We were just really into it [laughs] [...] at the time, we had photos where you would print them out and you'd get them developed and that's why I ended up with shoe boxes full of photos of us doing just weird shit. And yeah, I would keep everything. And I remember [peer] was always fascinated with my filing cabinet because I just kept everything that we'd done, mostly, in the filing cabinet. (Leigh, 2020)

This also shows a connection between documentary practice and preservation. The filing cabinet acts as an archival space which delineates these materials from others stored in housing. The recognition of the filing cabinet as an archival object in the Riot Grrrl Collection held by the Fales Library is explored by Lymn (2014, p. 329). Though the materials in the filing cabinet Lymn refers to were moved into more formal and more easily accessible boxes for retrieval, the filing cabinet is retained as an object, a trace of the originating context for the collection.

Ruth describes keeping posters and other materials both digitally and physically in her house "trans manor":

> I started instinctively just keeping a record of this ... trans manor is still full of posters, some on the walls, and some in storage, from the gigs because I've got physical copies of these posters and the revolt posters. It kind of seemed important. And then if people would take photos at the gigs I would keep the photos, and so we've got some of them on here, and some of them on Myspace (Pearce, 2019)

Participants sometimes utilised the terms "archive" and "records" informally, demonstrating that materials already held this status to them as individuals despite not being deposited in an archive service. Instead, the decision to keep materials together for future use gives these collections archival meaning to individuals. The archive does not strictly apply to materials which take a certain form, format, or exist in specific locations, but can be understood as a "floating signifier" which gives meaning to materials (Halberstam, 2005, p. 170).

In some cases, digital files or physical materials were given additional context, through the addition of extra information or organisation (e.g., separating materials into folders with labels). The following page contains two images taken from the Not Right website (Not Right, 2012). The first is taken from the "lyrics" section of the site, for which each individual song is given a web page. The page for the song I selected ("intersectionality song") includes lyrics, links to background reading which informed the band as they wrote the song and digitised images of tabs. Figure 5 is one of the images uploaded to this page which includes typed lyrics, the chords and guitar riff for the song.

The digitised materials on this page give context to the song. Context is a key concept within archival practice, particularly the ideas of provenance and original order which mandate that archivists respect the arrangement and administrative context that underpin the creation of records (Cook, 1997, p. 21). A comparison can also be drawn between these terms and Hall's concept of "pre-history". Hall proposes that

For(a)ging Histories

ABOUT MUSIC GIGS **LYRICS** PHOTOS ZINES
UK RIOT GRRRL

INTERSECTIONALITY SONG

Had a troubled childhood
Something on my mind
Pain through teens, self-hatred grows
I know my freakish means

Now I have the power
Standing on this stage
Look at me, look at me
Perform transgender rage

Had a loving family
Went to a good school
Had it so damn lucky
Abled body, abled mind too

Middle-class white girl
Standing on this stage
Look at me, look at me
Perform transgender rage

This complex is performance
Such privilege is a pain
Even hard-offs have it easy
In their own way

This one is for all those
Who can't be on this stage
Look at me, look at me
Perform transgender rage

This one is for all those
Who can't be on this stage
Look at me, look at me
Perform transgender rage

Transgender rage
Transgender rage
Transgender rage
Transgender rage

Reading etc.

My Words to Victor Frankenstein Above the Village of Chamounix: Performing Transgender Rage (Susan Stryker)

Intersectionality and marginalisation within feminism (somekindofbecca)

White Privilege: Unpacking the Invisible Knapsack (Peggy McIntosh)

Middle Class Privilege (Jane Van Galen)

Social Model of Disability (Wikipedia)

Figure 5 Screenshots of lyrics for "intersectionality song" and list of links to reading (Not Right, 2012)

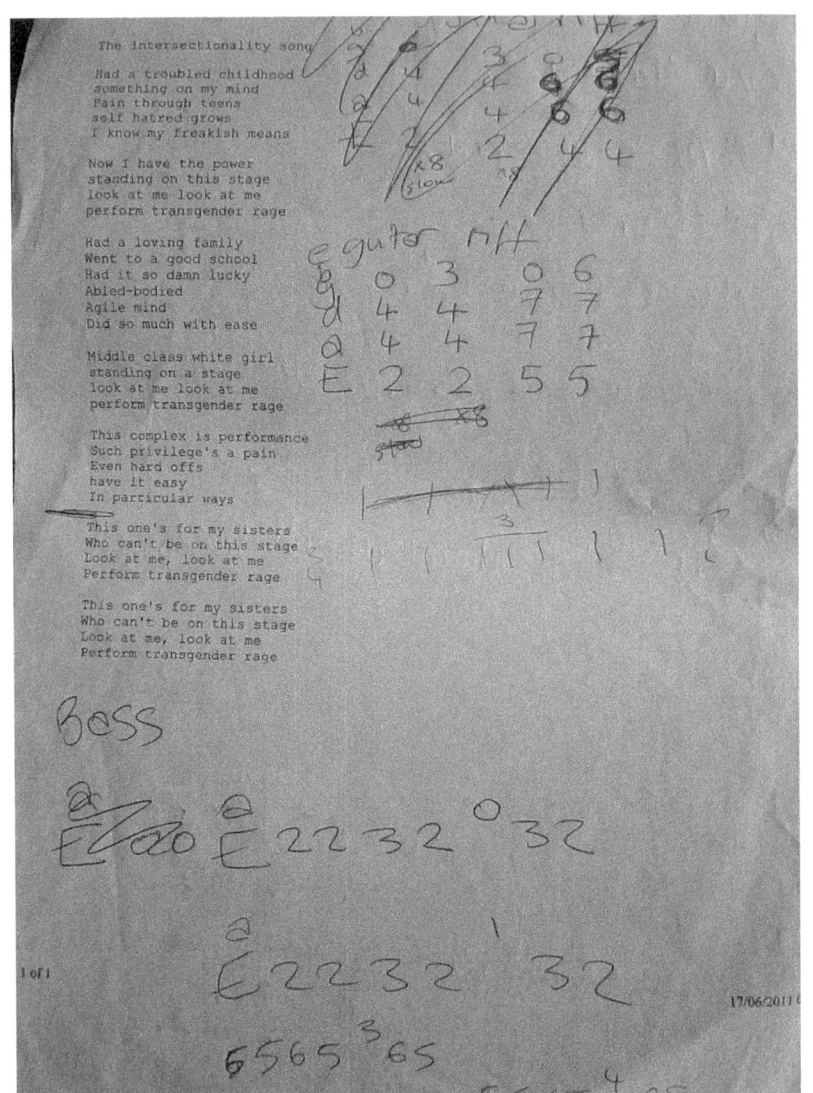

Figure 6: Digitised guitar tab and notes (Not Right, 2012)

> No archive arises out of thin air. Each archive has a 'pre-history', in the sense of prior conditions of existence. (2001, p. 89)

All archives have a background context and an ideology that underpins its construction. Returning to the Not Right website, what is visible on the website is effectively a "pre-history" of a song—including the process of songwriting (illustrated by tabs and chord notes) and the references which make visible the politics underpinning the song's writing (and the links between lyrics and other texts). The inclusion of digitised notes and tabs with songs also makes visible the process and labour beneath the production of DIY music, once again highlighting the behind-the-scenes labour of making music.

Another intervention often taken by participants was the migration of files, particularly born digital records held on platforms. Migration of materials is undertaken by archivists doing digital preservation work (McKinney, 2020, p. 13). Migration is used to maximise the long-term accessibility of formats, particularly proprietary formats which are more likely to become obsolete—such practises engage with the fragility of files stored on ever changing technological devices (Gaur and Tripathi, 2012, pp. 293–294). In this study acts of migration were sometimes undertaken when digital platforms closed or ceased to be used within the community. For example, Ruth described moving a folder of digital fliers for her promoting activities between Myspace and Facebook. The action to extract files, create a new space on a second platform and add basic information to each image illustrates a desire for the materials to persist and remain of use. Of this work, Ruth said that

> I shifted it all over because I wanted to keep a record. And I think the way I thought about it at the time, [it] was like just showing where we'd come from. (Pearce, 2019)

Others were aware of the need to think about how to migrate digital materials. For example, of the use of Instagram to create the "Leeds DIY" archive, Tayyab said that

> I know that people are using Instagram as a platform for archiving in lots of interesting ways... Whenever Instagram dies, hopefully there will be a third party app online where I'll be able to like, pull all the pictures and still have a collection, import it to whatever new it needs to go. Because Instagram is not going to last forever. (Amin, 2019)

Thus, whilst Instagram was viewed as an informal storage platform for archival materials and provided an access point for other people, there was an awareness that work would have to be done to move materials when the platform closed.

The work to move or digitise materials was done manually and was thus reliant on an individual's capacity and willingness to do this work. There is a parallel here between the informal actions taken by participants and digital recovery projects, which are explored by Earhart in the context of literature. Earhart writes that digital recovery projects are "labours of love" motivated by an urge to disseminate hard to access materials (p. 66). Case studies exploring the work of digital preservation in an organisational context demonstrate the continuous labour required to keep up with digital preservation work (Gaur and Tripathi, 2012, p. 296).

Routine management of archival content is often undervalued. For example, Ben said that

> it feels like a thankless task sometimes if you're doing just archival work as opposed to doing like a zine or a show (Perkins, 2019)

In relation to LGBTQ archives, Sheffield also describes the tension that occurs when

> excitement gives way to a recognition that archival work is labour, that it requires an investment of time and money and that our community's ideas about who we are and what we want to be change over time? (2020, p. 4)

Routine tasks like migration of digital files are invisible labour embedded in the background of DIY music. Whilst this section has identified ways in which some of this work does happen, this is not a priority in comparison to more urgent work.

There is more to keeping than a simple holding of materials, especially when this work is personally motivated. Archival theory has engaged with the emotional dimensions of record keeping relatively recently (Caswell and Cifor, 2016; Cifor, 2016; Laurent and Hart, 2018; Douglas and Alisauskas, 2021; Rosen, 2021). Although all actions I have identified are infused with affect, the rituals of keeping, moving and organisation of archives speak most strongly to the idea of care work. Referring to record keeping work by bereaved parents, Douglas and

Alisauskas describe how making and caring for records enabled a continuing connection between parents and children who had passed away (2021). We can similarly look to work done to keep and organise records of closed spaces or previous projects as a small way to maintain a connection over time. The act of keeping is both logistically care work (to "take care" of records) and becomes an expression of care for what is represented in the records.

The informal work undertaken to keep and move materials in the previous examples suggests that materials were valued by participants, and that they undertook this work because they cared. Value is a central and contested concept within archival theory. Archival education has historically relied on Schellenberg's concepts of primary and secondary value to describe value for the creating organisation (primary) and for collective memory (secondary) (1956). These ideas have been criticised for representing value as universal and inherent rather than subjective and socially constructed (Brothman, 1991, p. 84). Many participants involved in this study held onto materials motivated by "felt" value. This was described as "nostalgic" or "sentimental". For example, Kaz reflected that:

> I already do [hold onto materials] a little bit, but I think that's just because I'm a sentimental person. I've got a roll full of posters from previous events and there was one stage where my bedroom had posters all over it, it got to a point where there were too many so I took them off [laughs]. (Scattergood, 2020)

Whilst affective value does not fit into traditional archival notions of value, it does fit into notions of value prioritised by community-led, queer and feminist archives (Reitsamer, 2015; Cifor, 2016). For Cvetkovich, personal collections formed by motivations comparable to the above form important sources of alternative knowledge (2003a, p. 8), particularly when otherwise absent in archives.

This section has demonstrated how informal processes of keeping and caring are undertaken following short-lived events, the closure of spaces or the end of a project. These materials are also sometimes organised, described, and migrated between spaces, which mirrored other dimensions of archival work (e.g., digital preservation, cataloguing and arrangement). These actions represent a disruptive and unconventional model of preservation, due to the keeping of otherwise ephemeral materials outside of formal repositories.

Forming

The formation of archives is an important action within activist communities. Hall describes this moment as "a significant moment, on which we need to reflect with care" (2001, p. 89). Appadurai describes the archive as "a deliberate site for the production of anticipated memories by intentional communities" (2003, p. 17, emphasis added by author). In contrast to the previous stages, the actions taken within this section were consciously archival. In this sense, the action to form archives represents an anticipation of future use by others and mobilises the materials within a broader framework of collective memory.

Individuals formed collections of physical materials which were compiled in scrapbooks or folders. Emma describes developing a practice of scrapbooking during her university years:

> there was a lot of talk there about documenting things and recording stuff for posterity, and documenting stuff as you went along. This has stuck in my mind, because as well people often say, oh, wow you've got good memory but I think it's easier when you've got all this documentation around you (Falconer, 2019).

The use of scrapbooking to form archives is explored by Eichhorn in the context of feminist archiving. Scrapbooks, as Eichhorn writes, can be understood as an "archival genre" which was utilised by women to document their lives before women's history was acknowledged in heritage organisations (2013, p. 32). Emma's collection of materials creates prompts for her own memory, and the practice of scrapbooking is a way in which to preserve paper-based traces within a context (in this year, within dated scrapbooks linking experiences to dates and locations). Emma described this work as "for the joy of future archivists", which indicates an awareness that the materials might be deposited in the future or used for historical research.

The collecting of material traces parallels collecting activities which are familiar in popular music fandom—for example record collecting, which was discussed by several participants. Maalsen and McLean extend the concept of the archive to encompass these material collections (2018). However, the ability to form these is reliant on having physical space in domestic settings, which was an issue for many participants (see chapter seven). For example, Alex reflected:

> With records, just the size of records takes up, like, I don't know, I'm just looking at my flat, maybe a tenth of the flat, I'm not joking, they're just a space consuming thing so you really have to assess what you're gonna keep or the walls start caving in. (Trapp, 2020)

In the desire to collect records, there is a similar desire to "capture" which Ishmael et al. situate as core to white Western archival practice (2020, p. 211), Straw identifies how record collections can be positioned as "public displays of power/knowledge" which are underpinned by male control, enforced through homosocial interactions and the exclusion of women from collector spaces (1997, pp. 4–5). The association between collecting in order to form archives and the production of power merits highlighting, especially as these collections can subsequently form the basis of histories and archives (Maalsen and McLean, 2018, p. 50). However, when (as in this study) collecting is done by people traditionally marginalised in these spaces, these actions can be situated as attempts to contest gendered practices and renegotiate the terms on which histories are made.

Some examples of collecting of born digital materials were also identified. Kaz referred to an instance of informal digital collecting that she undertook after seeing an all-day gig she organised documented via Instagram stories, which disappear after 24 hours of being publicly available online. As she says:

> You lose all that [content], that's really sad. I actually remember after last year's birthday gig, I had various friends who were playing the show, all of my Instagram stories for that day were all just stories of performances from the day and I was like, oh my god, this is magical and it's all going to disappear. So I put a call out I think on Twitter, [saying] if anyone's got videos of today please send it to me before they all go and a few people did just send me the videos on on Facebook. And it wasn't really for anything. It was just because I was so sad at the idea that I was going to lose everyone else's videos after 24 hours… so yeah people sent them to me and I did absolutely nothing with them but watch them again [laughs] (Scattergood, 2020).

In the above example, Kaz took action by asking individuals to send materials directly to her. This action ensured the persistence of the documentation, even if only for her use. In relation to the use of Facebook live by social movements, Sheffield describes how live-streaming technology disrupts broadcasting practice and enables movements to create records. However, the drive to create (or "recordmaking") did not "necessarily translate into recordkeeping"(2018, p. 101). These informal glimpses of gigs, communities and spaces are the most at risk of loss due to their ephemeral online lives and rapid inaccessibility. Individual actions such as the above are micro interventions to prevent what often feels like the inevitable loss of such traces.

Forming digital archives sometimes happened as part of routine re-organisation. The following screenshot shows the home page of organising collective Revolt's website which shows a tab in the header menu titled "archive", created by the collective. This is in addition to the standard "archives" side menu, which is a standard function that enables a user to browse by date to find previous posts. The archive section created by the collective is used to hold information from previous gigs and events. By moving a page into the "archive" section, the individuals consider the information valuable enough to keep and move it into an informal repository of sorts. This can be easily compared to the actions of archivists, who afford value by acquiring and moving archives in more formal repositories (Caswell, 2016, p. 8).

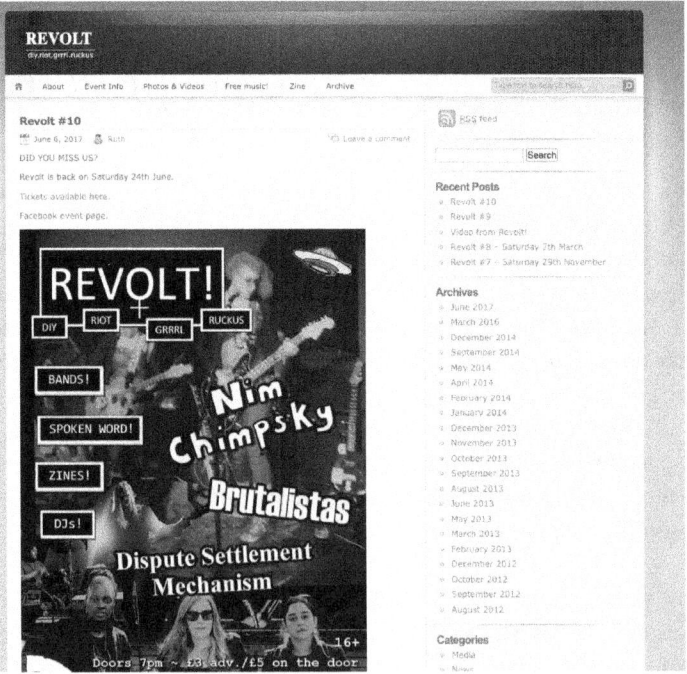

Figure 7 Screenshot from revolt website with "archive" tab in menu (Revolt, no date)

The preceding examples have demonstrated informal examples of forming. However, there were also examples of archives formed through purposeful history work. These included one deposit comprising materials relating to Ladyfest London and a personal archive to the Glasgow Women's Library, and a zine collection and organisational documents from the same context which were deposited at the Women's Library in London (see chapter eight). In relation to one collection, Nazmia described how collecting developed in response to a lack of awareness of the legacy of Ladyfest organising by a newer generation of organisers:

> in 2010, when they did Ladyfest 10 in London, I was quite cross with them, because they had it in The Garage and they just didn't acknowledge that another Ladyfest had happened there (Jamal, 2019).

McKay describes an ahistorical nature evident in DIY culture, writing:

To what extent does claiming newness equate or contribute to historicism? There is some evidence of a lack of historical awareness on the part of youth activists. A clear potential downside of youth can be its rejection of both expertise and history, of radical history which is often hard enough to narrate or recover anyway. (1998, pp. 13–14)

The above example demonstrates how newer generations of activists might not perceive history as a central part of activism. Although in general this thesis argues that histories and archiving are activist tools in DIY music, some of these projects were established precisely because newer generations had no connection with the cultural legacies of those that had preceded them. This could be connected to the need to be perceived as "original" in music cultures, which might lead bands to refer to themselves as "the first…" or similar, to demonstrate that they are groundbreaking and worthy of support. However, this language was perceived as dangerous by several participants. For example, Steph reflected:

> if you're the first–there has to be a second … it's very dangerous language, we try not to use that or say that we're the first of everything, because history is so … well not badly documented, but history can be very warped and we can lose stories all the time. So we don't really know who was the first of doing anything at all. (Phillips, 2019)

In the above example, Nazmia's frustration led to an action that made these easily lost or erased histories more visible so that others could find connections and inspiration from earlier generations of organisers.

Whilst individuals might be motivated to form archives, there was often a disconnection between these processes and the decision to then deposit materials within heritage institutions. As Leigh reflected about their decision to deposit a collection of materials,

> the process of recognising that this stuff belongs in there [the archive] is a bit of a weird process …. and I think it was a real slow burning one. (Leigh, 2020)

Although materials were clearly kept, valued, and cared for by individuals, the decision to deposit them within institutions was one which few pursued. In part, this can be explained by scepticism of institutions or a lack of understanding of the process (see chapter eight)—however, many participants expressed a lack of self-confidence in their own cultural output. For example, Aaron reflected:

> I never felt like what I was doing was like hugely important, because no one else outside of like our band or any other bands made me feel like my contribution to it was as important as someone else's, so it's hard to say if someone came up to me and went I feel like this should be documented and they could persuade me to do it, then I would do it. (Batley, 2019)

Lack of self-confidence may contribute to underrepresentation of DIY music in collections when individuals do not value their work. Aaron's comments suggest that this could be changed if there was more encouragement, which suggests that both peers and archive workers could improve the likelihood of deposit through more dialogue and support.

The actions explored in this section relate to circumstances in which cultural organisers are responsible for building archives. Halberstam refers to a "lack of distinction between the archivist and the cultural worker" (2005, p. 162). In the above examples, a community member often undertakes archival work to form a collection and ensure the survival of archival traces of activities they viewed as significant. These examples illustrate how community members act as archival agents in the intermediate stages between cultural activity and the deposit of materials, through gathering materials or using community networks to form archives prior to outreach from organisations. Institutions have played a much more minor and supporting role–though, crucially, outreach from organisations with aligned ethos' often motivated individuals to consider depositing materials before they had otherwise considered it as an option.

Sharing

This section explores actions of sharing information and memory within communities. This parallels access work undertaken by archive workers. Hedstrom describes how archivists

> construct a variety of interfaces between the past and the present through choices about what to keep, how to represent archival documents and collections, how to design systems for access, and who to admit or exclude from interactions with archives. (2002, p. 26)

Although appraisal and collecting are more commonly associated with the production of power, the construction of systems of access also implicitly excludes certain groups (for example, through requiring state ID documents). However, the access and use of archives are presented as key dimensions of activist archival practice (Caswell, 2014c; Sellie et al., 2015; Gordon et al., 2016; Ishmael et al., 2020). Common cultural activities including bootlegging, tape trading and downloading via peer-to-peer networks also demonstrate emphasis on sharing and access within music communities (Anderton, 2016, p. 89). Campbell also situates how remixing the archive (through DJing) enables dissemination to take priority over preservation (2021, p. 495). In this study, sharing was an action undertaken to pass on cultural legacies, information and connections to peers and future generations.

Firstly, I return to the Ladyfest London deposits discussed in the previous section. Individuals interviewed about these collections articulated desire for public access as underpinning the decision to deposit these collections. Bill reflected:

> we were very aware of the ways in which these histories are lost and that there isn't any evidence of those things having happened... and that's why we wanted to make sure that it was put somewhere that people could access it and... it would have a future. (Savage, 2019)

Nazmia described motivations to make the experiences of her and other QTBIPOC in UK DIY music more known and available for others to find:

> I just think that that's really important, if you're the only one who is at something, and then you're looking for the only one from the generation before ... I wanted to make that story of like me and [peers], and [organising collective] and all of those other people as

accessible as I knew how…. I wanted all of the ephemera to be somewhere so that someone else could dig through it and feel like oh, that's this thing that I did, or look at all the stuff that this person and these other brown people and black people went to. (Jamal, 2019)

In these cases, accessibility was crucial in combating the potential loss or erasure of these histories. Research in queer and feminist archives also indicates that those undertaking archival work in this context "emphasise access and community accountability over preserving documents in boxes kept "safe" from use" (McKinney, 2020, p. 13).

Lack of accessibility of materials was considered an issue by several participants–for example, a workshop participant reflected:

> If everything is just the stuff that we've kept ourselves and our own zines that we've picked up or the posters that we've got then it's just your stuff and you're not really sharing that with people and then that stuff gets lost.

The desire to share information shows an understanding that information has the capacity to empower individuals and transform lives, provided it is available and accessible when needed. Laberge writes that

> In itself, information is not valuable. Information only has value or power when it is used to generate knowledge. In this sense, protecting information does not produce knowledge of any kind, but rather creates the essential condition for such knowledge production. (1987, p. 45)

Access to information can empower individuals to produce their own knowledge and create alternative futures influenced by the past. Caswell also describes how archival practice can be a form of "imaginary" through which marginalised communities manifest and envision futures through collecting (p. 49). The importance of accessibility within this community context is clearly connected to the potential use of archives, for individuals searching for information to inform the development of alternative futures through connection with archival imaginaries.

Digitisation was viewed as a way to make materials more accessible to others. For example, of old master tapes relating to a past band (Die All Bears), Aaron said:

> it's not all available, like I found the Die All Bears master tape the other day. I have no more left of the actual cassette but I'm trying to find a way by which I can get it digitised to be able to put it up online.

Kirsty described how she was motivated to photograph some paper remnants which represented her band Not Right, planning to upload them to the band's website. This was used to provide access to information for band members and potential future users. As Kirsty said:

> We were like we'll scan these [tabs] and put them online... the sharing photos and recordings felt like it was more for other people, a sort of place, a repository for the memories of what we did... (Lohman, 2020)

In reference to lesbian feminist digitisation practice, McKinney writes that

> Deciding to digitise an object imagines new queer networks in which it might circulate, along with a different kind of life for the object. (2020, p. 157)

Returning to the processes of searching described in the opening of this chapter, digitisation can heighten the visibility of needed information through "facilitating scrolling, browsing and searching practices for lesbian and queer researchers, and community members, who still need these words and images today" (McKinney, 2020, p. 160). Digitisation as a practice anticipates future users, who might seek to connect with digitised resources. It can also be a practical tool motivated by the need to downsize and move regularly, a shared experience by many community members.

DIY music community members participated in informal practises of mourning, demonstrated through the sharing of memories on social media. Cassie describes how these practises often manifest around the conclusion of creative projects (in this case, the final show of punk band Doe):

> Punks do care about history, right... because we get so attached to like bands and venues festivals and stuff... and when they stop, we want to make sure that that experience, the band that we've loved for the last 10 years, that we remember all those amazing things. I went to the last Doe show on Saturday, and so many people were posting photos and videos just of the night, obviously, but also photos and videos from when they've seen them over the years, and hangouts that they've had with them, and tours that they've been on with them, and Doe themselves posted all these things over the years. (Agbehenu, 2019)

The conclusion of projects enables people to share their connection with a project, band, or space. In the above case, a final gig is an opportunity for a wider community to memorialise by sharing materials on social media. In reference to the use of digital media by social movements, Merrill et al. describe how platforms "provide opportunities for circulating memory" which they believe exceeds the archival (2020a, p. 16). Publishing materials in turn allows a community to build collective memory by creating links between memories (e.g., commenting "I was at that show" or adding further contextual information). The circulation of archival traces on social media creates opportunity for relationships and context to be added, producing networks and knowledge after the event or the closure of a space.

Verbal sharing of experiences is also a way in which community members connect, bond and pass on information and histories. This is also common in queer subcultures, who may utilise oral sharing of histories in the absence of traditional archival records (Ramirez, 2005). Cvetkovich describes how in response to these known absences

> memory becomes a valuable historical resource, and ephemeral and personal collections stand alongside the documents of the dominant culture in order to offer alternative modes of knowledge. (2003a, p. 8)

In the context of this study, Tayyab described these processes as "storytelling", describing them as follows:

> the you had to have been there kind of thing, is the ephemera of it... the conversations when you go to a show and you talk, did you see them at that time or did you see like that other band, or the act play at this show, that was a really special show (Amin, 2019).

Abdurraqib also refers to both writing and verbal sharing of memories as a type of archiving, writing that:

> I had moments at shows, moments in live music that I wanted to relive again and again, and I realised that the only way I could do that was by archiving them somewhere even it's just in a waffle house after the show. Like, speaking the memory of the show into the air is also an archiving. (2017)

Through such practises, sharing of memory becomes part of the socialising that underpins UK DIY music communities. These practices are intimate and embodied, and situating them as archival places them within an understanding of heritage that is capacious and located, as Joseph and Bell write, "in movement, in the body, in language in proverbs, in the aspects of our lives that lie beyond gross sensual perception" (2020, p. 523). People themselves become "living repositories" (Joseph and Bell, 2020, p. 521) who carry forward memory and legacy.

This section has explored the action to share information, memories and archival traces within DIY music communities. I began by exploring examples of sharing that were facilitated via more familiar forms of archival access. The desire for increased accessibility underpinned decisions to deposit materials, as participants were often unable to otherwise facilitate access to researchers. Following this, I explored actions which were motivated by the desire to share information and memory but did not conform to traditional notions of archival access. These included digitising and publishing materials online (see also chapter seven) and sharing memories in social settings. The latter formed an important part of community building and bonding between peers.

Referencing and use

The final action identified through interview data was the re-use of memory, cultural legacies, and archival traces. This was commonly undertaken through cultural production—for example, in zine making, lyric writing, photography or film making. The relationship between musical practices and use of the past is not exclusive within this community context—for example, Joseph and Bell describe how the music practice of dubbing can be viewed as an archival activation of the past:

> The dub engineer repurposes both recorded sound and electronic technology in ways that neither was originally designed to support; this creates a new, unique performance, rearticulating the past in the present. (2020, p. 522)

Musical practices such as remixing are situated similarly (Ishmael et al., 2020, p. 213; Campbell, 2021). For Campbell, a "remix" praxis enables the redistribution of existing (and inaccessible) knowledge and archival materials (2021, p. 489). Campbell also proposes that remixing archival materials is an inherently subjective and creative process, which stands in opposition to the "objective detachment" of archival traditions (2021, p. 495).

In the following examples, I return to Chidgey's concept of "citational practices" (initially cited in chapter three) to examine the practice of referencing the past through cultural production. In relation to the creation of cultural memory in feminist zines, Chidgey uses citational practices to

> refer to a range of textual strategies that work to underpin which actors are being invoked in zine articles and artworks, which texts are being cited, and what mnemonic practices and aesthetics are used to create common understandings between producers and readers. (2013, p. 663)

Chidgey describes how contemporary feminist zines utilise repeated references to art, zines and texts from the early riot grrrl feminist punk movement. This strategy, often commonly employed in the naming of zines, club nights and organising collectives, enables riot grrrl to be used "as a site for memory and reminiscence (or nostalgia) and as a means for current identification and celebration" (Chidgey, 2013, p. 664). Citational practices can also contribute to processes of canonisation, through which specific activists persist through repeated circulation and citation within communities. Thus, it is almost important to acknowledge the exclusionary potential of these practices.

To explore the use of citational practices, I begin with an example relating to black feminist punk band Big Joanie, in combination with data gathered from an interview with singer Stephanie. Following this, I go on to provide a second example from my own zine project. I utilise these examples to demonstrate how referencing is undertaken within cultural production, and the underpinning political motivations that motivate individuals to cite to prevent erasure or to emphasise the contributions of previously marginalised individuals.

Big Joanie are a black feminist punk band who formed in 2013 as part of First Timers, a London-based festival through which marginalised people are encouraged to form bands and play a gig following access to community networks, skills sharing workshops and a platform at the concluding gigs. Since their formation, the band have frequently employed references to other Black women and queer people in visual design and songwriting. For example, in a press shot taken by photographer Pauline Hisbacq, the band are photographed standing in front of a print of singer, model, and producer Grace Jones (Mann, 2018). In the video for their song "Fall Asleep" (Big Joanie–Fall Asleep, 2018), the band are pictured walking along a canal with Debbie Smith, musician with 1990s rock band Echobelly. Steph describes the motivation behind these representation as follows:

the way that we think about music, definitely, because we've been doing [it] for, it feels like a long time, we're kind of music nerds [laughs]. I think in that sense of always thinking back to the music that we like, but also kind of our relation to that music and, creating a lineage for ourselves and placing ourselves as black women in that lineage and kind of seeing how it all links up. (Phillips, 2019)

Employing citation and reference through visual technologies enables Big Joanie to place themselves within a broader landscape of cultural production led by black queer and/or feminist musicians.

Citational praxis can be used to connect DIY music acts to others with similar political motivations or shared cultural identity. However, it can also be employed to represent connections between music and family or local community. On the cover of their debut LP Sistahs (Big Joanie, 2018), Big Joanie also utilised a family photograph of singer Stephanie's mother and aunt on holiday in Wales, during which they experienced racism from the landlord of their holiday accommodation. Steph describes the motivation behind including this image on the cover, writing that the photograph

> just reminded me of how I became the person that I became ... and just linking her acts, those everyday ways of tackling racism and linking it to what we're doing with Big Joanie and what we're doing, and everyone else. Just I can see the threads running through there. (Phillips, 2019)

By including the image of Stephanie's mother and aunt on the cover of the release, the band draw a link between their own cultural activism and the everyday activism undertaken by their family when moving through racist environments and encounters. In reference to feminist activism, Sowards and Renegar write that

> Feminist activism may operate in private settings, such as daily conversation or the internet. Such activist measures may go unnoticed, even though these individuals may be very proactive in their daily lives. (2006, p. 61)

Thus, as well as linking the motivations underpinning activism across generations and situating themselves in connection with earlier generations, the band also make visible forms of activism that may be maligned in histories and archives of activism.

The second example I will explore comes from my own creative practice. The zine project *Move Under Yr Own Power: Interviews with Women and Queers Making DIY Music* was used to begin this thesis (Fife, 2016, 2018). The image on the following page is taken from the second issue of the zine (Fife, 2018). The illustration includes a central illustration of myself, surrounded by the names of UK DIY music bands that I have connections with and/or have had influence on my own creative practice. The writing down of names was a way to acknowledge the cultural backdrop of my own music and an informal way to afford value to projects that have begun and ended without any other formal documentation to represent the collaboration.

The use of similarly informal practices of reference are explored in other cultural contexts. In relation to performance, Clarke and Warren also refer to ongoing practises of referencing, re-use, and representation:

> The work continues through oral accounts that are passed-on, rumours, hearsay, reviews and reinterpretations in print. It remains live through research, review, re-use, remediation, re-performance and re-enactment, circulating and recirculating in the cultural scene. (2009, p. 50)

Chidgey also suggests that individual zines persist beyond their limited publication span and circulation through being reviewed, quoted, and reproduced in other zines. As she writes,

> this "passing on" and reinscribing of past zine works into a new zine, becomes a form of testimony to the history of the zine community which is being created or contested. (2006, p. 11)

The visual and textual traces of DIY music reflect an activation of the archive undertaken through persistent referencing to projects, particularly those which are of personal significance but exist outside of mainstream history frameworks. Utilising these tools, we write histories through links and citations, even if they otherwise go unwritten in more formal history writing.

Referencing was also identified in digital spaces. Digital platforms were often used to create links between bands and cultural organisers. An example of this is the use of the "recommendations" section on artist pages held on Bandcamp, a digital platform used to share and sell music releases. This section was commonly used to create explicit links between projects. In some cases, individuals also used

For(a)ging Histories

Figure 8 Illustration from Move Under Yr Own Power: Interviews With Women And Queers Making DIY Music (Fife, 2018: p. 5)

websites to similarly reference other bands. Ruth describes how her band Not Right used their website to link to bands active at the same time which shared similar politics:

> we put on all the bands we could find who were active at the time at the same time as us, and then we kept a link, an archive of things we'd found on the internet. (Pearce, 2019)

Referencing through linking serves multiple purposes—in the absence of promotion in mainstream media platforms, these actions circulate music via individual efforts to increase accessibility. Following the conclusion of projects, these links remain and become documentation of networks and are used by historians to trace communities (see chapter five). Of films hosted on Facebook live by activist groups, Sheffield writes that

> Even if the original videos remain ephemeral in nature, they are bound to other records through individual and collective linking or referencing. (2018, p. 109)

Reaching back to Chidgey's concept of citational practices again, we can situate the act to link to materials (which themselves may be ephemeral) to document connections and preserve networks informally.

This section has explored actions to use and reference traces of UK DIY music. I began by exploring how the re-use of traces in cultural production is common within creative communities. Following this and using Chidgey's concept of citational practices as a framework, I explored how referencing is utilised as a strategy to enable the persistence of memory. I also identified how these actions are motivated by a desire to place projects and spaces in network with others, making visible the otherwise under-documented networks of influence and support in DIY music communities.

Conclusion

Referring to the use of Facebook live by social movements, Sheffield distinguishes the impulse to create records ("recordmaking") from archiving ("recordkeeping"), as the latter is focused on the maintenance of authentic, reliable and useable records and is largely not undertaken on digital platforms (2018, p. 101). Whilst I agree that there is a difference between creating records and the labour required to keep and facilitate access to them, this chapter has situated actions to find and create traces within the same landscape as work to keep, form and share archives. I have also decisively not created dividing lines between work done in institutions by professionals (e.g., access work) and communities, instead identifying the points of interaction between the two and affording equal value to individual actions. This lack of boundary situates these different forms of work within a collective endeavour to forge space for histories and archives of UK DIY music. Further examination of the relationship between communities and institutions is conducted chapter seven, which continues to problematise the borders between the two.

In reference to the Interference Archive, Gordon et al. describe their open access focus as "a foundation for education and mobilisation" (2016, p. 60). The data explored in this chapter demonstrates a similar politics around the connection between information, action, accessibility, and education. In my previous chapter I referred to Marian Wright Edelman's comment that "it's hard to be what you can't see" (2015) and its subsequent impact on DIY music communities, particularly those led by women, queer people and people of colour. In concluding this section, I find myself returning to this again as a phrase which explains why the accessibility, visibility and persistence of our own histories resonates so much through the data gathered during this research. In exploring these actions, I have identified the way in which the past matters within DIY music not because of any inherent reverence of preceding generations, but rather because the past communicates possibility for the future, in a way which connects to the archive as a source of activation (Halberstam, 2005; Carter, 2017; Joseph, 2018). These past traces communicated possibility through periods of isolation, disconnection and longing–forging spaces through communication, creativity and access to information.

Figure 9 Archival boundaries (original illustration)

Presence, Absence and Deletion
Digital Information in UK DIY Music

In 2019, Myspace confirmed the loss of 50 million songs that were uploaded to 14.2 million profiles on the website (DeVille, 2019). The files were deleted from its music player due to an error that occurred during server migration, with the materials affected (dating between 2003 and 2015) irrecoverable. After the news was released, I saw reverberations of emotions travel through my personal networks. Many peers grew up using Myspace, and uploaded music to the platform. I had deleted my personal Myspace profile years before the loss, but occasionally I still logged on to check on my old band's profile. When I did so, I would find memories of club nights, gig venues and cultural networks that had long shut down, dissipated, or run out of steam. After the announcement, I reflected about my own feelings about the loss on my research blog:

> the songs I wrote about crushes and depression and not being understood in my small town are a method of and record of some of my earliest DIY cultural production (via home recordings on my desktop computer). I don't have those recordings anymore, they too were long lost on another hard drive also lost in computer upgrades and laptop malfunctions. (Fife, 2019a)

Would we have kept those songs given the choice? What was significant about the loss of music stored on a platform that was long forgotten by many of us?

Contemporary journalism explored the loss–of his own early music, Pearson wrote that "it's entirely possible that those songs, as bad and poorly-recorded as they were, might not exist in any other format" (2019). We had naively assumed that the music stored on internet platforms would continue to exist in perpetuity, and the labour of the upkeep of this data would be accepted by corporations. We thought that digital materials had the potential to outlast physical traces, and that cloud storage was stable and reliable. Of the incident, journalist DeVille wrote "the lesson: Back up your files! Whatever cloud they're floating around in might dissipate someday" (2019). Pearson similarly stated "it's just one more reminder that if you let a corporation take care of your precious memories, you're headed straight for heartbreak, kiddo" (2019). For many, the loss was a hard realisation that important digital records were held behind forgotten passwords and on increasingly precarious and neglected servers.

I use this example as a starting point for this chapter because the cluster of issues and feelings articulated are illustrative of wider tensions about the preservation of archival traces in increasingly digital subcultures. The example was brought up frequently in research interviews as underpinning the desire to preserve or collect archival traces of DIY music. An example of this is in the below interaction from a group discussion at queer punk festival Bent Fest, in which I asked participants to discuss what issues affected people within DIY music communities documenting or archiving their activities:

> there's lots to do with the way we store stuff online, like, a really big easy example is the Myspace music disappearing, all that music on Myspace that probably had a lot of DIY creativity just going…and yeah so I think it's about time that we collect our own things. (Participant C, 2019)

Although documentation and archiving of activism from within is a long-standing practice, the insertion of social media platforms into this practice is much more recent (Smit, 2020, p. 101). This chapter therefore explores the relationship between DIY music spaces, digital platforms, and information networks, examining how this relationship affects the production of archival traces of UK DIY music.

In this chapter, I follow Gillespie's definition of digital platforms as

> sites and services that host, organise, and circulate users' shared content or social exchanges for them. (2018, p. 254)

Theorists have described the ways in which digital platforms and technologies have changed the organisational structure of activist movements (Sharp, 2006; Flinn, 2008; Gillespie, 2018; Sheffield, 2018). Poell and van Dijck write that "the intensive use of social media transforms the organisation and communication of protest" (2018, p. 2). Sharp also highlights the use of free and/or open-source software by networked participatory communities to create culture and social change, drawing attention to the connections between "technological innovation and social change" (2006, p. 19) and the embedded blending of "subjective and intersubjective practices in a self-reflexive process of knowledge production" (2006, p. 21). Similarly Kwame Harrison writes that "many recent underground music scenes have utilised new technologies in conjunction with a strong Do-it-Yourself (DiY) ethos to recruit, shape, and sustain their followings" (2006, p. 284). The accessibility and networked nature of these technologies enables movements to build across substantial geographical distances.

As Quinn and Papacharissi write, these platforms (often unintentionally) "sustain digital traces and relational memory maps of evolving connections between individuals in everyday life" (2018, p. 2). Digital platforms are also used purposefully to create, and circulate memories, in actions which parallel archival work (see chapter four). Those who activate the archival potential of sites are positioned as memory agents (Smit, 2020) who mobilise networks to collect and activate traces. However, as this relationship has become increasingly inextricable, activists and theorists have identified the dark side of our reliance on corporately owned platforms (Flinn, 2008; Hicks, 2013; Reading, 2014; Noble, 2018; De Kosnik et al., 2020). There is a now growing uncertainty about both the mid- and long-term accessibility of materials created through citizen journalism and activist use of record-making technology (Sheffield, 2018, p. 101). At this point in time, it is essential for research to critically explore these tensions.

The following sections utilise interview and discussion group data to analyse how DIY music communities relate to digital platforms as potential sources of documentation or archival practice. I begin by outlining the links between digital platforms, memory, and cultural activism. I then go on to illustrate the ways in which DIY music community members utilise digital platforms for informal memory practices, which assert their presence in history. Following this, I explore absence of information, particularly focusing on instances where digital information exists but disappears or is made inaccessible. Finally, utilising recent examples from the context of my research, I examine deletion of information and the subsequent impact on communities. I argue that these platforms offer opportunities, challenges, and threats to DIY music communities, and the precarious balance between these is often felt by those undertaking work on these platforms.

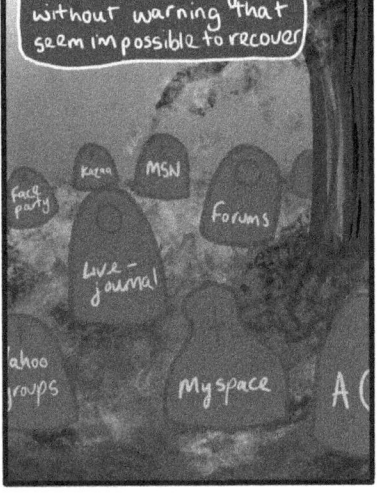

Figure 1 Digital graveyard

Digital memory and cultural activism(s)

Historically, activist communities have often adopted digital technologies to construct archives and democratise cultural memory practices, with researchers situating many of these projects within the field of community heritage or cultural memory (Allard and Ferris, 2014; Petro, 2015; Smith, 2016; Palmer-Mehta, 2018; Poell and van Dijck, 2018; Sheffield, 2018; Smit, Heinrich and Broersma, 2018; Correa et al., 2019; Chidgey, 2020; Smit, 2020). Archives are created using unconventional sources and methods–these include Twitter hashtags (Jules, Summers and Mitchell, Jr., 2018); Facebook groups and pages (Yaqub, 2016; Smit, Heinrich and Broersma, 2018; Gibbons, 2019); media articles (Palmer-Mehta, 2018); YouTube videos (Kølvraa and Stage, 2016), with some theorists asserting that even the internet itself can be understood as an archive of sorts (Block, 2001). These projects demonstrate a "promiscuous deployment of the title archive.... [which] presents particular challenges to conventional practice for both archivist and user" (Long et al., 2017, p. 63).

The use of digital platforms to create archives is also a focus of those researching community-led archives (Caswell and Mallick, 2014; Caswell, Cifor and Ramirez, 2016; Ferris and Allard, 2016; Mutibwa, 2016; Smith, 2016; Saber and Long, 2017; Cowan and Rault, 2018; Moore, 2020; Popple, Prescott and Mutibwa, 2020a). In the context of work undertaken by the South Asian American Digital Archive, Caswell and Mallick use the term "digital participatory microhistory project" to describe

> any programmatic activity that uses Internet based technologies to encourage community members to directly create short records for inclusion in an archives. (2014, p. 77)

These projects utilise widely accessible digital technologies to "empower the communities whose histories they seek to document and preserve". The resulting projects demonstrate how "commonplace technologies can be liberatory tools for archival activism" (Caswell and Mallick, 2014, p. 83). Although other community heritage researchers have identified how funded digital archival projects have become inaccessible due to a lack of technical expertise or funding (Prescott, 2020, p. 253), the possibility provided by digital technologies nonetheless continues to be emphasised in theory.

In reference to fandom cultures and digital memory, De Kosnik describes the work of "rogue memory workers" (2016, p. 2) to create archives and make accessible vast quantities of information and memories via the use of accessible digital technologies. Rogue memory workers make use of distributed digital networks to enable

> non-hierarchical and open participation in online communities, the rapid sharing of ideas and resources" (Knobel and Lankshear, 2010, p. 10)

Through the use of these technologies for information sharing, individuals can collectively produce and share knowledge, without the barriers and outside of traditional knowledge production structures (Knobel and Lankshear, 2010, p. 10).

Digital archival projects afford value to documentary traces outside of traditional archive spaces but often while utilising the language of these traditions (e.g. archives, catalogue, archivist). Archival theorist McKemmish proposes that documents become records when they are preserved by professionals, linked to related materials and described in archival catalogues. As she writes,

> Through these processes records come into being, and acquire their quality as evidence, both recording and shaping related events. (McKemmish, 2005, p. 9)

This view centres the archive professional and the traditional archive in the making of archives and records, rather than thinking about different spaces in which these processes (assigning value, linking materials and being cared for) can be undertaken. In contrast, De Kosnik's "rogue archives" are defined by

> constant (24/7) availability; zero barriers to entry for all who can connect to the Internet; content that can be streamed or downloaded in full, with no required payment, and no regard for copyright restrictions...; and content that has never been, and would likely never be, contained in a traditional memory institution. (2016, p. 2)

As Cotera writes in relation to chicana feminist archives in the digital age, this radical prioritisation of accessibility recognises

> the archive not as a static repository but as an active site of knowledge production that could realise the emancipatory potential of its central subject. (2015, p. 783)

These digital archives acknowledge the value of history and archives for current activist communities–as tools of empowerment which enable connections, networks and cross-generational information sharing.

There are overlaps between the politics of De Kosnik's "rogue memory workers" (2016, p. 2) and DIY cultural production. Research about zine communities has highlighted similar motivations–for example, Chidgey writes that

> zine makers themselves act as memory agents using informal memory work methods, including self-reflective first-person accounts and strategic use of cultural and autobiographical ephemera, to critically and creatively theorise the world around them. (2013, pp. 662–663)

Rogue memory workers and memory agents are overlapping concepts which explain work undertaken (in both digital and analogue contexts) by individuals and communities to preserve or communicate legacies of activist work. As a zine maker and community peer, my own experience as a member of these communities echoes these bodies of research. DIY cultures and rogue memory workers share a motivation to assign value to their own histories, a commitment to sharing and accessibility of information as well as a mistrust of capitalist structures and institutions as holders and creators of cultural memory.

The intersection between cultural memory, social movements and social media has been researched by several scholars (Poell and van Dijck, 2018; Smit, Heinrich and Broersma, 2018; Chidgey, 2020; Merrill, Keightley and Daphi, 2020b; Smit, 2020) Smit et al. discuss the role that social media sites served in processes of organising and memorialisation following the shooting of unarmed teenager Mike Brown in Ferguson in 2014. As they write, the moderator of the page was

> an important agent for memory work on the site. He consciously set the agenda by providing the topics for discussion, moderating and deleting material, and drawing from experience or selecting from the vast amount of available (social) media content. (Smit, Heinrich and Broersma, 2018, p. 3126)

The moderator, in the case of this article, can be thought of as an archivist, in the sense that they take responsibility for selecting, appraising, weeding, and maintaining a digital repository of memory. However, whilst a moderator can exercise power within the context of an individual page, the overall power over moderation of content lies with

Facebook's moderation team, interface, algorithms and mechanics (Smit, Heinrich and Broersma, 2018, p. 3123). This tension is described by Poell and van Dijck as awkwardly positioned between "techno-commercial platform strategies and activist tactics and values" (2018, p. 7). As well as social media, other authors point to self-made memorial webpages as alternative locations for individual memorialisation practises, particularly vernacular commemorations which may or may not align with national public memory narratives (Hess, 2007, p. 827).

Digital technologies enable new forms of cultural memory to emerge in tandem with the development of activist networks. However, research also indicates that activist and organising groups utilising these tools have left little trace behind due to the precarity of digital technologies. As Flinn writes,

> for those unorthodox and direct action groups which organised themselves via chat rooms, text, e-mail and password-controlled sites, any archival traces of their protest and articulation of an alternative position on anti-poverty campaigns have probably already largely disappeared. (2008, p. 116)

This is further exacerbated by "the transitory nature of many, particularly local, campaigns" which means that

> even those groups who are not deliberately seeking to avoid detection and surveillance are likely to slip into obscurity without leaving much trace except perhaps on independent media sites and perhaps in the local press. (Flinn, 2008, p. 116)

Flinn's analysis indicates that ephemeral and transitory branches of activist movements are less documented and subsequently less recognised within histories of these movements (2008, p. 115).

Since Flinn's article was published, there has been extensive media reporting relating to the repression of LGBTQ or other radical content via search algorithms on YouTube (Hunt, 2017) as well as the censorship and removal of "adult" content on Tumblr in 2018 (Romano, 2018; Waterson, 2018). The latter, which rose in profile partially because it was understood as "a safe space for subversive deviance and unrepressed explorations of identity and sexuality" (Romano, 2018), was widely criticised for implementing a policy that censored much of the cultural output of queer communities (Thrasher, 2018).

Scholars have also addressed implicit racism embedded in content moderation algorithms and search engines (Hicks, 2013; Noble, 2018). As Thrasher writes of Tumblr, processes of moderation are "subjective, culturally specific, and utterly political" (2018). The repression of cultural content, community networks and information by and for marginalised groups is not accidental, but rather the result of technological structures created through white heteropatriarchal ideologies. It is as such no surprise that the content and archival traces that disappear from these platforms is that which is made and circulated by radical and marginalised communities. The implications for the cultural memory stored on these platforms is drastic–particularly the potential for erasure of information about the contribution of marginalised communities to DIY cultural activism. As such, it is crucial that any analyses of rogue digital archives also account for the risk and precarity of these digital traces.

Prescott proposes that by exchanging the traditional archive for a digital platform owned by a corporation "there is a risk that the community archive may have exchanged one form of power relation for another that is much worse." (2020, p. 258). This sentiment speaks strongly to the close but tense relationship between communities and digital platforms identified within this section. With many questions and concerns still unanswered, within the next sections I continue to explore the ways in which social media, digital platforms and websites are utilised and resisted within the context of this research. While the following relates to a specific and localised context the issues and practices discussed are applicable to many related communities, particularly other forms of grassroots activism and/or cultural communities making use of digital technology.

Presence

This section explores how the community of this study used digital platforms to undertake memory work. Rather than aligning with corporate goals, the creative re-use of corporate platforms such as Instagram and Facebook displayed by the following examples can be understood as a form of resistance to archival traditions and hierarchies of value. The examples in this chapter illustrate individual actions taken to maintain information about past cultural spaces and activities via the utilisation of social media and other digital platforms.

The first example I will discuss is the Instagram account @LeedsDIY, which was set up by Tayyab Amin. The account describes itself as a "leeds music + culture calendar and archive" (Leeds DIY, no date). The account was established in 2018 and serves multiple purposes: to promote events happening in Leeds, and to document and collect visual traces of the Leeds DIY music scene, including fliers, posters, video and photography. This dual purpose aligns with the utilisation of social media platforms for memory explored by Smit, who writes that

> Serving a dual purpose—sharing now and keeping for later—this practice is simultaneously communicative and archival. (2020, p. 101)

@LeedsDIY grew out of an existing Facebook group of the same name. Local community network Facebook groups enable organisers to promote events and activities to an already engaged audience, as well as bypass the advertising income driven algorithms often used by Facebook pages.

After running the Facebook group for several years, Amin became sceptical of the platform's drive to mine community pages for advertising income. As he says:

> if you run a page on Facebook, you'll know that in order to reach your own audience of people that have liked you, you have to pay for that essentially…. Facebook is not your friend and it's obviously a big corporation…, there's no need for it to be friendly to like local independent scenes. There's no need for it to nurture that stuff, you know. (Amin, 2019)

Amin's comments reflect what Linchuan Qiu refers to as "the shift of platform operations from mediated sociality and participatory culture to commerce and stock market performance" (2018, p. 2). As well as monetising community services such as Facebook events and pages, social media corporations profit from the information stored and the free labour put into such platforms (Linchuan Qiu, 2018, p. 7)

Rather than entirely move away from social media, Amin instead chose to set up @leedsdiy on Instagram as an alternative space to collect and display digital traces as well as promote ongoing activities. Utilising social media to amplify information is common in cultural industries, and can increase the audience or impact of initiatives (Flew, 2018) Amin was motivated to use digital platforms to undertake this work after seeing other platforms utilised to share information:

without social media these different essentially archives of specific trends or specific phenomena wouldn't exist because they never would have had the critical mass to exist. It also happens in things like databases like the one called writers of colour, [where] you can look for marginalised writers who can write about specific beats … that stuff wouldn't exist without the critical mass [of] social media, and us using it in a creative way rather than the way that they want us to use it. (Amin, 2019)

Similarly, Rob commented on the potential of these platforms saying that

there are creative ways of making use of these things as well… we can't throw the baby out with the bathwater … but we do have to think about it. (Hayler, 2020)

Writing about the tension between mainstream and alternative media in 1990s dance music subcultures, Thornton writes that

the idea that authentic culture is somehow outside media and commerce is a resilient one. In its full-blown romantic form, the belief suggests that grassroots cultures resist and struggle with a colonising mass-mediated corporate world. (1995, p. 116)

Whilst Thornton's analysis relates to different types of music journalism, we can translate this persistent desire to remain outside of corporate structures to the context of digital platforms. However, as the above quotes suggest, there is possibility and opportunity in making use of these networked technologies, whilst remaining aware of their limitations.

My next example in this section relates to the adoption of more informal memory practices through functions on Facebook and Instagram, particularly the #tbt hashtag ("throwback Thursday") on Instagram and the "on this day" memories function of Facebook. In the following quote interview participant Aaron discusses his motivations for sharing memories via social media:

I moved countries, and I left behind a lot of where I'm from. So…. I've had to start from scratch because I don't have a history here. And unfortunately, social media has been really good and reminded me of what I left behind [laughs]… And I could maybe reshare that gig flier that someone did that had my band name on it. Or I can reshare that really great photo that Joe did of us when we played DIY Space for the first time. I absolutely love that photo and absolutely love posting it, because you know, we look great, so I'll take every opportunity I can to post that again and again and again because I want to remind myself just as much as let everyone else know that this was me four, five years ago... (Batley, 2019)

For Aaron, the underpinning motivation to engage in these informal memory practices is deeply personal. These affective dimensions have also been articulated by researchers in other community heritage contexts (Baker, 2015a; Cifor, 2016; Long et al., 2017). Kuhn's examination of the family photograph album highlights how photographs hold felt meaning for individuals (2010, p. 305). Although Kuhn's analysis relies upon the use of material photographs for memory work (typified by an individual always carrying a photograph with them), we can see a similar value assigned to the recirculation of a digital image here. Of images prized in this way, Kuhn writes that

> This talismanic photograph embodies something of immeasurable and almost incommunicable value, and it speaks of a present as well as a past, or pasts. (2010, p. 305)

Although Aaron does not "own" the photograph in question, the re-sharing of a photograph or digitised flier continues to attach meaning to the photograph and provides an opportunity to reconnect with a community which is now located at a distance. This potential for archival materials to provide connection for communities is also identified in community heritage research (Flinn, 2007, p. 159).

The practice of sharing and engaging with memory via social media platforms can be situated as an act of "communicative memory" (Assmann, 2011). Communicative memory, initially explored by Jan and Aleida Assmann, is situated separately from cultural memory (which is produced via the circulation of texts and the cultural canon). As Assmann writes,

> communicative memory is noninstitutional. It is not supported by any institutions of learning, transmission, or interpretation, nor is it cultivated by specialists or summoned or celebrated on special occasions. It is not formalised and stabilised by any forms of material symbolisation. It lives in everyday interaction and communication. For this very reason communicative memory is of fairly limited duration. (2011, p. 18)

Communicative memory is typified through intangible, non-hierarchical and often grassroots forms of history making (e.g. oral history, performance, rituals), which are facilitated through communication networks. As these practices occur outside of institutions and rely upon social communities, these can be disrupted when these networks are displaced. This concept has subsequently been employed by researchers exploring memory in hip hop communities who describe how lyrics are used to give voice to those marginalised within society (Putnam and Schicker, 2014, p. 95). Although not consciously archival, the recalling and resharing of memories creates meaning for those in DIY music communities and ensures that otherwise un- or under-documented experiences continue to circulate. Assmann writes that "repetition is a form of preservation, of memory" (2011, p. 24)—although referring to performance rituals, this sentiment speaks to the way in which this community engages with memory on social media.

My final example relates to the utilisation of an existing platform to create records of former and active DIY music spaces and bands. In the following quote interview participant Colette describes using Wikipedia to create and update webpages for venues and bands:

> I'm quite into Wikipedia, so I occasionally go... and edit band stuff, I think that's quite cool... DIY Space or Power Lunches have a page on Wikipedia and bands like Trash Kit and Big Joanie have a page on there... I quite like the idea of that beavering away information (Colette, 2020).

In the above example, Wikipedia was used to create sources of information about spaces and bands which were immediately accessible to others, potentially persisting into the future. Using Wikipedia as a source enabled Colette to contribute information that can form "a living memory of the moments, people and places that might disappear and be forgotten" (Saber and Long, 2017, p. 92). The utilisation of this platform to document queer and/or feminist punk bands can be situated as an intervention both into the underrepresentation of women and queer people on Wikipedia and the lack of information about DIY music communities in other more formal historical sources.

However, there are issues embedded within Wikipedia's structure and culture that prevent the use of the platform for the above activities. Theorists have problematised a utopian vision of Wikipedia due to issues including gender biases (Reagle and Rhue, 2011). Scholars also identify the deletion or flagging for deletion of content by other users with "misogynist infopolitics"—for example, information about sexual violence flagged for being written in a "biased tone" (Peake, 2015). Colette described some of the challenges of using Wikipedia to create pages when there is a lack of existing authoritative sources to underpin information:

> I tried to make a page for a record label that I thought was brilliant. And it got deleted because it wasn't credible enough. Or you have to really like fight your corner. (Colette, 2020)

The emphasis on values of neutrality, authoritative sources and objectivity in Wikipedia editing is raised by Peake, who describes these battles as "lawyeristic manoeuvres" which "replace expertise about subject matter with expertise about Wikipedia's rules" (2015). Although the context of Peake's article is different to this study, these largely invisible struggles directly impact on what information counts and is made available via this platform.

Given the tensions identified in the preceding sections it is necessary to ask why we continue to use these platforms for these purposes, instead of engaging with alternatives. In Colette's case, the justification for using Wikipedia related to making information widely available on platforms which are understandable and accessible to most people:

> If people only have like rudimentary digital literacy skills and don't have a university database to search for things or something… Wikipedia has like a really high impact on like search results, so it comes up pretty high. Like, you know, versus like your own little website

Wikipedia has been used by social movements to develop knowledge sources as a movement develops (Twyman, Keegan and Shaw, 2017, p. 1400). These practices combine dynamic collaborative editing with networked documentation of evidence as events occur. The immediate visibility and accessibility of the resulting content is needed for individuals searching for information and community (see chapter four), and leaves behind a trace for those looking for histories of DIY music. In reference to community music archives, Baker and Huber describe how archiving is "as important for the memory practices of "the present"" as potential future users (2015, p. 122). The facilitation of access to information via digital interfaces also confronts traditional forms of access, which can require understanding of archival systems, processes and administrations that intimidate (Stoler, 2010, p. 9).

Some interview participants believed that digital platforms could broaden how archives (and their contents) were understood. Cassie said that

> I can't think of anything that people are doing that's not mainly based around digital methods. But maybe that's a really exciting thing because ... when people think about archiving, they think about boxes and boxes of dusty documents, when actually the archiving of our experiences and our culture like there's so many more options now about what that looks like. (Agbehenu, 2019)

Digital memory work also contributed to the redefinition of the role of archivist and/or curator. For instance, Tayyab reflected:

> And curating... it's actually key here cos you know, two of the words that have like really like rose to prominence this decade are content and curation ... while those words are portals to kind of harmful mindsets about information sharing, at the same time there's something democratising about everyone being the curator now. (Amin, 2019)

The playful engagement with and re-envisioning of archives and/or curating in this context destabilises the "borders" of archival practice and discourse (Ishmael, 2018, p. 270), instead re-producing archival traditions from different positions. This potential is significant because it shifts discussions about how we are included in the archive from discussions of inclusion, representation or recognition (which separate us from "the archive" from the outset) and towards transformative visions of the archive which are situated as part of decolonial archival praxis (Ghaddar and Caswell, 2019, p. 72). Risam's work in postcolonial digital humanities emphasises the potential for digital platforms to intervene in and remake "the worlds instantiated in the digital cultural record through politically, ethically, and social justice-minded approaches to digital knowledge production" (Risam, 2018, p. 4). Rather than working with and/or in archives established within alienating traditions, digital platforms offer the potential to start again, on different foundations.

This section has explored how individuals utilised digital platforms to assert the presence of DIY music spaces, communities, and creative projects. Digital memory work was undertaken through the establishment of consciously archival spaces, which were used to both promote current events and leave traces behind for future users. Individuals also engaged with more informal ways to document and share information, including sharing memories on social media platforms and adding information into larger platforms (e.g. Wikipedia). Digital platforms were used so that information could be easily encountered and to maintain accessibility to traces. This aligns with scholarship exploring memory work on social media within social movements, which indicates that sharing of memory "may help mobilise individuals into action, legitimise their cause, historically situate their struggle, and create a collective identity" (Smit, Heinrich and Broersma, 2018, p. 3126). These projects and actions asserted cultural value and added depth and meaning to traces, which in turn enabled individuals to regain some sense of control over their histories.

Absence

The preceding sections of this chapter proposed that social media and blogging platforms have afforded DIY music communities new space to share archival traces in ways which make creative use of the networked and participatory nature of platforms for subversive purposes. In many ways, this section explores the later life of these materials after momentum and energy from these projects has run out. Utilising quotes from interviews, I explore the extensive digital labours these projects rely on, and issues of absence, inaccessibility and sustainability that affect the longevity of these individual actions.

As I search for now long-gone promoting collectives and cultural producers online, I find myself frequently clicking on broken links or greeted by error messages. I search for social media profiles and am told that the profile "no longer exists", words which seem to erase the existence of communities unintentionally and violently. The instability and inaccessibility of web history is an issue for a community that relies on digital platforms for everything from socialising and organising to memory work. Most traditional documentary traces of DIY music spaces are now digital, including recorded music, posters/fliers and correspondence between individuals (Jones, 2018, p. 117). This can be situated within what Milligan refers to as the broader "medium shift in how we document our lives, societies and cultures" which instigated the establishment of the Internet Archive in 1996 (2019, p. 4).

In chapter three, I introduced Earhart's concept of the "digital recovery project" to explore alternative forms of canon-building (2015). Digital recovery projects were utilised by literary scholars and activists in the web

Figure 2 We don't exist (original illustration)

2.0 era to digitise and provide access to texts that had been maligned in Western canons and subsequently gone out of print (Earhart, 2015, p. 62). However, the rapid creation and expansion of digital recovery projects was short-lived and many sites have subsequently disappeared or are now decaying due to a lack of upkeep and interest (Earhart, 2015, p. 82). Although the paper-based archival record is subject to decay over time too, in a digital environment this happens rapidly and in an unpredictable and potentially more devastating manner. The knowledge of the decaying and dissolving of the optimistic digital spaces of web 2.0 frames this section's examination of the afterlives of digital content.

Information stored on digital platforms is not reliable, even when sites were initiated by those active in DIY music communities. A participant in an early discussion workshop reflected that:

> It's funny, there's things that you google to find out what year they were and then they're not there now, if it was a gig a year ago it'd be there, it's really unhelpful. (Participant C, 2019)

The above comment happened during a mapping activity undertaken with attendees of Bent Fest and illustrates the challenges of writing histories of DIY music spaces when there is a discontinuity of information. The participants in the workshop are reliant on digital information and utilise the internet as a source. As much of this information is relatively recent (in this case, less than ten years old), participants in this workshop were surprised to discover that these sources had already become inaccessible. When sources are lost, it is not only the information which disappears but the potential for communication between different generations and sub-sections of the community. As Aleida Assmann writes in relation to communicative memory,

Communication between eras and generations is broken when a particular store of common knowledge disappears. (2013, p. 4)

The loss of information negatively impacts a community's ability to understand its history, connect with those from earlier generations and learn from previous projects (see chapter three).

Emma described how the costs of server upkeep led to her taking the site for her former promotions collective offline:

> we actually had quite a fancy site, but I'm no longer doing it and the hosting is coming up for renewal and I'm not going to pay for another year, so that's going to be gone soon. But I mean, I've got it all

backed up. But you know, it won't be available publicly on the web anymore. (Falconer, 2019)

Emma showed awareness about web archives (the Wayback machine) and committed to storing the website as files on her own storage—thus preserving the website in some way. However, by taking it offline, she temporarily removed capacity for public access to the information on the website. The maintenance of a "live" website is an economic commitment which is often unsustainable in the long term. In another interview, Colette reflected about a website for a previous band that had since been deleted due to the cost of hosting:

> Frau had a really good website that [bandmate] kept updated and like put all our gigs on and had our past gigs which she just eventually just stopped paying for the domain for that, so that doesn't exist anymore. (Colette, 2020)

In many other cases, similar websites have disappeared without any trace remaining behind and without being deposited in a web archive. To illustrate this, the website for Power Lunches (a former DIY music space cited by many of the London-based interview participants in this study as significant to their own creative development) is now offline, despite the venue closing only slightly more than four years ago. As a result of this, a comprehensive source of listings and communications about the space has ceased to exist, unarchived. As Hess writes in reference to memorial websites, websites are often subject to "the weathering of time" –

> while the edges don't chip and the text seems as fresh as the day it was produced, some memorials are simply erased from existence by their lack of maintenance and payment of fees for domain space. (2007, p. 821)

In these cases, the absence of these digital traces is caused by economic and logistical factors. As the domain name for this (and many other websites) is not a UK domain (e.g. .co.uk or .org.uk), the website was not automatically captured by the UK Web Archive, unless individuals had awareness of the option to nominate a site directly.

Social media platforms like Instagram and Facebook promote cultures of daily updates, stories and live broadcasting which should, in theory, provide more representations of UK DIY music communities. However, many participants in this study referred to an ongoing inaccessibility of web traces, particularly those from the early and mid 2000s. Of this issue, Ben said

> social media helps a lot because of this just need to document everything …. that there's more of an archive and we're kind of exposing more of these things in little pieces and stuff … but then that could disappear, like… the great rapidshare mediafire years in the late 2000s, loads of those have already gone … we had a thing where we had everything, and then it's gone again, but then it isn't at the same time, it is still there, but it's… less accessible. (Perkins, 2019)

Emma similarly referred to Facebook's search functions, stating that

> if people aren't doing paper fliers for gigs, and it's only a Facebook event, could you find a Facebook event from three years ago? I couldn't. (Falconer, 2019)

The shift from paper to digital fliers and posters (or no fliers at all, and just a Facebook event) leave the cultural memory of an event firmly in the hands of social media platforms. As Milligan writes,

> having all this material saved does not mean that it will be accessible—not only does the data need to be stewarded, but it also needs to be discoverable. (2019, p. 6)

When information is preserved (even if only for the short term) on digital platforms, there is no commitment to make that information readily accessible after its immediate use for current organising has passed. These issues with inaccessibility of content were already noticeable to individuals looking for events in recent history.

These examples highlight a key issue with web-based sources, which is the rapid pace at which content can change, due to either individual action to take websites offline or larger scale platform changes instigated by corporations. As Brügger writes

> The problem with the Web is its ephemerality: content is frequently either updated or removed permanently, and layout, design and forms of interaction are changing rapidly. After just a short period, the Web of the past is likely to have disappeared, and it is only available if it has been archived. (2018, p. 197)

Brügger's concerns are shared by archival theorists who highlight the importance of rapid collecting practices and archival interventions in order to preserve traces (Flinn, 2008; Sheffield, 2018). However, there is little evidence of heritage organisations doing web heritage work within music subcultures, with recent initiatives (both institutional and community-led) focused on past decades rather than current communities. This retrospective focus follows expected archival timeframes, in which collections are acquired years or decades after events occur (Sheffield, 2018, p. 119). Meanwhile, individuals within DIY music communities lack the archival skills to manage web content, which heightens the lack of control that participants felt over their archival traces.

In some cases participants undertook small actions to prevent the absence and inaccessibility of born-digital information. For example, Rob reflected that

> nothing lasts forever, especially digital formats and platforms. And as I get older, and you see things, you see things ebb and flow, you might start thinking more about that. (Hayler, 2020)

Rob expressed an ongoing concern about his reliance on WordPress to host his music blog. He chose to print a physical copy of all the posts (3,000 pages of content in total). This mitigated feelings of anxiety and ensured the content would survive in another form. Although the act of printing out digital content may feel like a rudimentary response to archival professionals, it nonetheless represents an attempt to preserve and maintain control over digital information that would otherwise likely disappear.

Along with inaccessibility of information, another issue which has consistently been raised as part of this project is the amount of work required to keep digital archives alive and active. In reference to the development of a Canadian trans feminist digital archive, Cowan and Rault raise concerns about how these platforms "rely on the unpaid labours of users of these scenes to also produce their content" (2014a, p. 476). Over the course of our interview Tayyab frequently reflected on how he was unable to commit the amount of labour required to produce content for @leedsdiy:

> I don't really have the time to put into it, which is a shame but in theory, what I'm hoping to do is to continue uploading stuff, and then making a story for every month, so you have a calendar for that month, it's difficult just because I don't have the time to do it. (Amin, 2019)

It is noted that at the point of finishing my PhD, the site has ceased being updated. Alongside producing content for these platforms (which also function to share information about current activities), creators may need to migrate content, fix broken links, pay for hosting or server space and/or create back-ups to keep these sites alive. Research has focused much more on the emancipatory potential of personal digital archival practice, and as such "the digital labours involved in their after-lives" (Cowan, McLeod and Rault, 2014) often goes unacknowledged or unaddressed. In the cultural context of UK DIY music spaces, this is particularly important to acknowledge as many community members manage multiple commitments in paid work, activism, creative practice, and families. As Tayyab reflected, "participation [in DIY music] is a little bit of this, a little bit of that, a whole bunch of different things that I'm juggling" (Amin, 2019). Chapter four identified how archival work is often invisible labour, and here it is clear that this routine work can also be a low priority in comparison to other competing commitments.

Discussions also illustrated the potential absence of born digital traces (and particularly web heritage) from community-based and more formal collecting activities. As previous chapters have indicated, many individuals seek to collect, keep, and move with personal archival collections of paper-based materials. However, the inclusion of web-based and born digital archival materials in such archives was less common. When asked about the web-based information about their involvement in DIY music, Leigh said:

> Oh, yeah, we had a MySpace. And I think all of the fliers and stuff were on there as well. But I don't know if I kept anything particularly digital around that time. (Leigh, 2020)

Although individuals are aware of the utilisation of digital platforms and internet technologies to document UK DIY music, they were less likely to assume that those traces are archival in any way. As such, these materials are less likely to be contained within any personal archiving projects.

Throughout conversations that happened as part of this project, I was surprised to find that few people were aware of web archiving, particularly the UK Web Archive (UKWA), through which it is possible to nominate your own website for archiving. The UKWA only archives websites with UK domains unless individuals submit their website for archiving. This would exclude many of the sites identified through interviews which often had .com domains. Whilst many individuals who participated in interviews were aware of the British Library's Sound Archive (and had been reached out to for releases), the same was not true of the UKWA. The below interaction between myself and blogger Rob typifies this:

> Rob   They, some fellow at the British Library wanted copies of all the music
>
> Kirsty The sound archive?
>
> Rob   The sound archive, of course ... I did mention the blog. And I said, look, if you're archiving, if you're interested in archiving this stuff, then there's a lot here for you to look at, if only to pick out things that you might be interested in, contacts and stuff. I don't know what they've done with that, if anything. (Hayler, 2020)

Improving awareness of institutional web archives could counter what otherwise seems like inevitable loss of digital content, without requiring additional labour from community members. Chapter seven explores how interviews provided an opportunity for me to make use of my boundary spanning role to provide information and advice about web archiving to individuals.

This section has explored long term implications for access to and preservation of archival traces of UK DIY music on digital platforms. The switch to predominantly digital record creation causes absence and inaccessibility in many ways—absence of communities using digital platforms in traditional archive collections, absence or inaccessibility of information due to the cost and labour involved in its maintenance, inaccessibility of information after current use, and absence of web heritage in personal archival projects. These absences impact on history writing, cultural memory and on the sharing of information between generations of DIY cultural activists, producers, and organisers. Building on this, the final section of this chapter explores instances in which information and digital traces are deleted from platforms as part of moderation and/or community management protocols.

Deletion

I begin this section with a personal experience, through which I initially became aware of practices of deletion and moderation of content held on digital platforms. In February 2019, I was organising the third Weirdo Zine Fest, a zine fair for radical and marginalised cultural producers. Around the same time, peers were co-organising the final Bent Fest (a UK-based queer punk festival) and a birthday music-based all-day event for the DIY feminist collective Girl Gang Leeds. We had all used social media extensively to promote our past events, making the most of Facebook, Instagram, and Twitter's user bases, sharing cultures and networks of groups and communities. The first time I organised Weirdo Zine Fest, the event received around 2,000 RSVPs, press coverage and hundreds of visitors, all of which I can attribute largely to practices of sharing, liking, and engaging through social media.

In our position as cultural organisers working in DIY music, each of our relationships with these online corporate platforms felt uncomfortable. Social media commits to many of the same aims as DIY cultures—both aim to centre participation, sharing, intimacy and autonomy in cultural production. However, the former utilises all the above to make money and build business via capitalism. As Jones writes,

> DIY has often been concerned with the pernicious impact of the music industry on both consumers and producers, and social web platforms have offered new, alternative means of circulating music outside of these traditional structures. However, multinational corporations such as Facebook, Google, and Twitter hold significant cultural and economic power of their own, and their practice is shaped by their own commercial imperatives. (2018, p. 16)

Pelly has also pointed to the use of these platforms by police and other authorities to monitor and subsequently close illegitimate DIY spaces (2018). Working on these platforms felt undeniably useful for extending audiences and bringing new people into DIY music spaces, so we accepted the temporary necessity of working with and through them. However, the paradoxical nature of this relationship was felt by interview participants. For instance, Ben said:

> You have DIY labels paying Facebook for advertising space, in a way that they would baulk at doing [for] the old media villains and stuff like Maximum Rocknroll having these kind of things about no major labels no Murdoch no Vice that kind of thing, but then you're existing on these very strange platforms…

Thus, the relationship between DIY music spaces and social media platforms is challenging and tense, however still nonetheless intertwined.

In 2019, the algorithmic moderation practices of social media affected each of our organising groups. In the weeks leading up to our events, after months of digital promotion and outreach, we each received notifications that stated that our events "violated community standards" and had been removed without a trace. Community standards, often invisible to most users of social media, dictate the types of content which exist on these platforms and, as a result, what content is deleted or flagged as inappropriate (Poell and van Dijck, 2018, p. 553). The need to impose these rules is presented as a legal obligation, but often disguises a darker ideological position. As Gillespie writes the

> responsibility of curating the content and policing the activity of their users... [is] not simply to meet legal requirements, or to avoid having additional policies imposed, but also to avoid losing offended or harassed users, to placate advertisers eager to associate their brands with a healthy online community, to protect their corporate image, and to honour their own personal and institutional ethics. (2018, p. 255)

The moderation of digital platforms is done in the interests of advertisers, capitalist corporations and legal obligations, rather than the individual users of platforms. As such "these corporations have a structural economic interest to systematically police the activity and content on their platforms in ways that do not always correspond with activists' politics of visibility" (Poell and van Dijck, 2018, p. 553). It is unreasonable to expect that platforms in such positions can remain impartial when influenced by these different stakeholders.

In our case, the loss of the event meant more than the loss of the information about the event, which could be easily reproduced. We each also lost access to a network or community that had built up via RSVPing to the event page. Kaz from Girl Gang Leeds describes the experience of the deletion of this information on the collective at the time:

> We had a really big really important Facebook event deleted last year... it was leading up to our second birthday party, which is our most expensive event of the year because it's the only time we do an all dayer where we've got a full day of bands to pay and we've got a venue to pay, we've got food to pay for, we've got usually a cake, a photographer, all sorts of stuff that we don't normally have. And it's very, very reliant on people knowing it's happening, people buying

> tickets….for me it wasn't just about losing like a Facebook event, when you say to people at first it doesn't really sound like that big a deal, but it was like we had a really strong following on it. I think we had about 2000 people on it and I was like, oh my god, that's 2000 people that might think this event isn't happening anymore, they're not going to see any updates. They're not gonna buy tickets. I'm gonna lose money and that's what it came down to. (Scattergood, 2020)

In the process of losing these events, we had lost connections, information and the result of a lot of cultural organising labour. We set up appeals via Facebook's internal processes, and then started to rebuild what we had done before. Each of us reached out to one another as the deletions happened to verify whether we had all experienced the same. While we waited for further information from Facebook, we debated whether this had happened because of targeted reporting (each of our events were explicitly inclusive of trans people and sex workers) or whether the events had been deleted by an anonymous algorithm. We received no communication beyond the initial notification and, ultimately, never received any clarification about the precise reason behind the removal of our events.

Kaz describes the emotional and logistical impact of this deletion on the collective:

> it made us realise how vulnerable we were and how reliant we were on this thing that is not really in our control. And we'd never thought of it like that before. I think we'd always just been like, yeah, this is our way of communicating stuff, this is the way we promote our events and it had never really occurred to us that that was gonna be an issue... I'd like to say that now we're better but we're probably not, we probably do still rely on definitely the Facebook event, and like Instagram and Twitter, in the same way as we did because it's free and it's accessible to us. But yeah, it definitely made me think twice about like oh god, we're really reliant on this thing. (Scattergood, 2020)

When asked about feelings about anxiety around the deletion of material held on digital platforms, Rob similarly said:

> I'm concerned about WordPress or Bandcamp, or Twitter or being part of the digital economy. There's a logistical reason to be concerned because it all could just be turned off. And there's a political reason to be concerned because you know, the overlords are listening [laughs]. (Hayler, 2020)

Both of these quotes are clear illustrations of what Saber and Long refer to as "the anxiety of the digital" (2017, p. 93)–feelings of vulnerability and uncertainty connected to the lack of control we possess as users of these platforms. Recent writing by Zuboff has also indicated that the "emancipatory promise of the internet" has also provided "important shelter for surveillance capitalism's ability to root and flourish (2019, p. 30). The lack of control and negative affect we all experienced through these experiences helped us understand that these platforms will never be safe spaces for the information we create or the communities we nurture.

This wasn't the first time we had all seen evidence and information relating to DIY music deleted by social media platforms. In 2014, queer feminist music collective LaDIYfest Sheffield reported the deletion of their Facebook account via a Wordpress blog. In their blog post the collective wrote about feeling grief over the loss:

> this account has taken us four years to build and, although there's something embarrassing about mourning the data stored by a capitalist virtual social network, it still feels like a pretty huge loss. (LaDIYfest Sheffield, 2014)

The deletion of the LaDIYfest Sheffield account was caused by a crackdown on the use of pseudonyms on social media platforms, enforced by "real-name policies" which required "users to identify themselves through their legal name" (Poell and van Dijck, 2018, p. 553).This resulted in the mass deletion of accounts which had not previously conformed to these guidelines. The grief over the loss of the account was partially caused by the loss of the organising networks and community that had developed over the course of the account's existence, but also by the loss of the digital memory of the collective's existence.

Exploring the impact of the above policies on protest movements, Poell and van Dijck write that

> for many activists it is important to remain anonymous, whereas social media platform owners—generally American corporations—have a strong interest in knowing users' real identities, which can be monetised more easily. (2018, p. 553)

Haimson and Hoffman also refer to this "administrative and largely inflexible notion of "real names"" as being destructive to trans users and survivors of abuse who (amongst others) may need to use different names to their legally assigned (or "dead") names for safety or to affirm gender identity (Haimson and Hoffmann, 2016). The aforementioned authors highlight the negative impact that deactivation and deletion have on activist organising groups as well as causing negative emotional impact on individuals in marginalised groups. Looking at the above example it is easy to see a similarly disruptive and negative impact on UK DIY music organising groups.

Another example of the deletion of the web heritage of UK DIY music referenced during my research interviews was the closure of Yahoo's GeoCities websites across the 2000s and 2010s. Between 2009 and 2019 a number of journalists referenced the gradual closure of GeoCities by Yahoo, noting the networks and content that would be lost with the websites (Gilbertson, 2009; Bastone, 2018). As Bastone wrote in 2018,

> essentially a web hosting service that made it easy for anyone to build their own websites, GeoCities became a thriving digital metropolis of rudimentary HTML pages devoted to personal hobbies, quirks and pastimes. (2018)

As well as the content held on Geocities websites, Gilbertson noted the impact on the online networks which once flourished in those spaces–as he writes

> sadly, when sites disappear, whether they're artefacts like Geocities or more modern examples like Pownce or Ma.gnolia, there's never a way to recover the lost connections between people. (2009)

GeoCities and website hosting platforms from the same era (e.g. Angelfire) provided important points of connection and information for participants. For example, Aaron describes finding information on these websites in the early 2000s:

> when I got into riot grrrl… the internet was kind of coming to the fore, like 2000, 2001. And the only way to really know anything about riot grrrl was to look up on the internet, and that's when you discovered all the weird Angelfire websites and stuff that had references to it.

In many cases, inactive websites were viewed both with amusement (due to unsophisticated web design which typifies GeoCities websites) and with appreciation, as their persistence nonetheless enabled individuals to find community and find out more about the history of DIY music communities.

These websites (some still active, and others deleted or closed down) represent individual or small-scale attempts to witness and "to assign significance to one's own life and the lives within one's community" (DiVeglia, 2012, p. 78). As well as creating opportunities to memorialise the DIY music spaces and communities authors valued, these websites created valuable space to speak back to dominant narratives of DIY music communities, which is particularly important in the context of movements with tense relationships with mainstream media, cultural memory and popular culture (e.g. riot grrrl). In the case of riot grrrl, Strong writes that individual memory "plays a vital role in the maintenance or changing of social structures, in this case patriarchy" (2011, p. 399). In reference to memorial websites created following the September 11th terrorist attacks, Hess writes that

> the vernacular voice [of memorial websites] competes with these other official voices to represent the events of September 11th. Consequently, users witness the competing value structures and interests inherent in public memory. (2007, p. 819)

The websites from earlier DIY music communities form sources of connection, information and memory that are valuable and transformative for the above interview participants. In many cases, the information on those websites provides an opportunity for individuals to talk back against the disappearing women of music histories (Strong, 2011).

As the above examples suggest, the deletion of information held on digital platforms is a significant issue for UK DIY music communities. The closure of platforms such as GeoCities, deletion of information on Facebook and Tumblr, and the loss of data on Myspace music poses a significant threat to the cultural memory of UK DIY music communities. By exploring instances of deletion of information and digital traces of UK DIY music, this section has identified the emotional impact of such processes on cultural organisers and community members. As well as the loss of information itself, the shift to digital networks and organising practises leaves UK DIY music communities without control of their information or how it is preserved and used.

Conclusion

Utilising the server migration that led to the deletion of most of the recorded music held on Myspace in 2019 as a starting point for a critical analysis, this chapter has explored the connections between DIY music spaces, communities, information, and digital platforms. I began by situating this community within a broader context of activist organising, highlighting the impact of "the volatility and precariousness of the digital" (Saber and Long, 2017, p. 81) on activist memory. By exploring the relationship between digital platforms, information, and UK DIY music communities, I have been able to identify challenges, opportunities, and threats to the cultural memory of these communities that manifest in this context. The value of web heritage in UK DIY music is not to be underestimated–in many cases, Facebook pages or Tumblrs may be the only information persisting beyond the active years of very ephemeral spaces and projects, especially as traditional material traces are predominantly digital in nature (e.g. fliers and posters). The precarity of this information in turn, as well as the risk of deletion, inaccessibility or closure of the sites holding it, requires urgent intervention to prevent loss of this cultural memory. This includes a shift in the value afforded to these materials within communities and heritage institutions, sharing of knowledge and tools which enable individuals to archive their own web heritage, and active outreach from heritage organisations to collect these traces (where they are equipped to do so).

Figure 3 Ground collapsing 1 (original illustration)

Unstable Alternatives

Figure 1 Flier for DIY Space for London fundraiser gig (2012)

I find the digital file for the flier on the preceding page when scraping the media library of a website for digital assets to deposit with the DIY Space for London archive. The words generate feelings of sadness as I remember the energy, drive, and rage that underpinned the fundraising for the space at the time. As I scroll through the contents of the website's media library, I find traces of much more that is now gone. London's grassroots and DIY music spaces from the 2010s are represented–Power Lunches, The Grosvenor, T-Chances, and others which are now closed. House shows and squats dot amidst the more formal (yet still temporary) spaces–195 Mare Street Social Centre, Eileen House. The latter, a squat in an office block in Elephant and Castle, was temporarily claimed from the hands of property developers and Boris Johnson by a coalition of collectives called the Self-Organised London Group in 2013 to act as an "anti-gentrification centre" (Past Tense, 2017). The DIY Space for London collective were one of groups based there, throwing benefit shows during 2013. Hopping between tabs, I find that this squatted space hosted queer cinema nights, a Spanish-English language exchange, benefits support, a people's kitchen, and political theatre (along with, apparently, punk shows). The juxtaposition of a wide variety of activist events, gatherings and activities is common in DIY, autonomous and community-led spaces, which often provide affordable access to space for a wide variety of purposes. The loss of just one of these spaces thus impacts not just DIY music communities, but a much broader subset of grassroots collectives and organisers.

Another one down.

Figure 2   Flier for DIY Space for London fundraiser gig at Eileen House, 2013

I didn't know anyone involved in DIY Space for London in 2012. I had just moved to London in 2012 as a zine maker and blogger, starting a postgraduate course around the same time. Over the following year, I got to know individuals from the DIY music scene in London. The excitement for the DIY Space for London project was infectious–at the time, London was in desperate need of an autonomous space that could function

Figure 3 Selection of fliers for DIY Space for London fundraiser gigs, 2013

for multiple purposes—activist meetings, zine fairs, punk shows, film screenings, club nights, banner painting, clothes swaps and more. Those involved from the onset of the project had seen the closure of many temporary punk spaces and squats, and sought the stability, accessibility and autonomy that had not been otherwise available. What followed the inception of the project was a burst of fundraising activities, represented by a series of fliers on the following page.

The first time I walked into DIY Space for London was slightly before opening at a small gathering for friends and family of the volunteers and co-operative in September 2015. A friend showed me around the space, which felt huge considering the 50-capacity basements we otherwise clustered in at the time. The promise of the space was overwhelming. Jones writes that within the cultural context of DIY music, smaller spaces are often afforded value—he refers to this as

> prizing the intimacy of a small venue, and the temporary community created within it, as an end in itself, rather than seeing it as a stepping stone. (2018, p. 14)

Though what had been created was a small space, it seemed like an end to a long journey towards a community-owned and operated space. It felt like more than enough for the future.

The story of the space is a familiar one. The first generation of organisers burnt out quickly, with few members of this first generation retaining active involvement behind the scenes. There were internal conflicts that caused further rifts. The housing crisis forced many out of London, including me. In 2020 during the COVID-19 pandemic, the venue's lease was due for renewal. A combination of difficulties meant that the renewal was not granted, and the volunteers then active in the space then dismantled a space that had only opened 4.5 years earlier. Another one down.

This initial exploration of a series of traces from the space presents many experiences that will be familiar to any reader with history in DIY cultural activism. In the following sections I identify a series of intersections of precarity which affect the production, preservation, and deposit of archival traces of UK DIY music. I define these intersections as precarious networks; precarious spaces; precarious traces; and precarious lives. I will argue that this combination of short lived and close-knit networks, rapidly closing physical spaces, undervalued and precariously stored artefacts and unstable housing and work contributes to the loss and disposal of records of these communities and spaces. Previous chapters of this thesis have demonstrated that information matters to those involved in this research, and that many are taking informal action to ensure the persistence of their individual and collective memories. However, data gathered through interviews also indicated that the ability to act was heavily affected by external factors, particularly those caused by living under austerity, gentrification, and the gradual erosion of state support. By exploring these intersections in more detail, I will make visible socioeconomic factors which put not only these histories and archives at risk, but those of many other musical communities in the UK.

Theorists have regularly argued that we should consider music communities in relation to the socioeconomic, political, and geographic context in which they emerge, which is particularly evident in explorations of music in deindustrialised cities (Cohen, 1991; Spracklen, Henderson and Procter, 2016; Kenny, 2019). In his discussion of the punk scene in Washington DC, Azerrad describes how punk bands formed and dissolved rapidly due to turnover in government workforce which affected the population (2012, p. 377). Socioeconomic circumstances affect our ability to make music and access equipment and resources, the support available to new cultural spaces, and the sustainability of our community endeavours. This chapter furthers this thinking by arguing that socioeconomic circumstances further impact on what remains of our communities.

Precarious cultural networks

DIY music centres around a culture of performance and congregation within physical spaces. The combination of socialising and performance within small spaces provides an opportunity for the development of local networks, through which bands, organising collectives, tours, projects, and other collaborations are formed. Leonard's exploration of 90s riot grrrl subcultures makes use of the word "network" to describe a community because "it identifies lines of interconnection" without suggesting a leading singular voice (1997, p. 231), a sentiment which is also relevant in this context. The use of networks to nurture creativity is similarly aligned with Leonard's context, in which a combination of zines, spaces and gigs within these networks are used to encourage involvement and build confidence amongst young women traditionally marginalised in punk spaces (1997, p. 240).

These small local networks connect with others with similar ethos' based in other localities through invitations to travel to share line ups and attend larger festivals, creating national (and sometimes international) networks which regularly cross paths. This national network is demonstrated by the following quote from Kirsty, who reflects on experiences of travelling across the UK:

> You suddenly find yourself in a situation that you live in Coventry, but you can hop on the Megabus up to Leeds, walk into Wharf Chambers and people are like, oh, hi, it's Ruth and Kirsty from Not Right, and you're like, this is bizarre [laughs]. But you know, then it feels like we're actually part of something, that we can wander around the country and know people and be on the same page with people in terms of what we're doing culturally. (Lohman, 2020)

Musical networks that transcend local geographies are described as "trans-local networks" by Kruse, who describes how individual and disparate scenes are connected through "broader systems of cultural production and dissemination" (2010, p. 629). The sense of informal community network visible in the above anecdote connects to other research about music cultures, including that of Joseph, who writes that "music… has a specific community-building capacity through the affective atmospheres it can produce" (2018, p. 17). These networks not only enable musical collaborations but provide space for communities and friendships to develop over time.

The formation of informal networks such as the above are not exclusive to DIY music. In relation to lesbians involved in AIDS activist collective ACT UP/NY, Cvetkovich describes "the more ephemeral network of friendships and publics that accompanied its vast archive of graphics, documentaries and papers" (2003b, p. 430). The author describes close and affective connections between members of the organisation:

> The women talk about going dancing in the clubs with the men after meetings, developing beloved friendships and even romances, and building rituals and traditions such as a queer Jewish seder; they describe a wide array of affective networks that underpin activism. (Cvetkovich, 2003b, p. 437)

McKinney similarly describes how feminist networks provided a combination of practical and emotional support, the latter an essential part of nurturing history and archival work undertaken by those marginalised in society (2015, p. 323). In Cvetkovich's context, bonding and developing friendships was a survival strategy and a way to provide support and care to those they were connected to through activism. I can think of many parallels in my own history–sharing brunches for people staying at my house after a gig, the ready sharing of skills, knowledge and equipment between peers, the many dance parties, and after-show gatherings at houses and after doors closed at a space, the spare seats in cars to festivals and all-dayers, and many more. These social aspects of cultural activism are both logistically essential (without mutual aid providing floors to sleep on and free meals, touring is prohibitively expensive for the average DIY band), and a commitment to a culture which seeks to sustain involvement and widen access through small caring gestures and connections.

National networks in turn become international networks when bands tour in different countries, when peers relocate and/or through the use of digital technologies. International networks have also historically been nurtured through zines and publications via letters columns, personal ads, and correspondence networks (Fenster, 1993; Leonard, 1997; Mussell, 2012; McKinney, 2015; Stead, 2016). Mussell describes ephemeral publications as forming a crucial part of an international "information economy" (2012, p. 78), allowing information to be stored and circulated in cultural networks. In relation to 20th century feminist newsletters, McKinney describes how a publication's network "facilitated collaboration across space, with people who were otherwise different to know about, let alone reach" (2015, p. 310).

Although DIY cultural networks have been developed through publications and in physical spaces across generations, new digital platforms have enabled the proliferation of networked spaces and online friendships across geographical boundaries. Referring to online fan communities, Lothian writes that

> As fan cultures migrated online, they used digital media to reproduce what the legacy archival and participatory spaces of zines and conventions had made possible: not only lovingly created responses to objects of fandom, but also interpersonal connections and cultural networks that exceed any given media property. (2013, p. 546)

Although researchers have identified the significance of online message boards and other digital spaces in the development of music and fan cultures (Kruse, 2010; Lingel et al., 2012; Lothian, 2013), these digital networks have remained largely unarchived. In turn, despite ethnographic studies that highlight the ways in which social networks underpin DIY music cultures (Downes, 2010; Griffin, 2015), these informal and affective social connections are rarely documented in archives and records of UK DIY music. The remainder of this section considers reasons why networks are underrepresented in archives and histories of DIY music, drawing attention to the ways in which information about networks is frequently held outside of repositories.

The affective and informal nature of DIY music networks can be lost because it is rarely consciously documented as part of cultural production. For example, in the following quote Steph describes the existence of a network of black feminists active in London:

> I was in a black feminist group who were supposed to have like a website and archive, but it all fell apart, and so there isn't really any evidence that there was a really important black feminist group operating in London, that actually brought out some [of] our best black female feminist thinkers ... it was this meeting of all these brilliant women, but now there's no archive that it happened. (Phillips, 2019)

In the above example, the network went undocumented by peers but persists in living memory and through verbal storytelling practices. This highlights the capacity of oral history as a tool to represent networks within histories and archives of UK DIY music. The use of oral history within music subcultures is not a novel idea–there are now a plethora of punk oral history books (Robb and Craske, 2006; McNeil and McCain, 2016; Warfield, Crasshole and Leyser, 2021). Oral history is described as complementary to the DIY ethic–Turrini, for example, writes that the two in combination "are primary components of punk's "cultural toolkit"" (2013, p. 61). However, what existing research into punk oral histories does not highlight is the capacity for this method to make networks more visible in archives and histories.

Finding historical networks in DIY music is a game of discovery, conducted through liner notes, fliers, social media interactions, Facebook event attendees and Wikipedia pages. In the following quote, Kirsty describes her own experience of tracing networks in DIY music using sites like Discogs or Wikipedia:

> online archives of all sorts of different scenes are just absolutely amazing [for] tracing these things like, I hear a band in the list of a couple of other bands, and if I know one of them, then chances are

I'll be able to work out the musical connections or theme connections that mean that somebody listed those bands together, and then I can find all those other bands and find who was in that band or what person linked these bands. (Lohman, 2020)

Those of us with history in movements are often able to read between the notes and travel through links to uncover these networks, "reading between the lines of connections" to produce meaning (Spracklen, Henderson and Procter, 2016, p. 148). For those outside of these communities (or those seeking to connect with previous generations) this tracing of networks is a challenge. As the above quote indicates, the sources used to follow networks from the recent past are not traditionally "archival"–Discogs and Wikipedia, for example, are databases which hold information but do not necessarily consider the long-term preservation of such information as part of their remit. Network data (gathered via dialogue and analogue methods) can be used in network analysis projects of punk communities (Crossley, 2008, 2009, 2015; O'Shea, 2014; Watson, 2020), but when digital, the representations of these small networks will only be kept for as long as the platform can make use of the data. The information representing these networks is therefore more precarious than information held in archives due to the platforms on which it is currently discoverable.

Archival collecting and history writing practises can also undervalue the role of networks in DIY music. Chapter one of this thesis explored how the selective tradition has informed collecting and history writing practises. Through this process, histories and archives can be centred around those with "significant" achievements, impact, or a particularly productive cultural output. The focus on cultural outputs and commercial success minimises different forms of work done by others in DIY, which are as essential to the operation of DIY music communities. For example, Colette reflected that:

> the brilliant thing about DIY in punk is that, especially when you book a tour, you've maybe got a contact via someone but you don't know the person, you get there and they've made you really amazing food, they've made a brilliant poster, they put you up in this house, they've done [a] really good job, and then if you put then put their band on or whatever[...]there is something to be said about recognition of people working really hard at something that is .... DIY and they believe in it. (Colette, 2020)

Of queer and feminist performance art, McKinney and Mitchell write that

> This process-driven, behind-the-scenes labour is often hard to document because it's work that happens in the background, before any engagement with the public takes place. But "getting the job done" represents so much of what queer art making and queer activism actually entail. (2019, p. 8)

Whilst it is easy to focus on the outputs of cultural production–and indeed, these material objects are often the easiest to locate–the labour and networks that underpin this are at least as crucial in these histories. A focus on "achievement" and "productivity" in histories by centring releases and performers not only attaches capitalist notions of value through production, but also further contributes to the erasure of those who work "behind the scenes" and the underpinning networks of DIY music. McKinney also refers to the way in which "activism is most often written into history as big events and public spectacles, which renders quieter infrastructures invisible" (2020, p. 8). A focus on outputs, then, is not exclusive to DIY music, but is endemic within wider histories of activism which undervalue the labour and underpinning infrastructure of such communities.

This section has explored the precarity of DIY cultural networks, highlighting the ways in which networks often go undervalued and underrepresented in histories and archives of DIY music, due to a focus on the "products" or outputs of cultural production and the lack of documentation representing networks. When networks are documented, it is done via online databases rather than in more formal records, rendering this information precarious due to the platforms on which it is held. In turn, digital manifestations of networks can be subject to quick closures after conflicts in spaces and collectives, leaving little formal documentation of networks.

Precarious Spaces

In *DiY Culture: Party and Protest in Nineties Britain*, McKay writes that "short or long term, space is a prerequisite for community" (1998, p. 28). For networks to function, access to space is essential–without physical spaces that can serve as venues for gigs or digital spaces to live stream, it is not possible for bands to perform. Without access to social spaces, networks, projects, and communities do not develop. However, many of these spaces exist precariously, perpetually on the brink of closure due to factors in the current permacrisis climate. Although DIY cultural spaces have historically been fleeting spaces, the potential impact of the ongoing permacrisis environment on community recordkeeping is currently underexplored.

The last decade has seen the rapid development of several new autonomous spaces in the UK. Alongside long-established social centres (such as the Cowley Club in Brighton and the 1 in 12 Club in Bradford), crowdfunding initiatives and grassroots fundraising has enabled the opening of new spaces including DIY Space for London in 2015, Partisan (based in Manchester) in 2017, CHUNK (based in Leeds) in 2013, and Glasgow Autonomous Space in 2016. The opening of these spaces was reported on in music journalism (Welsh, 2015; Amin, 2017; Moloney, 2019). Amin refers to how such spaces display "a DIY attitude that prioritises communal support, autonomy and self-sufficiency over metrics such as popularity and capital" (Amin, 2017). Though such ethos' are admirable to many, they also render spaces more financially precarious than their more commercial equivalents (small music venues). Spaces following anti-capitalist ideals have always faced these threats—for example, in her analysis of feminist archives Eichhorn writes that

> In a state where such objectives [profit and money-making] trump all other social and political goals, initiatives driven by anti-economic mandates... are naturally vulnerable. (2013, p. 10)

Although some spaces may be purposefully precarious (as will be explored later), it is important to note that economic threats which force spaces to close are perpetuated by outside forces (e.g. landlords, councils, police) and cannot be situated under this same umbrella.

The motivation for the establishment of autonomous spaces comes from a desire to have control over the spaces in which DIY music networks operate. Otherwise, local cultural networks can be reliant on the use of more hostile spaces or temporary spaces to host gigs. Nazmia mentioned the use of a local community centre in Elephant and Castle (Pullens) by queer feminist cultural organisers in the early to mid 2000s, describing an abundance of affordable spaces that could be used for putting on gigs before the gentrification of certain areas of London:

> that was part of why we could organise in the way that we were doing. At the time, there were loads of venues, loads of venues that we used that have closed down now. Loads of community centres

that we could use that were really cheap. I think Pullen's was like 12 pounds an hour... and it had a kitchen! (Jamal, 2019)

However, although these spaces were remembered fondly by participants, current organisers are less able to make use of comparable spaces due to tightened restrictions on squatting, the closure of community centres and the gentrification of many inner-city areas. These issues drive communities to pursue establishing autonomous and more permanent spaces.

Squats and temporary spaces also faced regular threat of closure by authorities due to their semi-legal or illegal status. For example, Colette stated that

> Traditionally squats and DIY spaces are often very non-legit, they're often either not following fire codes... maybe running an illegal bar, not saying that any space I've ever been involved in has done this [laughs], but definitely in the US most DIY spaces are, they use the ask a punk thing, where the show won't be written on the flier, you'll have to ask a punk to find out whose house the gig's at or whatever, because they're illegal and they'll get shut down and there's different laws around it. (Colette, 2020)

The concept of "ask a punk" refers to a commonly understood practice in which information about the precise location of a gig or space will not be formally documented in order to prevent closure by police. Peers are expected to read subcultural aesthetic codes (e.g. jackets with patches, band t-shirts, dark clothing etc), email a host or ask via social networks to gain the information needed. The passing on of information occurs when a correspondent appears "authentic" (Beer, 2016, p. 27). This code explicitly contradicts the motivation to make information accessible discussed in chapter four, demonstrating a tension between wanting DIY music spaces to be available to the right people but unfindable by authorities.

The above quote illustrates how, in the case of illegitimate music spaces, information may need to be passed on verbally to prevent spaces being shut down. In this sense information is what Ferris and Allard describe as "strategically ephemeral" and "allowed to "disappear"/be forgotten/drop out of public circulation" (2016, p. 197). The passing on of information verbally was also discussed in chapter three, in which information about abusers was circulated in this way to protect peers and prevent prosecution of survivors (Bowcott and Snapes,

Unstable Alternatives

Figure 4 Ask a punk (original illustration)

2019). Social media platforms have also been used to gather information about groups, sometimes leading to the indictment and arrest of activists by authorities (Farivar and Solon, 2020). Explorations of protest movements highlight how information about data tracking now forms part of safety guides circulated in advance of protests (Boyd et al., 2021). Sheffield identifies how

> activists may self-censor to the extent that they delete content from their social media accounts to avoid persecution or remove their accounts entirely, rendering them inaccessible to both authorities and their social networks. (2018, p. 112)

A lack of documentation or publicly available information can be crucial to protecting communities and individuals, and contributes to preventing the precarity of these spaces, albeit also making them harder to trace through the archive in the future.

Participants often referred to feelings of anxiety and fear that DIY spaces would close, even when they were otherwise legal and more stable as organisations–for example, Steph reflected:

> It's a very unstable society that we've built [laughs]. As much as been so nourishing, it could just crumble any minute. I always went to Power Lunches, and now that's just gone, and we don't really talk about it anymore. And I don't know if there'll be an archive of the gigs that went on there, and the bands and scenes that formed there. It was a centrepiece of the scene... but it's hard to do that, and then you have wait 20 years and do a retrospective, if the people remember what was going on. Things disappear so quickly, and bands disappear so quickly, and people move away and so, things just don't feel very set in place, in this city at least. (Phillips, 2019)

Even before the coronavirus pandemic, several newer DIY music spaces faced regular threat of closure, due to financial precarity and gentrification. For example, of the closure of Power Lunches in 2015 due to rent increases, Welsh wrote that

> Power Lunches was an autonomous space that did everything on its own terms, but it's getting harder and harder to do that in the U.K. any more without sawing off your own head to make the rent. (2015)

DIY Space for London also regularly shared moments of financial crisis in the lead up to their closure in 2020, particularly during months in which bookings were less frequent and bar income unreliable (DIY Space for London, 2018). The precarity of such spaces is heightened by reliance on volunteer labour, particularly reliance on volunteers who themselves are leading increasingly precarious transitory lives in cities (see next section).

So far this section has focused on the precarity of DIY music spaces which exist physically. However, DIY music networks have also created digital spaces including message boards, listservs, and social media groups. For instance, in the following quote Bryony describes the use of online message boards by hardcore punk communities in the 2000s:

> I often felt like it was a space to certainly read and learn a lot about, like I learned a huge amount from punk message boards. And a lot of stuff, it's that weird, situated tacit knowledge that is never going to be on Wikipedia, because it's just weird stuff from zines that have been transmuted, that people have typed up onto message boards. (Beynon, 2020)

In Bryony's case, the message board was a virtual version of a punk space. Despite also manifesting the issues rife in physical venues (misogyny, homophobia, and a lack of accountability, for example), message boards provided information and community for those who needed it. Message boards were also widely used because of their relatively unsupervised nature (Lingel et al., 2012, p. 159). The online message board could in many ways replicate the intimate community of a small grassroots space, combining communication networks with a perception of privacy from authorities.

However, although both message boards and Facebook groups (which are used similarly in networks) form a central part of DIY music communities through serving as virtual alternatives to physical social spaces, they are often similarly at risk of closure or loss. This is due to multiple intersecting factors (see previous chapter). The first risk that I will explore relates to the risk of traces and content being lost when digital platforms change or close. For example, Emma says:

> There's the Wayback Machine, but it doesn't save the pictures, so there's gonna be a whole generation of stuff that's just gone because it was internet only. Or especially if you weren't hosting yourself… even when Tumblr had its heyday in the early part of this decade, give it five years, that's all going to be gone. (Falconer, 2019)

The precarity of digital spaces is heightened because of the risk of closure of spaces as digital communities continue to evolve and move between platforms. Whilst a message board or mailing list is controlled primarily by a moderator or website owner (which has its own risk), the spaces created using external platforms (such as Facebook) are ultimately controlled by organisations far removed from DIY music communities. These spaces can be seen as parallels to the temporary spaces created within venues without shared politics (for example when a queer club night is programmed in a function room at a pub)–though communities are able to temporarily occupy a space, they cannot control the venue or platform itself.

The precarity of digital spaces can also be heightened due to unsustainable working methods and internal conflicts. For example, Nazmia referred to an early UK feminist email list, which had "disintegrated over that period of time" due to conflicts in queer feminist community at the time. In an exploration of DIY queer feminist music cultures, Downes refers to conflict and overly close interpersonal working practises as a cause of decline in spaces and communities:

> attempts to produce DIY queer feminist music (sub)culture within informal collective structures risk (re)producing harm, exploitation and power relations between members, which can result in personally attacked activists relinquishing their involvement… This could result in the gradual attrition in the number of active queer feminist (sub)cultural producers in the UK and subsequent decline in collective spaces and communities. (2010, p. 245)

McKay also describes the way in which DIY culture can "blur the distinction between action and living" (1998, p. 27) through, for example, using spaces for performance, organising and living. This specific unsustainability, which is often caused by a lack of boundaries, overly close working relationships, the development of romantic relationships, conflict, burn out and insularity can cause spaces to collapse unexpectedly. When networks collapse due to these conflicts, spaces in which they operate can be affected (sometimes causing their closure). This is especially the case in digital spaces moderated or funded by one individual. In such instances, not only do spaces collapse but information relating to their existence can also disappear, making reconnecting with them or seeking accountability for past actions much more difficult.

Precarious traces

This section explores how precarity intersects with archival traces of UK DIY music spaces. Throughout this section I make use of the term traces to refer to what remains after performance, spaces and events. In relation to queer performance in archives, Muñoz refers to traces as "a kind of evidence of what has transpired but certainly not the thing itself (1996, p. 10). I engage with the term "traces" because it also suggests absence, ghostliness and/or loss, each of which resonate with previous chapters and research into queer and feminist archives (Mitchell and McKinney, 2019) in which archival records are also rare.

Although DIY music culture encompasses more than performance alone, live music is core to its operation. Performance in the archive is most commonly explored in the context of archiving theatre, dance and live art (Muñoz, 1996; Jones, 1997; Schneider, 2001; Clarke and Warren, 2009). The ephemeral nature of performance challenges the concept of the "privileged "saveable" original" (Schneider, 2001, p. 101) that underpins heritage collecting practises. Performance leaves behind little in the way of meaningful traces–for instance, Leigh reflects about band Jean Genet's performances during the 2000s:

> One of the things that they would do [would be to] just put a keyboard demo on and then just dance around with no clothes on and be hilarious… they created the space and everybody created the space … if you just had the music as an object, and just had the sheet music or the keyboard you wouldn't get, that's what I mean about that kind of objectification of DIY music culture …. I find [it] really strange. (Leigh, 2020)

In this example, though elements of the performance could be collected it carries less meaning without additional context (for example, the environment of the performance or interactions between audience members and performers). What is tangible and possible to collect is an inadequate representation without more intangible elements also included. Alongside this, as Istvandity writes,

> the material objects of music, including recordings of performances, are particularly vulnerable to lose because of their precarious nature as ephemeral, consumable, and ideally, replaceable. (I 2020, p. 4)

This is echoed by Baker and Huber who refer to "the apparent 'disposability' of popular music and… popular music's mass produced items"

(2015, p. 115). The "space" created by performance (e.g. the relationship between environment, performer, technologies and audience) is intangible and not possible to replicate in collection, and the material objects that could provide a connection are viewed as disposable and therefore not of value.

Paper-based ephemera was described as valuable by participants. Ephemera is frequently used as a loose "catch all" term for "primarily paper-based materials designed by their creators for short-term use" (Reichard, 2012, p. 38). For those in this study, traces including posters and fliers were often described as holding archival value. For instance, Cassie said:

> I've always loved looking at old fliers and tickets... I've seen loads of the riot grrrl stuff from America, the hand drawn and photocopied fliers that they would make, and I think that stuff is really important. (Agbehenu, 2019)

Some participants held onto ephemera as an informal memory prompt. Emma described how these materials can be overlooked as records:

> I suppose we probably think of photos, recordings and videos being the main thing but it's the ephemera as well. For example even the simple cheap fliers like that [shows fliers], like there was one I was going to find that–a friend was going to give me a flier for his gig and realised he'd forgotten them so hand drew a crappy one. And I kept it and stuck it in the scrapbook. (Falconer, 2019)

Fliers continue to be made and circulated in addition to the use of social media for promotion. These forms of ephemera are recognisable as modern references to older subcultural practices.

Archival theorists have proposed that ephemera is undervalued by archivists (Burant, 1995). However, cultural theorists have argued that ephemera can provide access to stories, narratives and representations of everyday lives (Heathcott, 2007; Mussell, 2012). In relation to Black queer archive Rukus! Ajamu X et al. describe how ephemera can be undervalued by both heritage professionals and community members:

> As far as I know, this was the first time that we had talked about heritage in relation to our sexual identity, within the context of the UK. So people would say, "it is just a flyer." And so they would dismiss it. (2009, p. 285)

Ephemera can fall between the cracks of community and institutional collecting when viewed as for short term use alone. This could also be heightened when ephemera is contemporary and not yet viewed as having potential future significance in an archival context.

In this study, a combination of experiences of impostor syndrome and the modern nature of traces had a negative impact on whether traces were viewed as "worthy" of archiving. For example, Alex reflected that:

> I find it really hard personally to understand the value of things that I do... I want to put on shows, I want to organise stuff, I want to go out, but I personally find it a really big struggle to do something like archive it and remember it because I think it's just a different skill set and a different way of being that I think maybe some people like, maybe people kind of living outside or like lower class people might find difficult to do. I don't really know how it's linked, so I think there's just complex psychological barriers like that. (Trapp, 2020)

In the above quote, it is easy to see how an individual's thought process can lead to a devaluing of materials that might also be devalued by heritage organisations. An examination of the data collected through interviews with individuals who self-identified as working class suggests that in particular these peers struggled to see their traces as of value in a longer term sense and would be less likely to deposit materials unless explicitly encouraged to do so by others.

Paper-based ephemera used to be a reliable archival trace of DIY music. However, digital marketing is now the primary way of reaching audiences. Although many promoters and bands still produce ephemera, this is also reliant on financial resources or access to free printing via workplaces. As Kaz said,

> I often just print stuff at work and go and put a handful in places that I know will take them... it's always hard to balance that sort of stuff with full time work as well. (Scattergood, 2020)

The switch to digital marketing has caused a noticeable drop in the amount of paper traces produced, and therefore able to be physically kept, by community members. For example, Bryony reflected that

> I know personally [in] my archive box, there's a real drop off at the point ... which you can see in the fliers, at the point when social media, even from Myspace onwards, when that became like a bigger thing, I tend to then have less and less fliers. (Beynon, 2020)

These informal personal archives show the immediate impact of a move towards born digital record creation. The status of these archives is also affected by a lack of understanding of how to archive digital materials (beyond saving a copy on a personal drive, for example), and the different skill set required to undertake such work.

So far in this section, I have focused on traditional forms of ephemera–however, attention must also be given to digital ephemera, when these records are under threat of loss due to their precarious storage, as the previous section suggests. The rest of this section considers digital ephemera and digital traces of UK DIY music as a contemporary equivalent. I give particular attention to ephemeral audio-visual traces produced on platforms including Instagram stories and those created using live-streaming technologies.

I will begin with an example from my own archival traces. On the next page is a reproduction of a blurred photograph taken of my first gig in a UK DIY band. The photograph is published on Twitter after a worker at the venue (Power Lunches) noticed two of us drinking while our drummer played a solo. My phone camera is filled with similar pictures, taken in dimly lit venues to share via social media or to help me to remember a band. I revisit this picture occasionally, retrospectively affording it value because it was the start of a journey within DIY music. My emotive response to the photograph is similar to that discussed by Kuhn in her examination of the use of family photographs in memory work. As she writes, photographs are traces which enable "the activity of meaning making" through figuring in a network of discourse between past (the representation) and present (my relationship to the photograph and recollection of the memories it evokes). The picture itself is nothing special, but it makes me feel something because of what I associate with the image itself. In relation to live art Clarke and Warren write that "our homesickness for the scene's commencement returns us to its archaic traces" (2009, p. 48). Homesick is an apt description for the combination of feelings engendered when reviewing these traces, remembering fleeting moments of empowerment.

In the case of my band, other evidence exists. We continued playing for a few years, releasing tapes and merchandise, then disbanded. We all kept hold of some materials that document our existence, although haven't deposited any of them in archives. For others, this isn't the case–for example, in an interview Ben reflected that

Figure 5 Twitter post from @powerlunches (Power Lunches, 2013)

if a band play three gigs or they play First Timers and never again, and the only record of that is on their mate's Instagram account, or it's ten seconds with some gifs over it or a few pictures, where does that go? but then … that's not to say we shouldn't think that's less important, I think it's just there's a bit more of an anxiety of how is this archived? (Perkins, 2019)

Tayyab described the status of videos of performances and gigs held on YouTube that document songs that are not recorded or otherwise documented in any way:

They mainly pop up through YouTube and then they die out because they can't get the critical mass, right? There are so many songs that I like that just only exist on YouTube. They never got released. They never got mastered or engineered and put out there, like that just never happened. It only exists on YouTube… There's no real way to like archive it. (Amin, 2019)

Though photography and video is not commonly thought of as "ephemera", digital photography or video taken for short-lived publication on

YouTube, Snapchat or Instagram stories could be said to be ephemeral due to its likelihood future deletion or inaccessibility. It could also be argued that such material is intended for "short term use", although this is dependent on the motivation of the creator in question.

The precarity of such digital traces continues even when published–for example, when a video is published on YouTube it will only persist for as long as the creator and the platform support it. Precariousness of digital traces is also enhanced by where it is stored. Current work in the archive sector to migrate and digitise sound recordings is motivated by the knowledge that newer media formats require much more urgent interventions to prevent the permanent loss of materials (British Library, 2019)=. Though cloud storage might seem to be a way to avoid such loss, high profile incidents such as the Myspace Music server migration discussed in the preceding chapter indicate that reliance on cloud storage can cause much more extreme losses. Individual storage of files on personal computers and hard drives also renders traces at risk of loss due to a lack of backing up of files. Web heritage is also at risk when web pages are stored in individual servers rather than web repositories.

Over the course of the coronavirus pandemic in 2020, during which time many physical DIY music spaces were closed, communities made more intensive use of digital technologies to replicate both the experience of watching performances and the social networks of a small DIY music space. Promoters and record labels including Specialist Subject, Divine Schism, Girl Gang Leeds, Bent Fest, Youth Anthems coordinated synchronous live "gigs" using livestreaming technology. These were run on platforms like Instagram live, with text-based chat used by participants to communicate. In some cases, performances were made available for streaming after the "live" gig finished–however, on Instagram live this was only for a period of 24 hours and if the performer/host elected to do so. In some instances, hosts downloaded videos and re-uploaded to their profile's feed, but again, this was uncommon. After this point in time the content effectively disappeared for host and user.

I refer to this example because it speaks to the urgency or perhaps the impossibility of archiving digital ephemera. The use of live broadcasting has been examined within research about social movements and digital technology. Sheffield describes how Facebook live videos are

> by default entangled with the Facebook platform and require immediate and complicated interventions to ensure that they are fixed in

any way that might make it possible to preserve them or use them again in the future. (2018, p. 117)

During this period, several coronavirus related collecting projects were established. Though the representation of "everyday life" was a key priority for many collecting bodies, no UK-based heritage organisations were engaged with documenting live-streaming in music cultures, and certainly not that done by DIY music communities. The combination of the short lives of these digital traces, a lack of digital archiving skills within communities, and a lack of institutional interest in music cultures renders these materials easily lost.

Precarious lives

Many of those working in DIY music spaces face an increasingly precarious existence due to combinations of insecure work, housing, family and relationships, as well as austerity measures including benefit cuts, the reduction of mental health provisions and an increasingly privatised NHS. In *The New Poverty*, Armstrong explores the impact of such combinations, writing that the millennial generation (which is the age bracket in which I and many DIY cultural peers occupy) find it harder "to have the security to settle, find stable communities, buy some property and raise their own family" (2018, p. 59). Recent media reporting also emphasises the housing vulnerability of millennials (Savage, 2018; Hill, 2019) and the disparity between those with access to housing via familial wealth and those who do not (Lott-Lavigna, 2019).

Reliance on shared accommodation means that many individuals now need to fit all of their belongings into a single room. Referencing the millennial generation, Savage writes

> Their living space is also declining. Each person living in the private rented sector now has on average eight square metres less space than they did in 1996.... Just under one in 10 households headed by millennials in their late 20s now live in overcrowded conditions. (2018)

The lack of access to stable housing was extensively reflected on throughout interviews. The ephemerality of DIY music spaces intersects with personal experiences of precarious life to create a climate of socioeconomic and creative anxiety. For example, Steph reflected:

> It definitely makes everyone feel very anxious… everyone's already very anxious [laughs] and it's just adding on to it. I think you just don't feel very in control of your life, like you can do what you can do, the rent goes up and no one can afford to live here anymore than this band goes or that venue goes, and that's just it, and you just have to deal with it and make do. (Phillips, 2019)

In this quote the lack of control that community members feel is explicit–this rapidly changing environment means that not only is a space closed before the community wants, but the scene in itself is transitory, dispersed and regularly rotated when individuals are forced out of areas and cities by gentrification. This means that on top of spatial precarity of music venues and social centres, creative projects are also short-lived, as are social circles and relationships.

Housing precarity was discussed frequently by participants. Kirsty reflected that moving house due to taking up fixed term contracts meant that she had to dispose of materials that might have otherwise been kept:

> The points where I've thrown stuff away has been when I've been forced to move house again and again and again. And as rents continue to rise and wages continue to effectively drop, and neoliberalism takes hold, the trend is more people in houses and [being] less able to keep hold of stuff. I guess that's thinking about just people keeping hold of stuff. Not yet thinking about actually making its way into any forms of archives, whether they're kind of more official or less official. (Lohman, 2020)

Bryony also reflected:

> It's probably also worth noting… if you're evicted or made homeless, are you really bringing, dragging your archive with you?… The fact that everyone's housing, at least in my universe, is so precarious at the moment, the need to just purge and chuck things out definitely has impacted like the health of an archive. (Beynon, 2020)

In relation to queer and feminist archives, McKinney and Mitchell write that their "keeping is a burden" (2019, p. 11). Peers told me that belongings were frequently reviewed and disposed of in order to make moving regularly more possible and due to constraints of living space. The personal archive, in this sense, is a burden for many, but particularly those without reliable income and housing.

The intersection of precarious lives and archives raises questions not only about whether any physical traces will remain, but also how we value what does persist. For many in this study, the informal personal archive is a small collection of gleaned scraps, objects and music connected to their own history of involvement. These are unconventional heritage objects–for example, some participants cited pieces of ceiling from a venue, others obsolete technologies, and many cited disposable ephemera as central. As an example, in the following quote Joe describes the contents of his own archive (held in a collection of folders in his room)

> I literally do have an archive… there's a lot of stuff like fliers, mainly setlists in this one, mementos, you know from gigs and stuff like that, notes from friends and things like that which I started collecting like a long time ago, just like picking up setlists and things like that. From my gigs that I've played, lots of gigs that I've been to, broken tape in this one… Like this one in there that is a piece of the Tenterhooks ceiling which was a DIY venue in Dublin until about 2016. We played the closing show and someone kicked the ceiling in and I kept a piece of the ceiling … and then in this one I've got some other funny stuff … This was, you can find a video of Dawn of Humans playing Static Shock weekend in 2014, and this is the mirror is hanging off the lead singer's penis as they play [laughs]. (Briggs, 2019)

This collection of materials relating to predominantly DIY and hardcore punk in the UK could seem unusual to an outsider, but nonetheless holds value and importance to those with personal histories within this context. McKinney and Mitchell write that "feminist performance leaves peculiar types of "documents" behind, and this is part of its queerness" (2019, p. 11). There are parallels between this context and that of UK DIY music, in which the objects collected often present challenges to traditional notions of the record but have meaning to those involved.

Those with stable housing were more able to form archives. It is important to note that the deposit of materials at Glasgow Women's Library discussed in my preceding chapter was enabled by access to stable housing by the depositor, Nazmia. As she reflected,

> the reason that I had an archive of stuff was because because I had very stable housing, my parents owned that flat. I lived there for 13 years before they sold it… I just used to hoard everything, like

a lot of the meetings happened in my house, or I would just bring stuff back afterwards, so I had boxes and boxes and boxes of shit. (Jamal, 2019)

These deposits were often motivated by a desire for permanence and long-term stability for collections, which it was not necessarily possible to guarantee by depositing in community-led archives or by maintaining custody within the originating community. For instance, Nazmia reflects on the decision to deposit with the Glasgow Women's Library:

> We decided, because the Women's Library in London was where the initial deposit for Ladyfest London had gone, and they were about to shut down, and all of this stuff went into the LSE archives and you can't get to it so I was like I don't want to put it there. And the Feminist Library has always been quite precarious… they have damp, and I was like, well, they're great and I love it, but also … the first Ladyfest in the UK was in Glasgow, Glasgow has got fucking purpose-built, well it wasn't purpose-built at that point, it was in the old building, but they had a lesbian archive, and a women's library. (Jamal, 2019)

Concerns about the sustainability and longevity of community-led archives are common—Baker and Collins write that these popular music heritage organisations are often "at risk of closure due to the difficulties of sustaining their archival practice in the medium- to long-term" (2015, p. 478). Given the ephemeral and precarious contexts in which such archives emerge, it is perhaps not surprising that the creator of an archive wishes to prioritise a service which can commit to long term preservation and access duties.

Persistence and loss

The preceding sections of this chapter have explored intersections of precarity which affect the production, preservation, and longevity of archival traces of UK DIY music. If there is one clear connecting experience between all of those who contributed data to this project, it is that we have all directly felt anxiety over the loss of spaces, projects, networks, and archival traces. Although it is tempting to end this chapter having concluded that precarity has a drastic impact on what remains of our communities and spaces now and into the future, this final section examines the strategies individuals employ to resist the loss of these histories and enable their persistence.

I begin by describing my own journey to collect the archive I reference at the start of this chapter, using this example to explore how archives (in whatever format they exist) provide an opportunity for spaces to persist beyond an initial short-term existence. I then go on to describe how communities afford value to their activities from the outset of projects, connecting this to the concept of queer time developed by Jack Halberstam. Following this, I describe informal practices of sharing memories and mourning which happen over social media and in social gatherings. Finally, I describe how creative practice offers opportunities for individuals to creatively engage with loss and cultural memory. I argue that when viewed together these practices form individual methods of resistance against the precarity of DIY music networks, spaces, traces, and lives. By engaging in these practises, we express that, although short lived, these spaces have value and impact which persists beyond their conclusion.

In June 2020, I drive to London after messages about the imminent closure of DIY Space for London, and what to do with its archive. I am known to several people involved in the shut down due to my involvement in the space and this research project. The archive is part of a shared history and some members are anxious that the archive will be lost, though others view it as little more than more paperwork to get rid of before the lease ends. The "archive box" (as it was informally referred to by individuals during interviews—the archive grew larger over the years) was a way to afford value to the activities that were going on in the space at the outset of this project. As Bryony reflected:

> I think in the very early days, the first five or ten gigs or so, there was this, okay, well, there's the archive box and we've got this acid free paper box in the office and you put the poster in there, but that eventually fairly quickly fell away as a process, which means that, yeah, there is a box there, as I understand it, and it's partial. (Beynon, 2019)

In reference to archives of live art, Clarke and Warren write that

> The beginning of an archive and instituting of a collection is a founding act in the emergence of a discipline. In a critical state of emergency, the archive draws a frame around an emergent form. (2009, p. 48)

I remember conversations in that first year where peers discussed what went into the box, informally agreeing the scope of the collection.

In the end these more specific conversations fell away and the box wasn't strictly monitored. As new individuals became more central in the space and others stepped back, the archive was less central, and many didn't even know there was a collection. However, at the onset of the project the decisiveness that what was happening was important to archive was significant.

In *Rogue Archives: Digital Cultural Memory and Media Fandom*, De Kosnik writes that

> Cultural memory has thus gone rogue with respect to its own temporality, its own place in the order and timing of things. Engagement with cultural memory is therefore not only what comes after the making and distribution of cultural texts, it also now often precedes that making, or occurs at every step throughout the process of making. (2016, p. 4)

In many cases throughout this project, participants reflected on individual decisions to archive continuously both from the outset and throughout projects. In the case of DIY Space for London, this looked like the informal establishment of "the archive box" in the most secure room in the building (the office). In my own experience, this has taken the shape of a small suitcase filled with materials that bring back memories or connections. This sort of informal personal archive was common amongst participants, although whether it was considered to be an archive varied between cases. As an example, in the following quote Steph describes her motivations for collecting the traces of her own music history:

> I think people are always interested in our histories and what we're doing, so it's just to make sure you just take down everything. I mean, you never know what's important. I want to make sure that we save every poster and every item of merchandise and every t-shirt, because you never know … I think it's just about realising that what we're doing is very important, and will hopefully have an influence on people in ways that we might not be as aware of now, but we might as well take it seriously and note everything down now so we can be of use to someone in the future. (Phillips, 2019)

In reference to queer subcultural memory, Halberstam proposes that

> we need to theorise the concept of the archive, and consider new models of queer memory and queer history capable of recognising and racing subterranean scenes, fly-by-night clubs, and fleeting trends. (2005, p. 161)

Queer time and space, according to Halberstam, develops in opposition to time which relies upon traditional markers of life progressions including marriage, reproduction, well-being and housing stability. By assigning value to spaces which are/were very temporary, ephemeral, and closed (or under threat of closure) and doing so from the outset of a project, we make room for queer modes of significance which exist not only outside of these structures but the precarity that defines many of our lives right now. Archiving can thus be viewed as a form of resistance against precarity and ephemerality, and the resulting collections can "serve as a living memory of the moments, people and places that might disappear and be forgotten" (Saber and Long, 2017, p. 92).

Chapter four identified how making and caring for traces can enable a continuing connection with closed spaces or concluded projects. These forms of informal archival work underpin the experience of loss and grieving, both in music communities (Galey, 2018) and our personal lives. In their research with bereaved parents, Douglas and Alisauskas describe how

> Things—documents, objects, bodies, dreams—weave in and around these stories and are attached in different ways to the parents' work of grieving, loving, remembering and imagining. (2021, p. 8)

The use of archives and archival traces to both remember what is lost and imagine what could be speaks to the motivations of many participants. In their examination of loss, Eng and Kazanjian write that

> the politics of mourning might be described as that creative process mediating a hopeful or hopeless relationship between loss and history. (2003, p. 2)

This chapter has identified how little control was felt over the perceived inevitable loss and fragility of DIY music spaces and networks. However, archiving created an opportunity to process these past spaces and regain some control over their representation.

Creative practice was used to represent lost spaces, either through citation and repetition of names and ideas (as explored in chapter four), or by utilising visual mediums like photography. For example, Joe describes how photography can represent both space and performance in an image:

> This one [photograph] in the Lughole has, it had "we DIY", which is part of a bit that said like till we DIY, but it just says we DIY in the background, which you might not even notice. Yeah, like capturing a space, you know, because spaces don't last that long. Most of them don't, but there'll always be another one, but it's nice to know something about one. (Briggs, 2019)

Queer theorists have situated creative practice as another form of record keeping, particularly intersecting with the aforementioned concept of queer time. In an article exploring the poetry of Langston Hughes and its relation to the very temporal spaces of Harlem queer nightlife, Vogel positions Hughes' poetry as a record which

> inscribes a queer time consciousness that is impossible to archive under the official regimes of documentation and verification. The queer time and space of the afterhours club, in other words, is archived in the line of the poem, if not at the library at Yale. (2006, p. 400)

In the case of the above example, photography can enable persistence of spaces and communities beyond the closure of spaces or the conclusion of events and projects. Of community-led archival practice, Popple et al. write that

> Community archives are a means of forming and exemplifying community feeling in a world where the older forms of community such as workplace and locality have become less important and social connections are more dispersed, fragmented and fluid. (2020b, p. 8)

Creative practice, too, offers the opportunity to form, solidify and communicate the feeling of belonging and support that reaches beyond the closure of individual spaces and empowers others too. As Joe reflected, this communicates that "those things are replicable, or that there is a special energy [that] you can have, that you can create that special energy".

The strategies and practises named above do not necessarily guarantee that the histories of UK DIY music will persist, and certainly do not make space for them in more formal archive repositories. As De Kosnik writes of the creation of archives by fan-led cultures, although these practises "do not guarantee that they or their works will be remembered... they create the conditions of possibility for persistence and recollection" (2016, p. 17). As Steph reflects about her own experience, the least we can do is put a flag in the ground and say that we're here, because I hope that our work will be the legacy that we carry on, you might not make a lot of money doing this, but you can say I was here, and this is how I helped. (Phillips, 2019)

Though the utilisation of the tools identified in this section may not be conventionally archival, the individual and collective actions undertaken demonstrate a commitment to remembering stretching beyond the original spaces and communities involved. For those undertaking creative and cultural activism in such precarious times, the "possibility of persistence" is perhaps all we can hope for.

Conclusion

This chapter has demonstrated the ways in which intersections of precarity underpin DIY music and are felt strongly by all involved. Over the course of this PhD, DIY music spaces became at risk in ways I did not or could not anticipate. The level of digital precarity faced by content became explicit through incidents which are explored in the preceding chapter. The coronavirus pandemic has significantly affected both the cultural industry as a whole and the specific community context of my own research project, which has already seen the closure of two physical spaces in 2020 alone (as well as the halting of all physical live performance). A project that began as an attempt to better acknowledge and embed informal archival practices in UK DIY music spaces has become another exercise in salvaging and recovering what is left after the rapid and unexpected closure of several spaces in which I have close personal involvement. The impact of the pandemic on DIY cultures and the broader music industry is still to be determined, however living through this time has been devastating to many with jobs and creative livelihoods in this community context. The pandemic has also demonstrated how close to closure spaces are at any given point, due to the lack of financial safety nets and reliance on those in equally precarious living situations.

Although some of these risks identified in this chapter are long term (for example, issues caused by close knit networks and the rapid closure of spaces due to gentrification have frequently been discussed in relation to activist and DIY histories), several relate specifically to recent developments in society and technology. These intersections of precarity cause loss and prevent the preservation of materials within communities but also motivate people to take individual and collective action towards the persistence of these histories. These actions are often small in scale—for many, they take the form of informal verbal recollections at gigs or a folder of fliers in their bedroom. However, they nonetheless indicate a collective desire for something to persist beyond a short term and ephemeral first life. Though we cannot control the external factors which close spaces, disperse communities and preemptively end projects, we can value what has come and gone in ways that speak against the easy dismissal of the short-lived in histories and archives.

Figure 6 Ground collapsing 2 (original illustration)

Information Lives In DIY Music
Kirsty Fife

there isn't a lot left from the time spent in these spaces

toilet selfies

blurry gig pictures

scraps of setlists

Unstable Alternatives

...then I moved back to Leeds in 2016 after too many rent increases

packing up my stuff. always involves making hard choices about what I can hold onto.

if you move 17 times before 30 you end up getting rid of a lot of things

Archiving in/between
Exploring Relationships Between UK DIY Music Communities and Archives

The preceding chapters of this thesis have illustrated the impact of histories and archives on those working, creating, and organising within the context of UK DIY music spaces. Although much of this book has been devoted to questions about records and individual archives, the archive as an institution and an organisation has been largely absent from my discussions so far, despite initially forming an integral part of my PhD proposal. Archival theorists have identified working relationships between organisations and communities as critical within activist collecting projects (O'Meara, 2013, p. 120). In reference to the records of Canadian indigenous communities Delva and Adams write that developing and sustaining relationships can contribute to resolving systemic power discrepancies (2016, p. 165). Communities can contribute to archives through the deposit of collections, through crowd sourcing of metadata or participation in archival processes (Eveleigh, 2014). Collaboration between organisations and communities holds the promise to build more diverse collections, enrich those already held, and bring new forms of knowledge into heritage.

However, there are often unspoken dynamics in relationships between institutions and communities. The acquisition of collections to provide "counter-narratives" within institutions can subjugate individuals and re-inscribe dominant narratives, even when professionals intend otherwise (Sexton, 2020, p. 10). Archival practices of arrangement and description can enforce silences and cause further trauma to community members, particularly those from marginalised backgrounds (Wright, 2019, p. 343). Digital crowdsourcing projects have been criticised for their reliance on the unpaid labour of communities (Cowan and Rault, 2014a, p. 476). These tensions warrant further critical attention, especially in the under-explored remit of UK DIY music.

This chapter therefore places the dynamics between communities, information professionals and institutions in the centre of my analysis. In the specific context of UK DIY music, communities are often assumed to be anti-institutional because of the centrality of non-hierarchical and anarchist organising principles in DIY music spaces. Whilst this chapter does not attempt to counter the presence of anti-institutional attitudes in communities, I do wish to move beyond what Lee refers to as a "limiting dichotomy" (2017, p. 328), in which communities and archive organisations are automatically situated in opposition to one another. Instead, this chapter traces a pathway through these perceptions, to make visible not only the preconceptions and problems that underpin this rhetoric but also the progression of DIY cultural peers into information work.

The first section of this chapter examines outside perceptions of how DIY music community members related to heritage, particularly the dominant association between the punk ethos of "no future" and an ahistorical stance. I argue that this association is overly simplistic and presents both DIY music and heritage conservatively, erasing alternative engagements between the two. The second section explores work that has been undertaken within queer and feminist sub-sections of these communities (which are those in which I am more centrally involved). Utilising the concept of the "archival turn" as engaged with in various cultural contexts (feminism, queer subcultures, activism), I make visible different engagements with heritage in DIY music communities as a contrast to the dominant stance identified in section one.

The third part of this chapter engages with the figure often unexamined in archival research about community-led heritage—information professionals who also occupy roles and share histories with/in communities. Utilising the concept of third space subjectivity (Licona, 2005), I propose that when community members move into archival organisations, they can utilise their position to create different and more equitable relationships between communities and organisations. These relationships are not without power dynamics, but due to the more intimate connections between individuals can create the room to navigate these processes with more ease.

The fourth section utilises examples from my own practice to explore how collaboration between DIY music communities and organisations can work. Through an examination of my own practice and research about participatory archival practice, I highlight the romanticisation and misrepresentation of participatory archival methods within the heritage sector, and a related underestimation of the cost of labour and support from communities. This section aims to present an alternative model of practice which is no less flexible and collaborative but acknowledges the different positioning of (in my case) a paid researcher and an unpaid community member, bound in friendship and shared history. In this case, remaining accountable and responsible to my community involved being willing to take on a more sizeable amount of work, whilst remaining flexible to the many different directions this project took.

This chapter purposely does not demonstrate a single model for practice or "solve" the "problem" of how to work with DIY music communities. Much as chapter three demonstrates that there is no singular narrative of DIY music, this chapter resists the idea that there is a single way to collaborate "successfully" with DIY music communities. Instead, I explore how the subjectivity of the individuals involved in these processes (including the archivist, the community member, the community space, and the archive organisation) affect the creation and maintenance of an archival bond. My focus on methods draws attention away from the contents of archives and towards the relationships and dynamics that underpin their construction, management, and preservation. In this work, I am influenced by Smith's Uses of Heritage, in which heritage can be understood as a process and a series of actions (2006). By focusing on actions, dynamics, and relationships, I hope to contribute more nuance and complexity to existing research about relationships between archive organisations and communities, which relies on emphasising the difference between the two without examining the individuals engaged in such work.

DIY music, "no future" and heritage

There is a perceived disconnection between heritage and DIY music communities expressed within both popular culture and related scholarship. Utilising an analysis of "no future" as a punk philosophy in combination with interview data, I unpick this association, arguing that this opposition is reliant on conservative understandings of both DIY music and heritage and can potentially prohibit the development of mutually beneficial relationships. As I go on to elaborate, this can erase legacies of archival work undertaken by women and queer people within DIY music networks.

DIY music is typified by an anti-institutional politics. Punk researchers refer to an embedded "oppositional tendency, with a network of resistances to authority, to work, to conventional politics" (Davies, 1996, pp. 3–4). As evidence of this, researchers refer to the "no future" ethos of 1970s punk coined by The Sex Pistols (Nyong'o, 2008; Szkudlarek, 2017). "No future" references a lack of possibility for young people–in the context of 1970s punk, this referred to the politicised rejection of a formulaic British life (defined through nation and monarchy). As Davies writes of this first wave of punk,

> The only way to escape from a meaningless existence... seems to be to ally oneself and identify oneself with apocalyptic events. (1996, p. 13)

This allegiance with destruction is often referenced to demonstrate an opposition with preservation–as destroying is the opposite of keeping (Strong, 2018). The recent destruction of 1970s punk memorabilia by the son of Malcolm McLaren is positioned as a contemporary manifestation of the "no future" ethos–materials which held value were destroyed as a statement against the nostalgic representation of punk in heritage exhibitions (Press Association, 2016).

It is often assumed that incidents such as the above demonstrate a fundamental ahistoricism in DIY music subcultures. However, this lacks a nuanced understanding of the model of heritage resisted by these subcultures. Adams states that the reaction against history and heritage by the Sex Pistols refers to a specific and conservative model of heritage typified by the positioning of the

> "Heritage Industry"—from visits to "stately homes" to the immense popularity of Laura Ashley—... [as] a firmly established element of national life. (2008, p. 471)

In the above quote, it is not history or heritage that are inherently objectionable within this cultural context, but instead the utilisation of these tools to promote nationalist and elitist histories. In this reading,

Heritage is about the promotion of a consensus version of history by state-sanctioned cultural institutions and elites to regulate cultural and social tensions in the present. (Smith, 2006, p. 4)

Appadurai identifies how the potential of the archive to communities has been

> obscured by that officialising mentality, closely connected to the governmentalities of the nation-state, which rests on seeing the archive as the tomb of the accidental trace, rather than the material site of the collective will to remember. (2003, pp. 16–17)

A focus on authorised heritage can "obscure the possibility of subversive uses of heritage" (Smith, 2006, p. 49), rendering alternative community-led projects and alternative visions of the archive less visible.

Focusing on other sub-sections of DIY music communities enables us to find further alternative engagements with history or information. Whilst the term "no future" aligns with destruction, the continued building of alternative spaces and the developing of new sources of information demonstrate a commitment to supporting future generations and changing the world through the creation of alternatives. This commitment to imagination and world making is typified by the anarchist slogan "another world is possible" which describes "a permanent process of seeking and building alternatives" (Gilbert, 2008, p. 91). Alternative models of archival practice and history writing (e.g. history from below, oral history, community-led archival work) which also resist the reproduction of elite histories are aligned with the ideals of punk, rather than opposed in the way many otherwise assume. The subsequent production of books built on oral histories collected by 1970s punk subcultural peers is demonstrative of an alignment between punk and these archival methodologies (Turrini, 2013).

In the context of this study, there were concerns about institutional management of DIY music histories–however, these related to how archives were managed by organisations, rather than whether they should be kept in the first place. This often related to concerns about selective collecting processes (see chapter four) and perceptions of what was "acceptable" in these spaces. For example, Alex was wary of what it meant when queer punk artefacts are exhibited within museum environments:

> We should definitely be so careful of that, because again, institutions and everything will just take what they think is acceptable, what they want, and you have to be like, conscious of like who's in on that and consent in the way people's pasts are being exhibited. (Trapp, 2020)

These concerns about the existence of non-normative lives within very normative institutions are shared by many authors who explore queer histories (Hernández, 2015; Holmes, 2015; Lee, 2015, 2017; Nguyen, 2015). Concerns such as the above demonstrate a consciousness about the potential for heritage institutions to reproduce a "politics of respectability" which enforce absences and canonical narratives that benefit normative society (Lee, 2017, p. 337).

In the context of queer black sexualities, Kwame Holmes highlights the archive as a site of Western surveillance of non-normative lives (2015, p. 56). In this context, in which queer and/or feminist politics often overlapped with DIY politics, politics of respectability manifest through decisions about who is approached to donate materials and how these objects are represented through interpretation. There were concerns about surveillance of semi-legitimate or illegitimate music spaces, or the value of information about such spaces to authorities. These concerns stem from an understanding within activist communities that organisations collecting activist materials are not necessarily activist in politics. In reference to the Interference Archive, Sellie et. al write that

> these new collections do not always develop from an affinity between the institution and an activist group... Any archive can collect objects made by activists. But this process does not automatically signify that this collecting establishes a relationship between the archive and the community that it draws materials from. (2015, p. 456)

To illustrate this tension, we can look to the V&A Museum's Disobedient Objects exhibition, which included campaign materials relating to strike actions and was on public display during a period in which museum workers were lobbying for wage increases after reports of staff experiencing "working poverty" wages at the museum (Trade Union Congress, 2014). Because of this tension, the exhibition seemed to decontextualise objects from the radical politics of their originating context and could be argued to be a sanitised version of activism.

Participants were concerned about how the subjectivity and values of an archivist or curator could potentially conflict with those of community members. For example, Emma described unequal relationships between zine makers and curators:

> With zines I've known a lot of people feel a bit used by large institutions... we both know the museum sector can be very insular and old

school tie, and it can be a very, very narrow selection of people who actually get to be curators, who can have a very patronising idea of what the public or the proles want. (Falconer, 2019)

Uncertainty about the collection of DIY cultural objects does not relate to a complete rejection of history, but rather a concern about what happens when these objects move from a close-knit community circle into a less regulated space, in which they are managed by many different (and potentially anonymous) hands. In the context of zines, Nguyen writes that management processes (e.g. cataloguing, digitisation, publishing) mean that "the conditions for encountering our objects are radically changed years later" (2015, p. 12). In one of the workshops facilitated for this project, Sarah-Beth reflected:

> For me, it would be really important if I donated something to want to know what the terms of that were so how can other people access it? What are the opening hours? Do you have to make an appointment to go see it? Or even like… we're contributing something, and at the moment it's just in a storage box, but what if it becomes an exhibition? What if it becomes something that people have to pay to access?

In the above example, anxiety and distrust manifests not only about the initial deposit of an item, but its potential to move between contexts or different models of accessibility. Professionals without pre-existing knowledge of or experience within communities thus need to take time to embed ongoing dialogue and flexibility into their archival protocols when working with communities.

The previous examples have stressed ambivalent responses to the collections of DIY cultural objects which affirm tensions between communities and archive organisations. However, there were also positive reactions to outreach articulated by participants. For instance, Cassie describes her band Fight Rosa Fight's reaction to being approached by the British Library to deposit their recordings:

> I mean, we freaked out… I just thought what an amazing opportunity and of course we're going to say yes, cos we don't think of what we're doing is being part of music history in the UK, like we're this little DIY band. And when we started we were so shit [laughs] like we were so shit! And we just found the whole thing wild. (Agbehenu, 2019)

In this example, Cassie sees the outreach from an institution as affording her own work additional value, and she was eager to ensure other projects were similarly recognised. This aligns with Foucault's writing about the concept as an authorising and legitimising force (1972, p. 129), through the affording of value to a DIY music release by a perceived "expert" in a heritage organisation (Smith, 2006, p. 12). Existing research about music heritage has drawn attention to the epistemological power of "collections [that] are determined by volunteers and enthusiasts and based on their vernacular knowledge and expertise" (Baker and Collins, 2015, p. 984), drawing attention to the potential for such initiatives to improve wellbeing and feelings of belonging (Cantillon and Baker, 2018). However, experiences such as the above also demonstrate how, in the right circumstances, interactions between institutions and community members can engender positive responses.

The perception that there is an opposition between heritage organisations and communities could contribute to the amount of collecting currently happening within DIY music, especially from large institutions who might seem disconnected from communities. Participants had been primarily approached to deposit cultural outputs (e.g. zines, records, digital releases). These forms of outreach again demonstrate a (limited) institutional interest in the products of DIY music. As chapter one demonstrated, a focus on products of DIY music over process should be more closely examined. As Cassie reflected, there is also a lack of clarity about which institutions can collect materials into a larger body of work:

> Who is collecting this stuff? I mean, it's cool that you've got things like... Queer Zine Library, and radical book shops are like collecting stuff, but like who is pooling this stuff? (Agbehenu, 2019)

Cassie's question is incredibly important–how can we create the affective, nuanced, and diverse archive that has been described throughout this thesis if we don't even have awareness of who is collecting, or who will devote more substantial space to archives of DIY music? In this sense there is a huge potential for archive organisations to contribute positively to DIY music communities by (as a minimum) providing space and opportunity to create collections.

This section has explored the relationship between the "no future" ethos and perceptions about the relationship between DIY music communities and archive organisations. Using interview data, I have identified both positive and ambivalent responses to outreach from heritage organisations. Those who felt more conflicted about their potential

Figure 1 Unanswered questions (original illustration)

representation in heritage spaces did not display an anti-heritage or anti-historical attitude, but rather a wariness about how they would be represented and who would move into institutional heritage spaces. In turn, these participants felt more positively about grassroots initiatives or community-led heritage projects. These responses indicate that the relationship between community members and heritage is more nuanced than perceived by professionals.

When there is a dominant focus on one particular position about history and heritage (e.g. the "no future" ethos), inevitably other viewpoints and relationships are suppressed. In relation to zine scholarship, Licona writes that a focus on punk in DIY culture can in turn overemphasise the zine maker's status as a privileged subject and obscure the subjectivities of those from different positions (2005, 2013). In the context of the intersection of DIY culture and history/archives, a focus on a specific resistance to history is over-simplistic and can erase the significant work done within particularly queer and feminist sub-sections of DIY music to document and archive previous spaces, networks, and creative projects.

Archival turns and reorientations

Having established the problems with an (over)emphasis on ahistoricism in DIY music, I now move on to explore alignments between certain sub-sections of DIY music and archives. Utilising the archival turn in queer, feminist, and activist spaces as a central tenet of this section, I describe an increasing orientation towards the archive as a site of cultural and knowledge production for community members. This contradicts the discourse explored previously and surfaces practice that can be situated within a longer history of activist archiving.

In this remainder of this section, I discuss two examples of deposit of archive collections (one collection deposited at the Women's Library in London, and a second between London and Glasgow Women's Library) which were instigated by community members in the 2000s. Both deposits can also be situated as occurring within what Eichhorn describes as "the archival turn in feminism", in which (predominantly US-based) feminist cultural activists began engaging with the archive (and specifically, the work of archiving) as a source of power and representation (2013, p. 3). The close relationship between feminist activism and the archive has subsequently informed a large body of research (Chidgey, 2013, 2013, 2014; Reitsamer, 2015; Ashton, 2017; Cifor and Wood, 2017; Dever, 2017; Henningham, Evans and Morgan, 2017). Dever describes the relationship between feminist researchers and the archive as a "gravitational pull" in which archives are "sites of promise and desire" as much as they are power and privilege (2017, p. 1). Cifor and Wood propose that archives "can be understood as critical tools and modes of self-representation and self-historicisation" (2017, p. 3) for feminist activists. The archival turn in feminism signals the way in which the archive can be used as a site of knowledge production for community members, forming an integral part of current activisms and the imagining of activist futures.

The archival turn in feminism can be situated within a legacy of activist engagement with the archive (Hall, 2001; Stoler, 2010; Flinn and Alexander, 2015; Cifor and Wood, 2017; Ishmael, 2018), through which "the potentiality of archives and of the past (often a "useful past") [is activated] in engaging with the present and seeking to influence the future" (Flinn and Alexander, 2015, p. 331). In this context, the archive is a source of visibility and continuity for activist communities, creating connections across generations (Cifor and Wood, 2017, p. 5). Connecting archival work within DIY music to this legacy of activist archiving also reflects the extent to which activist movements create "parallel and overlapping histories" (Cifor and Wood, 2017, p. 5). Cifor and Wood describe crossover between feminist and LGBTQ archives and histories—relating this to my own community context, I would identify many individuals within DIY music communities as also involved in queer, feminist, left wing, union, environmental and/or housing activist networks. Through this lens, the relationship between DIY music communities and archives is less oppositional than suggested in the preceding section of this chapter.

The exploration of the following two examples is used to counter the assumptions about anti-historical ideals that were identified in the previous section. Through my discussion, I describe how these archives are formed within this community context and what the deposit felt like for community members. An exploration of these examples also identifies how integral community members are in the deposit of materials. Both cases subsequently led to deposit within institutional (albeit feminist) archival spaces, due to individuals relocating or struggling to continue to house materials. This indicates that, contrary to perceptions that DIY music communities may wish to retain custody (in line with a post-custodial model), archives can fulfil an important need for space by managing access and custody of archive collections (for example, in the relationship between the Rukus! Archive and London Metropolitan Archives (X, Campbell and Stevens, 2009).

My first example relates to a deposit of materials at the Women's Library in London by participant Leigh. In our interview, Leigh described a process of unintentional collecting that occurred during their own PhD research, in which they undertook oral history work within queer and feminist cultural activist communities:

> people were just trying to get rid of stuff, so I ended up collecting a lot of stuff ... I remember just like coming back with bags and bags of stuff cos I was on public transport, and it was just absolutely knackering and sweating carrying around all this stuff and then not knowing what to do with it, so I just put it in the filing cabinet with my other stuff ... not thinking that anybody would be particularly interested in it. I loved it, and like there was some great stuff there to kind of help contextualise people's stories. (Leigh, 2020)

In this context, Leigh (as researcher) received materials because of their position as a trusted person within these communities and because people didn't know what else to do with them. They were able to add them into an own informal archive (the filing cabinet), even though they otherwise initially didn't know how to make use of the materials, understanding that the materials did have value.

Following the completion of their PhD, Leigh deposited some of the collection at the Women's Library in London. This process was also instigated due to a house move, following which they were unable to continue to hold onto the collection. In the following quote they describe the process of deposit:

> I ended up donating that stuff to the Women's Library, I'm not even sure how that happened. I think they got in touch with me because they wanted to archive the Manifesta website ... and I think from that they were like also have you got other stuff and I was like I've got all this stuff, like what do you want and they were interested in it. (Leigh, 2020)

This quote illustrates how much larger deposits can sometimes follow on from an initial small request (to archive the website of an organising collective). Leigh described their awareness of archives around this time as minimal, due to a perception that early feminist cultural organising was not relevant to them in the present:

> I became aware of archives because of Feminist Archive North, but I always thought that was just like a load of fucking 70s bullshit, like it wasn't relevant to me or whatever... I just didn't really vibe with their kind of feminism

Subsequently after a positive experience as a depositor with the Women's Library they became interested in archival research, utilising it in their future research. Thus, the experience of depositing records which related to UK queer and feminist music histories then made archives seem more relevant and useful within current activism. This example illustrates how outreach from organisations can have longer term impacts on individuals through transforming their understanding of the contents and relevance of archive collections.

The second deposit of materials discussed within the context of interviews related to two separate deposits of materials–one deposit comprising materials relating to Ladyfest London and a personal archive to the Glasgow Women's Library and the second a zine collection and organisational documents deposited at the Women's Library in London. The former was deposited by Nazmia (along with her personal papers) and the latter collection by several collective members including Bill, who was interviewed about the experience. Nazmia described how community collecting events enabled the development of a Ladyfest archive that would subsequently be deposited at Glasgow Women's Library:

> We put on this event called the Ladyfest Herstorical Society at Lambeth Women's Project. And at that people brought loads of Ladyfest stuff, and I'd said that I would take it to put it in an archive. So there was an exhibition, and at that I bought all of the Ladyfest stuff I had in my flat, which was quite a lot of stuff, and... in 2007 for Ladies Rock we'd also gathered a shitload of Ladyfest stuff and other paraphernalia to decorate Lambeth Women's Project. (Jamal, 2019)

The gathering, collecting, and exhibiting of materials within communities speaks to the individual and collective labours described in chapter five. However, in this case the collecting was also undertaken with a preceding intention to deposit within an archive repository. In this case, a decision to deposit preceded any outreach from heritage institutions.

The second Ladyfest related deposit—a zine collection—formed organically through the collective's zine distro, which distributed zines and raised money for Ladyfest in the process. Bill describes how this process worked as follows:

> people would send me their zines [to sell] [...] And yeah, and so then we'd ask people would you like to donate a copy to go in the archives? We'd love it. And I can't remember how many we donated in the end, but it was the start of their collection. I think they carried on collecting after that… we gave them a kick start! (Savage, 2019)

Archival collecting, in the above example, was embedded in the everyday life of a zine distro, through which zines were bought and circulated. The formation of a small collection of zines (estimated at several hundred at the point of deposit) was therefore something which developed in the existing processes of a zine distro, requiring less labour than (for example) a collecting project which held specialist events or involved outreach. The collecting of zines was also undertaken as an intervention or action to "kick start" (in their words) the Women's Library into forming a zine collection (which hadn't been done before that point). In subsequent research of my own (undertaken as part of my MA research in 2013), Women's Library staff reflected upon how this collection had in turn developed into a much more substantial collection through donations and active outreach in the zine community.

This section has identified instances in which cultural organisers are responsible for building archives (intentionally or unintentionally) and for their eventual transfer to an archive service. Halberstam refers to a "lack of distinction between the archivist and the cultural worker" (2005, p. 162). In reference to activist archiving Sellie et. al also describe

> a difficulty in separating "users" from volunteers, or researchers, or to find distinctions between those who use the collections and those who contribute to, or are represented within them. (2015, p. 458)

This merging of roles is common both in the journey of community members into institutions (as is explored in the following section) and when community members instigate and undertake archival work in community spaces. In the previous examples, a community member often undertakes duties of an archivist to develop and build a collection to ensure the survival of archival traces of activities they viewed as significant. These examples illustrate that often community members step into this work before more formal archive institutions reach out, thus forming a crucial part in ensuring the safety of such materials. Community members form important agents in the intermediate stages between cultural activity and the deposit of materials, through gathering materials or using community networks to form archives prior to outreach from organisations.

This section has demonstrated how formal archives are formed within queer and/or feminist DIY music communities. These more formalised collections of materials should be situated within the same cluster of archival labours discussed in chapter five. Crucially, by focusing on existing examples of archival work undertaken within queer and feminist DIY music communities I have highlighted a parallel between these communities and other activist communities which engage with the archive as part of their activities. This provides an important counterpoint to the relationship with archives and heritage explored in the previous section.

In/between: Situated archivists and third space practice

The previous section of this chapter looked at collections instigated by community members, which later were deposited in institutional repositories. This section further considers community members in archival roles, but this time through the examination of those who also occupy professional posts as information workers. Utilising the concept of "third-space" subjectivity, I use my own position in this project to explore alliances between DIY music communities and information workers that can be formed through third space archival practice.

The subjectivity of the archivist is often underexamined in research which engages with the tension between communities and institutions. This research can overemphasise or create "binary distinctions between activists and archivists, between archiving and activism, and between active and neutral" (Flinn and Alexander, 2015, p. 332). Professionals are assumed to ideologically align with their employing organisations, and to serve as representatives of institutions. The positioning of the archivist as "servant" to their organisations and the archival profession (Greene, 2013, p. 329) is inadequate because of the assumption that professionals adhere to their employer's imperatives and ideologies. Instead, by examining the subjectivity and actions of individual archivists (and specifically those with shared histories to the communities they collect from), it is possible to make visible a pathway into the information profession which is motivated by activist intentions and which can engender alternative relations between communities and archive services.

Historically, archival education and theory has been centred around "intellectual methodological and racial homogeneity" (Ramirez, 2015, p. 340). Archival concepts including the record, time and evidence emerging from white and Western positivist traditions have been presented as universal in archival education (Gilliland, 2011). The archivist's goal is to act as a neutral and objective custodian of archive collection–Caswell writes that archivists "purport to be from nowhere, purport to serve no one but their employers, and purport to leave no fingerprints" (2019, p. 6). Through this (now heavily criticised) worldview, archivists are succeeding if we are barely or in-visible in our catalogues, processing and acquisition activities.

However, neutrality and objectivity have been problematised by archival theorists who propose that these traits disguise colonial violence and white privilege (Stoler, 2010; Ramirez, 2015; Findlay, 2016; Ishmael, 2018). An active acknowledgement and engagement with identity and subjectivity within archival studies can help us get closer to identifying "the heart of the reproduction of whiteness and the power of white privilege in the discipline" (Ramirez, 2015, p. 343). The concept of a universal politics of punk has, too, been rejected by Duncombe and Tremblay who describe it as disguising "the spectre of White privilege" (Duncombe and Tremblay, 2011, p. 12). Instead, these authors call for a punk ideology that engages with subjectivity and identity as a way to address the whiteness of the subculture. Therefore, understanding subjectivity not only helps to understand the position from which histories and archives are produced, but also helps us to unpick how specific ideologies come to dominate disciplines and sectors.

Through examining the subjectivity of an archivist, we can better understand the impact of their identity on the historical record. Caswell has called for the information profession to engage explicitly with the situated identity of the professional. Through this worldview, the archivist can be viewed

> as a socially located, culturally situated agent who centres ways of being and knowing from the margins. (Caswell, 2019, p. 7)

Caswell's concept of feminist standpoint appraisal is built upon a legacy of calls to embrace marginality as a position of power (hooks, 1989; Licona, 2005), and to focus on how individual position affects the production of knowledge. This also aligns with calls to "think of our archival practices and processes as critical interventions, as deliberate and conscious acts" (Wright, 2019, p. 345), which demonstrate the potential to transform structures and exercise resistance through our daily actions.

The rest of this section is concerned with the underexplored "in between" space that an archivist with simultaneous professional, community and activist responsibilities occupies. I identify how shared histories and identities can potentially create more equal and fertile ground on which to establish archives. This allows for further critical examination of the subjectivity of those working simultaneously in both spaces. How do we, as activists, community members, friends and professionals, balance between our respective responsibilities? How do pre-existing friendship dynamics affect the perception of institutions in communities? How does this change the circulation and production of power in archives?

Trust can be afforded to organisations when individuals of repute within a community take up paid positions (for example, as archivists, curators or librarians). In the context of my PhD, my own position within DIY music communities enabled me to jump over hurdles that other qualitative researchers might face–for example, I did not struggle to access participants. The same can be said for information and heritage professionals who occupy positions within communities, and thus face less resistance or scepticism when they begin collections in formal institutions. For example, Bill reflected that people in positions such as my own could potentially transform these interactions:

> archiving seems to sort of cottoned on a little bit to how it might collect this sort of material, right? There's people like you ... so that's how it's gonna change, isn't it? (Savage, 2019)

The employment of DIY cultural peers within organisations is an opportunity to put into practice different relationships between professionals and communities.

There are existing examples of how DIY music has moved into archival spaces through the positioning of subcultural peers as archivists, librarians and curators in organisations. For example, we can look at the development of the Riot Grrrl Collection at Fales Library, which developed partially due to archivist Lisa Darms' connection to women who had gone to Evergreen College in the 1990s (as Darms had). Of the collection, Eichhorn writes that "the collection only exists, however, because the donors identify with and trust each other on the basis of their much less public history" (2013, p. 96). The development of zine collections in the UK and USA also draws on a long legacy of zine creators who move into the information profession because of a passion for access to information that, in many cases, begins with zine making. Some individuals in this study worked in libraries or archives, and described their professional motivations as connected to a passion to share information and build community also found in DIY cultural politics. For example, Colette (who works in public library services) said that

> I think there's something inherently punk about… giving people information and opening up that information to people… when people get really stuck in dead ends and don't know how to contact gov.uk because of their settled status in the EU or searching for jobs and things like that… just opening up information and sharing information with people, that I think is really important… (Colette, 2019)

Instead of positioning information professionals in opposition to DIY culture, we should situate the movement of DIY cultural peers into the information profession within a longer legacy of information activism (McKinney, 2020) which centre the provision of information as a critical dimension of activist practice.

In "(B)orderlands' Rhetorics and Representations: The Transformative Potential of Feminist Third-Space Scholarship and Zines", Licona explores the concept of "third space" lived experience which can be used to situate subjects who write from the margins (2013). The concept of the "third space" is used to describe the experiences of those who cross borders (which divide space, identity, places and other elements into dichotomies or binaries) (2013, p. 105). Third space rhetoric is explored in an archival context by Lee, who applies this concept to queer/ed archival methodologies (2017). Lee proposes that we can use the third space to describe how

> archivists themselves might be considered dynamic, embodied multiply-situated subjects who move between and beyond this limiting dichotomy of professional/amateur. (2017, p. 328)

The concept of a third space can be used in archival theory to describe the experience and feelings of insider archivists, who navigate engagement and involvement with both organisations and communities. The utilisation of this theory within archival theory moves beyond the simple binary of community and organisation explored earlier and instead makes visible the specific experience of those situated at the "virtual and material intersections" of community-centred archival practice (Licona, 2013, p. 4). Previous research about community-led archival practice in the context of archival studies has reinforced rather than examined the borders between professionals and communities, effectively erasing the opportunity to better understanding the complicated position of individuals who occupy both spaces simultaneously.

Overemphasis on the difference and/or boundaries between professionals and communities can disguise the potential for new relationships formed through shared histories. As Licona writes, this

> Demarcating line of the border–not always a straight line–can obscure third space or fertile ground of unrealised potentials. (2013, p. 13)

The concept of a third space archivist can be utilised to describe "alliance formation" between individuals from marginalised communities and archival professionals. In these formations, as Moore writes,

> We can think of the archive, any archive, as a shared space, rather than a context between different places and spaces of different archival practices. (2017, p. 135)

When we think of the archive as a shared space, we are acknowledging the way in which a space is shaped by different subjectivities as well as organisational policies. In a space where archivists and communities share politics, history and identity, alliances and coalitions can then be relied upon to challenge the reproduction of dominant narratives and the erasure of specific experiences. In this situation the third space archivist can be an important agent in pushing for social justice, representation and change both within and outside of heritage organisations.

These alliances can in turn build trust, intimacy and empathy into archival relationships. Describing her own work with the Feminist Webs project, Moore describes how

> The movement of 'tacking back and forth' between professional and amateur practices, or perhaps between different professions – archivist, researcher, youth worker –… is also suggestive of the work of weaving a web. (2017, p. 141)

The image of weaving, creating and entangling that emerges through the imagery of the web is further described by Moore as blurring "boundaries of the inside and outside of the archive, and also those of academic/activist/archivist" (2017, p. 142). Caswell and Cifor also utilise the image of a web, describing archivists as "caregivers, bound to records creators, subjects, users, and communities through a web of mutual affective responsibility" (2016, p. 24). Research about community-led archives has also suggested that professionals who do not have pre-existing relationships within communities can build trust over a period of time through their actions (Zavala et al., 2017, p. 208)—in the view of the web, working together over time reinforces the relational structures or shared space between archives and communities.

However, there are further dynamics embedded in the relationship between a third space archivist and communities which should be made visible. Those with both professional and personal responsibilities can face pressure from both organisation and community. In relation to feminist geography, Cuomo and Massaro reflect that

> the concerns of trespass, misrepresentation, reduction, and finally awfulness haunt us as feminist scholars studying people in places that are close to our hearts. (2016, p. 94)

The emotional weight of undertaking heritage work within intimate community is significant—as McKinney and Mitchell write of their own experience doing heritage work in lesbian feminist circles, work can be "emotionally demanding" especially when histories are "charged with affect, infighting, and the often painful work of being a feminist" (2019, p. 11). More consideration should be given to the emotional impact of being positioned simultaneously in and between multiple contexts, as well as the space that it creates in otherwise challenging dynamics.

It is also important to discuss who moves between DIY music communities and into professional roles. These positions have been historically closed to those without a high level of postgraduate education, and researchers have highlighted how this restrictive route to progression can in turn reproduce patterns of whiteness and affluence (Ramirez, 2015; Schlesselman-Tarango, 2016; Espinal, Sutherland and Roh, 2018; Henthorn and Fife, 2018; Ishmael, 2020; Fife and Henthorn, 2021). Whist the employment of community members in the information and heritage sector signals progress, it does not entirely level power discrepancies. These racialised dynamics in turn manifest in the compilation of archival materials from DIY music subcultures (Nguyen, 2015, p. 18), or in institutional drive and desire to archive specific movements (e.g. the discussion of interest in riot grrrl histories (Cifor and Wood, 2017, p. 12). Ishmael writes that

> One of the by-products of whiteness is the way it shapes practice, and what is considered appropriate or professional, which as outlined, shapes the requirements for funding and associated value judgements. (I2020, p. 242)

The gatekeeping of the archival profession by a predominantly white sector also impacts on the potential of third space archivists—when those recruited continue to otherwise conform to exclusionary standards for professionalism, then the histories made, collected, and funded will continue to perpetuate the problems identified here (see also chapter three).

This section has also relied on an assumption that information professionals will remain fixed within their professional posts. Though there are few statistics to demonstrate the exact percentage of professionals working on fixed term contracts, research by Poutch indicated that 59% of new professionals in the sector were employed on short or long fixed term contracts (2016, p. 160), and a 2015 workforce mapping exercise by CILIP and ARA found that 24% of the entire archive profession was employed on a non-permanent basis (CILIP and Archives and Records Association, 2015). Redundancies and cuts to funding also negatively affect the development of social movement collections, due to a lack of capacity to build relationships (Griffin, 2018, p. 504). It is important to bring precarious employment and the impact of austerity upon the archive sector workforce into discussions of relationships between communities and institutions. This section has demonstrated how trust develops through sustained and intimate relationships between individuals and communities–however, when the sector heavily relies upon unstable employment of various types then these cannot develop, or the dynamics of a deposit may change substantially during turnover of staff. When staff regularly turn over in posts, the ethical nuances of a deposit (e.g. agreements to consult before exhibiting) can easily be lost or forgotten. More focus needs to be given to how trust can be sustained through the continuity of ethical practice, regardless of who occupies a particular post.

Collaboration, Participation and Labour

The final section of this chapter explores the dynamics of collaboration and/or participation in relationships between DIY music communities and archive organisations. DIY music communities are formed through networks of mutual aid and information sharing. The non-hierarchical and collaborative nature of these networks led me to initially explore participatory ways of working and researching at the outset of this project. However, the process of initiating and developing participatory methods in this community context led me to extensively reflect on the cost and labour of participation and collaboration when it happens between communities and institutionally-located researchers. This section returns to these terms for a more detailed examination in the context of this project's community. Through an examination of the dynamics of participatory practice, I problematise the over-reliance on these methods within archival research and research within DIY cultures. Instead, I emphasise how these processes are often still controlled within organisations or by the instigators of projects and underestimate the amount of labour placed on volunteers or unpaid participants.

In "The labour of being studied in a free love economy", Cowan and Rault explore the power dynamics of a research project and the production of a digital archive of trans, feminist and queer culture in Canada. In the article, the authors refer to

> the labour of being studied within an academic-cultural milieu that increasingly camouflages free affective labour as collaboration and research-co-creation. (2014a, p. 471)

The turn towards participatory methods in archives relies on an assumption that communities will jump at

> the opportunity to do this work for their own good, toward the promise of finally being recognised, noticed, written about and valued. (Cowan and Rault, 2014a, p. 473)

However, it is critical to examine who can afford to take part in these opportunities. In relation to crowdsourcing metadata, Flanagan and Carini write that

> Those traditionally adding metadata to library materials would be primarily white, middle class, English speaking, educated, "wired," and highly trained in the information sciences. (2012, p. 520)

In some cases, acknowledgement and recognition is enough for a community—but should that be the only reward we seek to provide? In examples such as the above, the emancipatory and democratic goals of participation are curbed when only those with time and resource can engage. Without appropriate compensation or resource, these projects reproduce knowledge from the position professionals wish to de-centre or challenge.

Participatory archival researchers have drawn attention to tensions between participatory ideals and pragmatic realities (Eveleigh, 2014, p. 212; Sexton, 2016, p. 171). Politics of specific communities can clash with organisational infrastructures and institutional processes already long embedded. Sexton writes that

> all interventions, including participatory ones, are always constituted and controlled by forces that constrain and limit both the facilitator's and the participants' ability to influence what is done. (2016, p. 154)

As someone situated in both an (academic) institution and a community, I have also felt scepticism and weariness when the words community and participation are employed by organisations that otherwise abide by the hierarchical and selective production of knowledge, archives and histories. Of participatory community engagement practices instigated from within universities, Kinpaisby asks

> why now? Why not before? What is this really about? What sort of aims and whose interests does this really serve? How is it representing what the community actually is? Then, how is it representing the sort of relationship we want the university to have with the community? (2008, p. 295)

The extent to which these initiatives really benefit communities is uncertain, and the capacity to speak back to processes can be limited in evaluation and reflection stages.

Participatory research and archival practice is presented as activist in nature due to its focus on empowering participants and creating a two way flow of knowledge between institution and community (Kinpaisby, 2008, p. 293). In relationship to participatory archival practice in web 2.0 environments, Eveleigh writes that

> Participation in this vein is promoted as a means to address troubling issues of marginalisation and representation, professional passivity and power. (2014, p. 213)

Participatory practice aims to resolve power differences and challenge inequalities, rather than create new issues. As a result, we do not problematise or interrogate the dynamics of these methodologies enough. My own unease over the participatory comes from both a knowledge of the above pragmatic barriers that exist within organisations, and from a wariness about the extent to which archival interventions often create additional labour and burdens for the community in question. In relation to critical feminism and archival practice, Cifor and Wood write that

> Creating safe spaces for discussion, mutual support and productive dialogue is vital, but one cannot ignore the ways in which minoritised populations are again tasked with the labour of change. (2017, p. 19)

Participatory processes can be instigated when communities or individuals intervene within institutional heritage—however, weight can be subsequently felt by those intervening when they are expected to transform organisations from the outside. Those doing this work can subsequently burn out and be left behind by organisations. Eveleigh also highlights how crowdsourcing can be viewed as "a wholly pragmatic solution to a lack of financial and labour resource" (2014, p. 215). Therefore, the position of labour (emotional, computational, physical, volunteer, or other forms of labour) in participatory archival practice contributes significantly to the manifestation of unequal power dynamics between researchers, professionals and community members.

The previous section identified how community members moving into professional posts can potentially transform relationships between communities and organisations or create relationships on different foundations. However, the dynamics of paid/unpaid labour are at work in many of these relationships and should not go unexamined. At the outset of my own work, I was asking my peers to regularly participate in lengthy participatory conversations in order to enable more collaboration in the development of my project. During those first few workshops, I realised that I was asking them to do more work, when what I felt most keenly was a desire for me to make use of the time and resources I had to take on the work of archiving. In reference to participatory action research methodologies, Kinpaisby describes

> being comfortable with difference, and using difference strategically when it's appropriate, and submerging difference when it's appropriate, and seeking commonality—solidarity—when it's appropriate. (2008, p. 296)

Participatory practice can lead to an unnecessary submersion of difference. The dynamics of friendship can help to "tackle head on the complex circulation of power between" individuals involved in a project (Sexton and Sen, 2018, p. 877)—however, it does not remove difference between individuals involved with a project. For me, working with awareness of difference (in time, capacity, payment, and labour) required flexibility and adaptation of participation based on an individual's capacity.

Throughout this work, it has felt like there has been an ongoing enthusiasm for this project and what has felt like a shared agreement that we should be archived (in ways which aligned with community politics and ideals). Therefore, where I saw myself as most useful was as someone who could bring together shared history in DIY music with knowledge of archival practice and archive organisations. In this role, I could encourage and coordinate deposits, empower people to do documentary work and collaborate through occupying the role of facilitator in between communities and organisations. Working as a facilitator located between and within organisations and communities is an approach which has been successfully undertaken by others working in activist contexts including the Occupy movement (Erde, 2014, p. 86). This shift in practice was responsive to the community I was working with, but ultimately shifted the project away from working within the framework participatory archival practice. The following section explores what the work of archiving looked like in this context.

Doing the Work of Archiving

The shape my work took evolved through the specific temporal circumstances that framed this research. In the first year, I focused my energy on developing several starting points for potential collaborative projects. The most successful of these was a collaborative timeline mapping workshop which happened at queer punk festival Bent Fest in 2019. The workshop utilised methods developed in Charlotte Cooper's *A Queer and Trans Fat Activist Timeline*, a project in which workshops at gatherings of activists enabled the creation and subsequent deposit of a timeline of fat queer activism. As Cooper writes of the workshop,

> people talked and wrote, asking for clarification and discussing events they were simultaneously memorialising. It was like a dialogue between the past and the present, a statement of memory. (2012, p. 63)

Other community heritage projects have adopted geographical mapping exercises in similar ways, including Lashua, who used collaborative mapping workshops to document the intangible heritage of Liverpool's black community-led music social clubs in Liverpool throughout the 1980s and 1990s (2015).

A photograph of the timeline in situ and the information on it are reproduced on the following page. The timeline is a time and place specific record of spaces that existed to nurture DIY music, co-created by people who participated in or ran them. By working collaboratively to create the timeline, we utilised an existing gathering and the deeply networked working practices of DIY music spaces to create an archival object. In the context of historical geography, Ashmore et al. talk about the experience of "working-with" in archival processing. As they write

> Working-with the owner of an archival collection… offers alternative forms of communal knowledge formation which are worthy of further consideration. (2012, p. 82)

In the context of this project, we were working-with and within Bent Fest in order to create a record. Those involved in both the timeline's

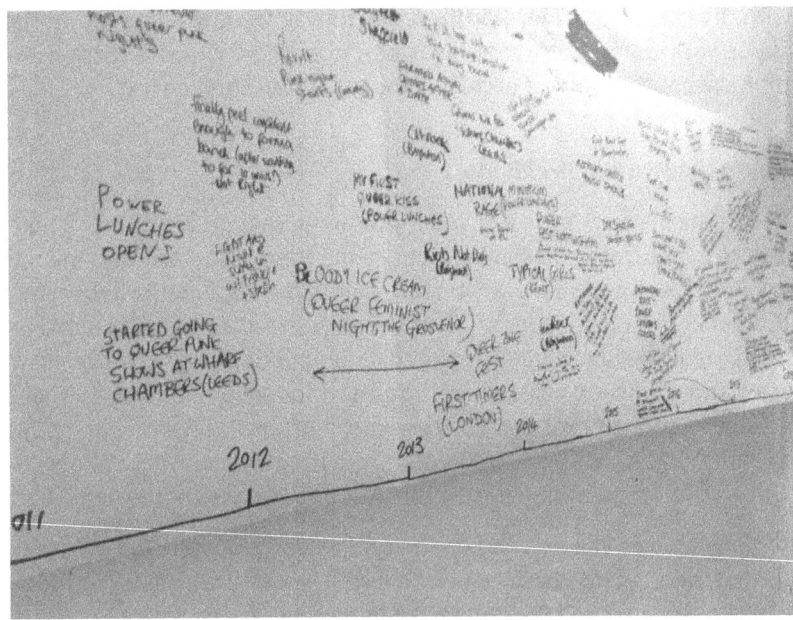

Figure 2 Timeline installed on wall of DIY Space for London during Bent Fest 2019

construction can be understood as having expertise gained via lived experience and previous participation. This connects to research about participatory and community archives by theorists including Gilliland and McKemmish who point out that these archives "may eschew a professional staff in favour of community experts such as Elders, veterans and community historians" (2014, p. 80). Undertaking communal, collective, and sociable history work through methods such as the above is an opportunity to embed documentation and archival work in the everyday life of spaces, and crucially with much less labour on the behalf of collaborators.

As the global pandemic escalated, it became clear that continuing to work via collaborative workshops and within existing events and activities at DIY music spaces would not be possible. This was caused by the temporary and permanent closure of several spaces, and the cancellation of almost all live events in 2020 and part of 2021. The beginnings of other potential collaborative projects such as the above were immediately paused, and instead it became more urgent to respond to the specific threats, e.g. the potential loss of informal archives that spaces had developed through their existence. This became another point at which participatory action research clashed with my work—Kinpaisby describes participatory action research as "slow research" which takes a substantial amount of time in order to develop shared understandings and common ground (2008, p. 296). Whilst arguably my shared history with the community in question enabled some shared understanding from the outset, for all the decisions in the project to have been made collectively I would have needed more time and resource. The juggling of multiple timeframes (the PhD timeline, participatory action research's slowness and the urgency and rapidly changing landscape of DIY music community) across one project is challenging, and ultimately the urgent work overtook the more reflective and contemplative elements of my project towards its conclusion.

The most urgent piece of archival work was undertaken in 2020 following the closure of DIY Space for London's physical space. Legal music spaces often have a landlord to whom rent is paid—once notice is given and the decision to vacate made clear, energies are turned towards the physical clearing out of a space. My existing history and "intimate insider" status (Taylor, 2011) in the UK DIY music scene enabled me to take on temporary responsibility for DIY Space for London's archive, and in doing so instigate conversations about its long-term storage following the clear out of the space. The rush of communication about the collection from multiple individuals highlighted concern and anxiety about the potential loss of the materials. The rapid action required in this circumstance could not map onto the more reflective and collaborative process of participatory action research, and in this situation, I took the lead in managing the collection, listing and subsequent deposit of the materials.

The decision to deposit materials was steered by me—and was heavily informed by my history with "the notion of the "archive"" and its structure, accessibility and form (Sexton, 2016, p. 198). The concern expressed by participants was primarily based around access to information—whether this information was in a formal archive repository or on a website was not considered important. This aligns with Smith's discussion about the importance of the use of heritage, which is viewed as at least as important as sites of heritage (2006, p. 46). Accessibility of materials (at least in a physical sense) is understood as critical within DIY music cultures, especially given that the sites of heritage (for example, physical spaces) were often already closed or lost to developers.

My decision to deposit some of the materials was spurred by a knowledge that without a permanent base, I would be unable to make the materials accessible due to my own lack of space and time to take on this responsibility. In this sense, in parallel with the case study of the Occupy movement's archives explored by Erde, efforts to keep the archive out of institutional hands effectively rendered it inaccessible (2014, pp. 82–83). In an interview article between Ajamu X, Topher Campbell and Mary Stevens the decision to deposit the Rukus! Archive at London Metropolitan Archives is discussed, and similar desires (for the archive to be held somewhere with resources) are articulated:

> I mean Marx said get your hands on the means of production. We're not holding it at Conservative central office now, are we? We are holding it somewhere which has got the facilities and resources to maintain it… And it's our archive; they're not owning the archive. (2009, p. 291)

The decision to deposit materials from this study can be situated within a modern post-custodial approach which reimagines "traditional archival orientations to support current realities of records and communities" (Zavala et al., 2017, p. 208). In my case, the need of the community in question was a safe and long-term space in which the materials could be stored and accessed.

Sharing Knowledge and Skills

The final examples of practice I will share relate to the dissemination of information and archival knowledge within DIY music communities. The interchange of information between archivists and communities is not a new idea. Stevens et al. propose that institutional services can be of use to communities through the provision of advice and training in areas including preservation, digitisation, documentation and copyright (Stevens, Flinn and Shepherd, 2010, p. 67). They describe this as a critical shift in relationships, writing that

> The one-way 'handing over' of records to the public domain is starting to give way to the 'handing on' both inside and outside the archives of a wide diversity of materials, knowledge and skills. (Stevens, Flinn and Shepherd, 2010, p. 61)

This shift in relationship and professional focus demonstrates an understanding that relationships with institutions could be centred less around the deposit, custody and control of materials, but instead around dialogue, community control and ownership (Zavala et al., 2017, p. 103). Writing about the development of the Australian Women's Archive Project, Henningham et al. refer to

> reframing relationships between archivists and communities... archivists being responsible for providing an infrastructure that facilitates community recordkeeping and archiving activities, to overcome barriers to discoverability and access. (2017, p. 103)

The archivist as facilitator is a reframing of professionalism that has been engaged with in activist and participatory archival contexts (Erde, 2014; Eveleigh, 2014). Erde proposes that communities and organisations collaborate through the development of co-operative networks to better enable sharing of knowledge and resources (2014, p. 87).

Researchers have also identified the importance of skills sharing within DIY cultures (Chidgey, 2014; Abtan, 2016). Chidgey proposes that a focus on learning and making in DIY culture enables individuals to "reclaim power in their everyday lives" (2014, p. 104). An examination of existing projects within DIY music communities makes a similar focus visible–for example, the First Timers collective (based in London) suggest that

> The skills we learn as d.i.y musicians are as often gleaned from those around us as they are from lessons (or youtube!) Making an effort to share basic skills through workshops or even just one-to-one hangouts takes the fear over not being good enough away. (First Timers, no date)

Skills sharing can also be an intervention in knowledge practices that otherwise enforce hierarchies and patterns of dominance (Abtan, 2016, p. 55). Sharing of information and knowledge can thus be an opportunity to intervene in existing hierarchies, social structures and to resist the reproduction of inequalities through different relationship models.

Those of us who have been involved in communities for longer periods of time often feel an affective responsibility to pass on connections, skills, and knowledge to others. For example, Cassie reflected

> I'm so lucky that I've met so many great people and so many friends that wouldn't we want other people to have that? And if we can pass that forward in any way, like this was what I was saying about the importance of like skill sharing. If we can do that, for years to come not just the immediate, like what workshop are we going to run next week, right? But what in like 20, 30, 50 years? (Agbehenu, 2019)

Not only is skills sharing already embedded within DIY music, but it can also be a way to encourage interaction between organisations and communities. By transparently sharing archival skills and knowledge, professionals can hand on the tools to archive histories that are already known to be important by communities. The following examples provide several short examples of the ways in which different research spaces provided opportunities to share skills and knowledge and encourage a more dialogical relationship between myself and participants.

The space of the qualitative interview proved to be a useful space in which interchange of knowledge happened naturally. Although interviews are normally viewed as a research method which enables the one-way flow of knowledge from participant to researcher, I found the existing relationships between participants and me enabled the interviews to develop into a more conversational and dialogic space.

Dialogic interviewing has been explored as a feminist interviewing tool which can engender a more intimate interview space and create co-constructed meaning (Bloom et al., 2020). The dialogic interview is also an opportunity for peer-to-peer learning, which has been explored in the context of higher education(Bloom et al., 2020). Qualitative researchers Sinha and Back also argue the case for "sociable methods" which value participation and dialogue–"working with rather than on participants" (2014, p. 475). In their context (working with young migrants) the use of more sociable methods was preferred as otherwise the interview format could mimic that of interviews with state officials. In my case, formal interviews seemed absurd given the close relationships I shared with some participants. Instead, a conversational approach emulated our social relations outside of this project–and provided the necessary space for me to be asked questions and pass on advice in turn.

Across my own interviews, I noticed the way in which these conversations led to participants affording more value to their own cultural output or their collections. For instance, towards the end of our interview Cassie reflected:

> would I even have thought about this if we weren't having this conversation? Or say I don't know you at all? Like, would I think about this as important? Probably not [...] I feel like you've made me think a lot about this, because I think music, particularly punk, particularly DIY punk, and playing in bands and being involved and all that stuff, is really transformative, like I can say that being in Fight Rosa Fight changed my life. (Agbehenu, 2019)

In some cases, I passed on more direct information about archiving. For example, I found that individuals generally did not know that they could refer UK-based websites for archiving via the UK Web Archive. In one case, I received direct feedback that the interview had enabled a participant to follow this route. The two above examples suggest that interviews can be used differently—instead of what might seem like a one-way transfer of "data", it can be an opportunity to have more lengthy and dialogic conversations in which information, resources and experiences can be shared between all involved.

The onset of the coronavirus pandemic provided an opportunity to develop a new strand of knowledge sharing activities–virtual workshops, which could be facilitated just with a Zoom license. For this project,

I chose to deliver a focused workshop on one area which particularly preoccupied participants–web archiving. Utilising my own research findings to develop training, I built a two-hour long workshop which I titled "Basic web Archiving Skills for DIY Cultures and Activists". These events were attended by a total of 140 people (which was the capacity of the events). One benefit of hosting a virtual workshop was the capacity to bring together individuals from projects across the world. The timing of the events in summer and autumn 2020 was particularly apt, due to the upsurge in interest in activist heritage following the widespread global protests of the Black Lives Matter movement. Participants attended on behalf of activist groups, zine libraries, community heritage groups, music collectives, as well as many who were motivated by an individual interest or concern (predominantly those involved in the specific community of my research).

Chapter three explored the development of my reflexive zine writing practice and the publishing of a series of autoethnographic zines in the series Adventures in Academia. Zines were also used to share information and knowledge about archiving. I produced two zines during the project—*Archive It Ourselves: Strategies and Tips for Documenting and Archiving DIY Histories 1 and 2* (Fife, 2019b, 2024). Content explored the value of traces of DIY culture, methods for documenting underrepresented histories, links and resources to support grassroots information work, and explanation of the process of depositing archives. These were disseminated via networks at zine fairs, stalls at events, online via social media, and via word of mouth.

The choice to produce knowledge and organise events outside of academic settings was a politicised one. Downes et al. call for researchers to engage with "alternative forms and forums of knowledge production" (2013, p. 118) and to develop "forums and networks that promote engagement and dialogue between activists, academics and academic-activists outside academic institutions" (2013, p. 119). My dissemination activities enabled the building of connections, sharing of knowledge, and dialogue between those producing information and those charged with the long-term custody of it (as well as those doing both simultaneously). Circulating archival knowledge outside of professional settings and in forms and language familiar to community members enabled peers to develop an understanding of archival processes which could either be used to develop grassroots archive projects or to empower them in decisions made to subsequently deposit materials.

Figure 3 Cover of Archive it Ourselves: Strategies and Tips for Documenting and Archiving DIY Histories (Fife, 2019c)

Conclusion

Throughout this project, participants and I have regularly talked about how "messy" DIY music is, due to factors I have explored elsewhere in this thesis (intimacy, friendship, conflict, harm, creative collaboration, a lack of boundaries between work and leisure, reliance on temporary spaces and unpaid labour). This chapter's examination of the archive as organisation, shared space and relational dynamic only further emphasises this messiness, which is manifested through overlapping personal, professional and community responsibilities. This overlapping of experiences and roles (e.g. archivist and subcultural peer) crosses the expected boundaries and borders between archive organisation and community, and in doing so creates useful and potentially fertile ground on which projects and collaborations can be formed. Though not without power dynamics and issues of their own, these relationships can also challenge the foundations on which traditions of archival practice are based. Using a subjectivity-focused framework for examining relationships between individuals, communities and archive organisations also surfaces more complex, interwoven, and nuanced understandings of the ways in which the three connect, overlap, and move in/between spaces.

Figure 4: Mess (original illustration)

Conclusion

The body of work presented here is a detailed examination of how UK DIY music spaces are documented and archived. Following the lead of cultural theorists concerned with the formation of archives in communities (Hall, 2001), I have argued for a conceptualisation of archival activity which takes into account how archives are formed, who forms them, and the circumstances from which they emerge (or, in many cases, do not emerge). By situating archives within a broader societal context, this project has identified the influence and (often negative) impact of heritage traditions, technological shifts, and socioeconomic circumstances on documentary and archival work in DIY music spaces.

Although the research for this project was conducted between 2018 and 2021, the foundations for this project were built in the preceding years. These were informed by my own fears and anxieties about the loss (or potential for loss) of spaces and communities that provided alternatives to exclusionary and capitalist music industry structures. There was no control over our lives, work, and access to spaces, despite desire to find and work to build alternatives. The ground I stood on was shaky at best. I tried to take small actions to document and hold onto those spaces, as did many peers. Nonetheless, it felt (and often still feels) impossible to see our future.

The duration of this project is a microcosm of the rapidly changing circumstances in which we operate. Three years is a short duration for a project, yet within this period we experienced multiple overlapping threats. These include the global coronavirus pandemic, rapid closure of DIY music spaces (The Mayor of London's Music Venues Taskforce, 2015), the loss of housing due to gentrification and the lack of tenants' rights in the UK, the loss and/or deletion of information held on social media platforms (DeVille, 2019), and cuts to cultural funding and income-assessed benefits which impacted on personal capacity, employment and the viability of spaces. My analysis has demonstrated how these threats simultaneously affect information and archival traces, personal livelihoods, and community spaces. Anticipating and mitigating the damage caused by these threats often takes precedence and leaves little space to develop long-term record keeping practices or ensure the safety of traces.

As community building becomes more difficult and less sustainable for individuals involved in UK DIY music, the heritage of popular music continues to be used in institutional heritage and tourism settings. At the point of writing this conclusion and during 2021's UK budget reveal, chancellor Rishi Sunak announced £2million of public funding had been allocated to begin the development of a new museum about The Beatles in Liverpool (Taylor, 2021). Following the announcement of the funding, Mark Davyd (of Music Venue Trust) criticised this decision writing that Liverpool's

Infrastructure of grassroots music venues, the places that actually inspired and developed the Beatles, is massively under invested in, crippled by the Covid crisis, and [is] in desperate need of support. (2021)

The allocation of this funding to this project means that a Beatles museum will join other existing spaces celebrating the legacy and impact of The Beatles in Liverpool (e.g. Beatles Story). The presence of one act will continue to dominate the landscape of music heritage in this setting, much as it does across other UK cities (for example, Joy Division and Factory Records in Manchester, Sex Pistols and The Clash in London). Meanwhile, the lives and cultural work of countless other music communities go unremembered, undocumented, erased and/or irrecoverable without further support, often due to manifestations of platform capitalism and the inherent instability of digital sources.

The allocation of government funding to the development of this space should be held simultaneously with other tensions in UK heritage sector—for example, former Culture Secretary Oliver Dowden's letter to national heritage organisations that warned staff to remain ""impartial"" and avoid ""taking actions motivated by activism or politics"" (Dowden cited in Kendall Adams, 2020). During a time in which national heritage institutions are being constrained from interrogating their colonial and racist pasts, what is being funded should be critically examined. Research has identified how the perpetuation of specific acts in music histories undervalues and erases the cultural legacies of different communities, acts, and genres (Nguyen, 2012b; Brunow, 2019). It is crucial to note that what dominates these narratives is too often white, male, heterosexual, and otherwise privileged. Without critical reflection, popular music museums and exhibitions merely reproduce exclusionary narratives and politics (Fairchild, 2021). Recent projects to establish archives for underrepresented music communities (Campbell and Stitski, 2018; The Kitchen Sisters, no date) and salvage remains from lost spaces (Pidd, 2017; Tailor, 2019) highlight how much has been lost through this dominance.

In my introductory chapter, I outlined three research questions. In the remainder of this conclusion, I summarise how my findings have answered these questions, before concluding with final thoughts about future research direction in this field.

How, af at All, are DIY Music Spaces Currently Documented and Remembered?

By resisting representing DIY music communities as in opposition to heritage, this thesis has made space for articulations of DIY forms of heritage, record keeping and archiving that often exist outside of the boundaries of the traditional archive. Chapter four utilised the framework of "unauthorised heritage" (Roberts and Cohen, 2014) to frame individual actions to create, keep, organise, share and use information. The emphasis on praxis in this chapter makes visible the "social and political labours of memory" (Merrill, Keightley and Daphi, 2020a, p. 14) in this context, surfacing actions which are motivated by memory, affect, and history, but rarely interface with formalised heritage activity. Chapter five's exploration of digital memory work similarly identified how digital platforms were utilised to hold and circulate information, which was assigned value by individuals but rarely moved into formal heritage spaces. The examples presented in these chapters demonstrate a need to push back against the perceived limits of the concept of the archive and the record and archiving as a practice and profession.

Chapters three, four, five and six demonstrated the affective dimensions of memory work. Community members utilised tangible and intangible practices to document, remember and connect through the sharing of memory and information. These practices included zine making, photography and film-making, podcasting, recording music, artwork production, and website building, which generated material or digital outputs, as well as intangible and ephemeral practices including performance, oral history and storytelling. Material forms of cultural production, which have historically been positioned as central in archives of activism (Hoyer and Almeida, 2021), often took digital forms in this study. This signals a change in form that impacts the shape and preservation requirements of archival collections from subcultural contexts, as well as the need to consider how technological shifts in society impact archival activity in communities.

How are External Factors in the Current Political, Technological and Socioeconomic Climate Affecting Documentary and Archival Activity in Current UK DIY Music Spaces?

I have often located DIY heritage as developing outside of institutional boundaries. Much as DIY music communities emphasise the value of creative freedom enabled by working outside the capitalist structures of the music industry, community-led information work often seems to flourish outside of the limits of the archive, the record and professional identity. However, chapters five and six identified how archives and information is easily lost when upkeep falls on individuals. Archiving is work, and for many in this study, this work is done alongside a myriad of other commitments. Although ostensibly spaces of leisure, DIY music spaces nonetheless rely upon forms of labour—for example, volunteer labour to run spaces and put on events, skills sharing, or emotional labour to nurture creativity. Our capacity to run spaces and events, build community, engage in cultural production, and construct and look after archives is affected by shifts in working conditions, personal stability, and state support. Our documentary and archival endeavours are often as short-lived as our spaces.

A focus on archives as sources inevitably renders the work done to form, care for and facilitate access to them invisible. This thesis has sought to centre labour in the analysis of archives, by focusing on the conditions in which they emerge and the impact of changing socioeconomic circumstances on communities, spaces, and archival traces. Researchers describe how collections are formed through forms of affective labour (Earhart, 2015, p. 66; Sheffield, 2016; Long et al., 2017; Taves Sheffield, 2020), yet archival labour itself is undervalued and underrepresented in both humanities scholarship and research about activist memory (Caswell, 2016, p. 10; Chidgey, 2020, p. 225). The labour of upkeep and lack of long-term physical and digital spaces to store traces was regularly identified as an issue by participants. In circumstances in which capacity and resources are this limited, there is potential for information and heritage organisations to support community work by providing access to space, sharing custody of materials, and sharing other resources and knowledge with community members.

Archives are affected not only by our individual lack of capacity to form, sustain and care for collections, but by the conditions in which archive services and heritage institutions currently operate. These organisations, too, face precarious existences under austerity. Griffin describes how working conditions and the financial precarity of archive services in turn affect the resilience of radical collections and the capacity of services to work in a meaningful way with communities (Griffin, 2018, p. 506). Chapter seven proposed that relationships can be transformed when activists move into and remain within professional posts in the information sector. However, the UK archive sector currently relies upon project funding from bodies like the National Lottery Heritage Fund to finance roles, which in turn restricts the opportunity for meaningful and long-term relationships to develop between archive services and communities.

This financial precarity can also reinforce the perpetuation of selective and uncritical narratives. In a discussion about museum decision-making under austerity, Rex describes mandates that museums will self-generate income to maintain financial viability (2020, p. 194). Rex describes how "museums [are] cast as a commodity instead of a resource" (2020, p. 196). The commodification of cultural and heritage is a consequence of neoliberalism, in which public services have been marketised, privatised and are viewed through their capacity to produce economic value. In these contexts, success is measured by "being compatible with growth strategies or selective narratives of place" (Rex, 2020, p. 201). One of the central tensions identified in this analysis is between economic exploitation of subcultural heritage and the originating communities, who receive no remuneration and are often being pushed out of areas and spaces due to rising prices and cuts to public funding. Under this climate, the heritage sector and DIY music spaces are similarly marginalised by politics which emphasise economics over community values and politics.

How do DIY Cultural Politics Intersect with Processes of Record Creation, Archiving and History Writing?

In an examination of Dutch punk networks, Lohman describes how "ideological aspects of punk came to affect the way in which punks understood wider choices in life" (2015, p. 359). This study has explored the way in which DIY politics and values influence how histories and archives were viewed and formed (see chapters three, six and seven). My analysis has identified how tensions between community members and organisations develop through clashes in politics and values. However, heritage does not just exist in organisations, and legacies of grassroots, bottom-up and community-led archival work are informed by politics which align with those held by many DIY music community members. This analysis has situated memory work done in DIY music communities within this legacy and identified ways in which archives can have a positive affective impact on individuals and communities. Chapter three explored how archiving and history writing could be utilised differently, identifying the potential for archives to become spaces of learning, accountability, dialogue, and meaningful representation.

At the outset of this project, I felt pressure to identify how DIY music communities related to these practices as a group. However, during my research it became clear that presenting a singular group position on heritage and archiving would be both untenable and unrepresentative of the diversity of views of participants. In her analysis of Dutch punk networks, Lohman asserts that attempts to understand subcultural practices through group practices lack nuance:

> To understand these complexities in the social world it is crucial to focus not only on group or social practices but also on individuals' practices and their conceptualisations, for it is through the meaning that individuals attach to their world that social practices have importance. (2015, p. 360)

As I argued in chapter seven, the representation of DIY music communities as uniformly anti-heritage is overly simplistic and can erase grassroots archival work done within communities and specific sub-sections of DIY music networks. DIY music spaces and networks are formed through the contributions of many hands. Spaces resist hierarchical organisational structures and the notion that one voice (and therefore viewpoint) holds power over others. Therefore, emphasis on plurality of voice and position is embedded into these communities and should be centred into any analyses as well. My project has sought to do this through identifying positions and politics which are shared and those which are contested internally within communities. The resulting analysis presents a more nuanced and complex picture of the relationship between communities, heritage organisations and archival practices, in which institutional representation, support and collaboration hold different meanings for individuals.

The data collected in this project nonetheless demonstrates that community members are concerned with the production of heritage. Chapter three explored how individuals criticised existing histories, exhibitions and collecting projects for erasing, misrepresenting, and uncritically presenting nostalgic narratives of subcultural involvement. This engagement with canonisation, historicisation and archiving demonstrates understanding of heritage as "not only a social and cultural resource or process, but also a political one through which a range of struggles are negotiated" (Smith, 2006, p. 7). Chapter seven identified how this resistance against selective traditions and institutional inequalities in heritage is commonly used as evidence of a fundamental and universal ahistoricism and anti-heritage stance. However, my analysis has pushed against this positioning by asserting the need for a more nuanced and critical complex understanding of these reactions, and which engages with the many different forms of heritage that can be produced.

This thesis contributes to the examination of power dynamics in relationships between communities and organisations in heritage. Using my own position and reflections, I have pushed against the simplistic representation of organisations and communities in opposition to each other. Chapter seven focused on the subjectivity of both information workers and community members, identifying how relationships between communities and heritage organisations are affected by the background of anyone occupying a professional post. This is most explicit when individuals with pre-existing background in DIY music communities move into paid posts in the information sector, or simultaneously occupy positions in professional and DIY networks. In this chapter, I described how these movements can transform relationships and blur perceived dichotomies between organisations and communities, instead enabling the formation of shared space. Explicit focus on the dynamics in individual relationships foregrounds possibility formed through friendship, shared histories, care, and ready sharing of space, knowledge, resources, and labour.

Future directions

Born-digital records and web-based archival sources (e.g. websites) remain underexplored in popular music heritage research, as well as research into DIY cultural heritage. The former has explored the use of digital technologies and platforms to create and host community-led archives (Collins, 2012, 2015; Collins and Long, 2015; Long et al., 2020), however significantly less attention is paid to the heritage value of born-digital records and websites. My study has identified how communities use digital platforms to store memories, document projects and share information, which indicates that websites in particular are often valuable sources for future preservation. Future research could explore these web-based heritage through the analysis of websites as primary sources, or alternatively utilise action research to improve awareness of web heritage initiatives in music communities or disseminate basic digital and web archiving practice in spaces. This is particularly urgent given the precarity of web heritage as identified in chapters five and six.

Whilst popular music heritage now represents an impressive body of scholarship, there is a minimal amount of this research which considers the production of popular music heritage from a critical standpoint. My review of existing research identified how certain music cultures are/can be marginalised within popular music heritage (Lashua, 2011, 2015; Khabra, 2014; Withers, 2014, 2015, 2017; Cantillon, Baker and Buttigieg, 2017; Reitsamer, 2018; Zuberi, 2018), which was further explored in chapter four of my analysis. Archiving is political, and the production of popular music heritage in both community and institutional settings is informed by government policy, funding mandates and politics of cultural value. Minimal literature has focused on the negative potential of influence of neoliberal politics on the representation of music in museum spaces (Fairchild, 2021), or on the potential for community projects to reproduce selective traditions and harmful notions of significance. This research has utilised critical archival theory to examine documentary and archival activity, and centred the perspectives of individuals marginalised in popular and alternative music settings. As a result, this research contributes to greater understanding of how the above groups relate to music heritage and utilise archives as sources of representation and resistance. Future research needs to balance the multiple potentials and dynamics that shape music heritage—resisting dichotomies between grassroots and institutional projects to instead focus on tensions, politics and values embedded in the production of heritage.

This analysis has centred activity and actions over archival sources, and as such identified examples of unauthorised heritage at work (Roberts and Cohen, 2014). Although authorised and self-authorised forms of popular music heritage are explored within literature, the concept of unauthorised heritage is harder to pin down and consequently the source of few articles (Strong and Whiting, 2018). Nonetheless, the concept resonates strongly both in my data, and within other music community contexts—for example, in analyses of the archival dimensions of remixing (Campbell, 2021). Future research could utilise this concept to explore other practices and examples of archival remediation through cultural production. This research could also address practices at work in music spaces (for example, display of archival posters) or on social media platforms through hashtags (e.g. #tbt and similar).

Methodological innovation is crucial in the future direction of DIY cultural research. My messy positioning—in/between community, professional and academic spaces—has been a challenge to navigate within the traditional framework of a PhD, which appears to require objectivity and distance in the pursuit of research validity. Instead of unsuccessfully attempting to make DIY cultural politics fit within this frame, I have instead used these values to inform my interrogation of traditions in practice and research, and to build my methodology. Much as my examination of archival praxis in chapter four aimed to push against the metaphorical and ideological walls of the archive by focusing on activity happening beyond their limits, my methodological approach has pushed against the boundaries of research validity by embracing and centring the affective and subjective dimensions of this project. Although I have succeeded in making space within the thesis format for alternative forms of knowledge production and creative responses, it is nonetheless important to acknowledge the labour of code switching and translating knowledge into multiple formats throughout the duration of a PhD. The tension between producing knowledge for the academy and the community often pulls researchers between two poles, one of which is still afforded more value and prestige. Future research should continue to push against these boundaries and utilise creativity and DIY cultural politics to inform work in methodology and analysis.

There are tensions purposely left unresolved at the conclusion of this project. I complete this analysis at a point when the future remains unclear, and the threats that motivated the development of this project persist and, often, continue to escalate. The threats we experience—digital reliance, loss of physical and digital space, dissolution of networks due to conflict, lack of resource and capacity, lack of record keeping practices in organisations, eroding cultural funding, surveillance by authorities—are shared by many other communities, as are the motivations to resist through creation, preservation and circulation of information and histories. Information is valuable to us because through it, we exist, we connect, we remember, we learn, and we build. Community members and information professionals face the ongoing challenge of undertaking and/or supporting this work in a hostile economic, political, and technological climate. In the absence of support and resource, we instead attempt to make our own tangled infrastructures, working between spaces, communities, and organisations to share what we each have, and to work towards an alternative that might one day survive.

Figure 1 Building (again)

Bibliography

Aasman, S. (2019) 'Finding traces in YouTube's living archive: Exploring informal archival practices', *Journal for Media History*, 22(1), p. 35. https://doi.org/10.18146/tmg.435.

Abtan, F. (2016) 'Where is she? Finding the women in electronic music culture', *Contemporary Music Review*, 35(1), pp. 53–60. Available at: https://doi.org/10.1080/07494467.2016.1176764.

Adams, R. (2008) 'The Englishness of English punk: Sex Pistols, subcultures, and nostalgia', *Popular Music and Society*, 31(4), pp. 469–488. Available at: https://doi.org/10.1080/03007760802053104.

Adams, T. and Holman Jones, S. (2008) 'Autoethnography is queer', in N. Denzin, Y. Lincoln, and L. Smith (eds) *Handbook of critical and indigenous methodologies*. Thousand Oaks: SAGE Publications. Available at: https://doi.org/10.4135/9781483385686.

Agbehenu, C. (2019). Interviewed by Kirsty Fife. 4 October, online.

Agostinho, D. (2019) 'Archival encounters: rethinking access and care in digital colonial archives', *Archival Science*, 19(2), pp. 141–165. Available at: https://doi.org/10.1007/s10502-019-09312-0.

Allard, D. and Ferris, S. (2014) 'The digital archives and marginalized communities project: Building anti-violence archives', in *iConference 2014 Proceedings*. Humboldt- Universität, March 4-7. Berlin: Berlin School of Library and Information Science.

Almeida, N. and Hoyer, J. (2019) 'The living archive in the Anthropocene', *Publications and Research* [Preprint]. Available at: https://academicworks.cuny.edu/ny_pubs/379.

Alto, M. and McKemmish, S. (2020) 'Is life a cabaret? A living archive of the "other"', *Curator: The Museum Journal*, 63(4), pp. 531–545. Available at: https://doi.org/10.1111/cura.12385.

Amin, T. (2017) *DIY in 2017: How Leeds, Bristol and London's scenes are striving to survive, FACT magazine*. Available at: http://www.factmag.com/2017/06/15/uk-diy-venues/ (Accessed: 30 October 2018).

Amin, T. (2019). Interviewed by Kirsty Fife. 28 December, Leeds.

Anderson, L. (2006) 'Analytic autoethnography', *Journal of Contemporary Ethnography*, 35(4), pp. 373–395. Available at: https://doi.org/10.1177/0891241605280449.

Anderton, C. (2016) 'Sonic artefacts: "record collecting" in the digital age', *IASPM Journal*, 6(1), pp. 85–103.

Angell Brown, M. (2021) 'Preservation's expanded field: The Hacking Heritage Unconference and the Fogarty Funeral', in S. Smulyan (ed.) *Doing public humanities*. London and New York: Routledge.

Anonymous (2018) *Wharf Chambers statement response–Abuse apologism and racism, wharf abuse and racism*. Available at: http://wharfabuseandracism.tumblr.com/?og=1 (Accessed: 26 February 2019).

Appadurai, A. (2003) 'Archive and aspiration', in J. Brouwer and A. Mulder (eds) *Information is alive*. Rotterdam: NAi Publishers, pp. 14–25.

Armstrong, S. (2018) *The new poverty*. London and New York: Verso.

Arroyo-Ramírez, E. et al. (2021) 'An introduction to radical empathy in archival practice', *Journal of Critical Library and Information Studies*, 3(2). Available at: https://doi.org/10.24242/jclis.v3i2.171.

Ashmore, P., Craggs, R. and Neate, H. (2012) 'Working-with: Talking and sorting in personal archives', *Journal of Historical Geography*, 38(1), pp. 81–89. Available at: https://doi.org/10.1016/j.jhg.2011.06.002.

Ashton, J. (2017) 'Feminist archiving [|A manifesto continued]: Skilling for activism and organising', *Australian Feminist Studies*, 32(91–92), pp. 126–149. Available at: https://doi.org/10.1080/08164649.2017.1357010.

Assmann, A. (2008) 'Canon and archive', in A. Erll, A. Nünning, and S.B. Young (eds) *Cultural memory studies: An international and interdisciplinary handbook*. Berlin and New York: Walter de Gruyter (Media and Cultural Memory), pp. 97–107.

Assmann, A. (2013) *Cultural memory and Western civilisation: Arts of memory*. 2nd edition. Cambridge: Cambridge University Press.

Assmann, J. (2011) 'Communicative and Cultural Memory', in P. Meusburger, M. Heffernan, and E. Wunder (eds) *Cultural memories: The geographical point of view*. Dordrecht: Springer Netherlands (Knowledge and Space), pp. 15–27. Available at: https://doi.org/10.1007/978-90-481-8945-8_2.

Attfield, S. (2011) 'Punk rock and the value of auto-ethnographic writing about music', *PORTAL Journal of Multidisciplinary International Studies*, 8(1). Available at: https://doi.org/10.5130/portal.v8i1.1741.

Azerrad, M. (2012) *Our band could be your life: Scenes from the American indie underground, 1981-1991*. New York, Boston and London: Little, Brown and Company.

Baker, S. (2015a) 'Affective archiving and collective collecting in do-it-yourself popular music archives and museums', in S. Baker (ed.) *Preserving popular music heritage: Do-it-yourself, do-it-together*. New York: Routledge (Routledge Research in Music), pp. 46–61.

Baker, S. (2015b) 'Identifying do-it-yourself places of popular music preservation', in S. Baker (ed.) *Preserving popular music heritage: Do-it-yourself, do-it-together*. New York: Routledge (Routledge Research in Music), pp. 1–16.

Baker, S. (2016) 'Do-it-yourself Institutions of popular music heritage: The preservation of music's material past in community archives, museums and halls of fame', *Archives & Records*, 37(2), pp. 170–187. Available at: https://doi.org/10.1080/23257962.2015.1106933.

Baker, S. (2019) *Community custodians of popular music's past: A DIY hpproach to Heritage*. London and New York: Routledge.

Baker, S. *et al.* (2020) 'Community well-being, post-industrial music cities and the turn to popular music heritage', in C. Ballico and A. Watson (eds) *Music cities: evaluating a global cultural policy concept*. Cham: Palgrave Macmillan, pp. 43–61.

Baker, S. and Collins, J. (2015) 'Sustaining popular music's material culture in community archives and museums', *International Journal of Heritage Studies*, 21(10), pp. 983–996. Available at: https://doi.org/10.1080/13527258.2015.1041414.

Baker, S. and Huber, A. (2015) 'Saving "rubbish": preserving popular music's material culture in amateur archives and museums', in S. Cohen et al. (eds) *Sites of popular music heritage: memories, histories, places*. London and New York: Routledge (Routledge Studies in Popular Music).

Bastian, J.A. and Flinn, A. (eds) (2020) *Community archives, community spaces: heritage, memory and identity*. London: Facet Publishing. Available at: https://doi.org/10.29085/9781783303526 (Accessed: 10 March 2020).

Bastone, N. (2018) *How to Visit the Last Remnants of GeoCities Before it gets Destroyed by Yahoo Japan, Business Insider*. Available at: https://www.businessinsider.com/how-to-visit-last-remnants-geocities-before-destroyed-2018-10?r=US&IR=T (Accessed: 25 February 2020).

Batley, A. (2019). Interviewed by Kirsty Fife. 24 November, online.

BBC (2017) *Blue Plaques celebrating your local music legends, BBC*. Available at: https://www.bbc.co.uk/music/articles/7f78803d-e6ae-469a-9e44-a243634a80db (Accessed: 3 December 2018).

Beer, K. (2016) *'It's my job to keep punk rock elite': information and secrecy in the Chicago DIY punk music scene*. M.S. The University of Wisconsin. Available at: https://www.proquest.com/docview/1867711163/abstract/C2C94DE54BFD467BPQ/1 (Accessed: 17 September 2021).

Behr, A., Brennan, M. and Cloonan, M. (2014) *The cultural value of live music from the pub to the stadium: getting beyond the numbers*. Edinburgh and Glasgow: University of Edinburgh and University of Glasgow.

Bennett, A. and Janssen, S. (2016) 'Popular music, cultural memory, and heritage', *Popular Music and Society*, 39(1), pp. 1–7. Available at: https://doi.org/10.1080/03007766.2015.1061332.

Bennett, A. and Peterson, R.A. (eds) (2004) *Music scenes: local, translocal and virtual*. Nashville: Vanderbilt University Press.

Bennett, A. and Rogers, I. (2016) 'Popular music and materiality: memorabilia and memory traces', *Popular Music and Society*, 39(1), pp. 28–42. Available at: https://doi.org/10.1080/03007766.2015.1061339.

Berg, J. (2018) 'Preserving music through reissues', in N. Guthrie and S. Carlson (eds) *Music preservation and archiving today*. London: Rowman and Littlefield.

Beynon, B. (2016) 'YCBWYCS', in S. Brown et al. (eds) *You can't be what you can't see: DIY musicians talk identity, gender and performing*. London: DIY Space for London.

Beynon, B. (2020). Interviewed by Kirsty Fife. 14 April, online.

Big Joanie–Fall Asleep (2018). London. Available at: https://www.youtube.com/watch?app=desktop&v=VscB7YNpeKw (Accessed: 15 October 2021).

Block, D. (2001) 'Broadcast and archive: human rights documentation in the early digital age', in *Florida State University conference on human rights*, Florida, pp. 1–21. Available at: https://ecommons.cornell.edu/handle/1813/2543 (Accessed: 7 October 2019).

Bloom, L.R. *et al.* (2020) 'Powerful methodologies/powerful pedagogy: autoethnography and dialogic interviews in a WGS empowerment self-defense class', *Qualitative Inquiry*, 27, pp. 689–699. Available at: https://doi.org/10.1177/1077800420948102.

Bly, L. and Wooten, K. (eds) (2012) *Make your own history: documenting feminist and queer activism in the 21st century*. Los Angeles: Litwin Books.

de Boise, S. (2014) 'Cheer up emo kid: rethinking the "crisis of masculinity" in emo', *Popular Music*, 33(2), pp. 225–242. Available at: https://doi.org/10.1017/S0261143014000300.

Bow, C., Christie, M. and Devlin, B. (2014) 'Developing a living archive of Aboriginal languages'. Available at: http://hdl.handle.net/10125/24612 (Accessed: 16 November 2023).

Bowcott, O. and Snapes, L. (2019) 'King Blues singer Jonny Fox suing five women over "sexual predator" allegations', *The Guardian*, 26 July. Available at: https://www.theguardian.com/music/2019/jul/26/king-blues-singer-itch-jonny-fox-suing-five-women-over-sexual-predator-allegations (Accessed: 10 December 2023).

Boyd, M.J. *et al.* (2021) 'Understanding the Security and Privacy Advice Given to Black Lives Matter Protesters', in *Proceedings of the 2021 CHI Conference on Human Factors in Computing Systems. CHI '21: CHI Conference on Human Factors in Computing Systems*, Yokohama, May 8-13.

Boylorn, R.M. (2013) 'Blackgirl blogs, auto/ethnography, and Crunk feminism', *Liminalities: A Journal of Performance Studies*, 9(2), pp. 73–82.

Boylorn, R.M. and Orbe, M.P. (eds) (2016) *Critical autoethnography: intersecting cultural identities in everyday life*. London and New York: Routledge (Writing Lives: Ethnographic Narratives).

Brager, J. and Sailor, J. (2010) *Archiving the underground*. Unknown: Self-published. Available at: https://doi.org/info:doi/10.5848/LB.978-1-936117-95-6_9.

Bragg, B. (2017) *Roots, radicals and rockers: how Skiffle changed the world*. London: Faber & Faber.

Briggs, J. (2018) *Screaming fatal truths II*. London: Makina Books.

Briggs, J. (2019). Interviewed by Kirsty Fife. 9 December, online.

Brilmyer, G. (2020a) *Proximity matters: disability, erasure and the archival bond of natural history*. Phd thesis. UCLA. Available at: https://escholarship.org/uc/item/98c6t32x (Accessed: 6 May 2022).

Brilmyer, G. (2020b) 'Towards sickness: developing a critical disability archival methodology', *Journal of Feminist Scholarship*, 17(17), pp. 26–45. Available at: https://doi.org/10.23860/jfs.2020.17.03.

Brinkmann, S. (2018) 'The interview', in N.K. Denzin and Y.S. Lincoln (eds) *The SAGE handbook of qualitative research*. Fifth edition. Thousand Oaks: SAGE Publications, pp. 579–599.

British Library (2019) *Save our Sounds | Projects, The British Library*. The British Library. Available at: https://www.bl.uk/projects/save-our-sounds (Accessed: 17 August 2021).

British Standards Institution (2016) *BS ISO 15489-1:2016 Information and documentation — records management*. London: British Standards Institution.

Brothman, B. (1991) 'Orders of value: probing the theoretical terms of archival practice', *Archivaria*, 32, pp. 78–100.

Brothman, B. (2006) 'Archives, life cycles, and death wishes: a Helical model of record formation', *Archivaria*, 61, pp. 235–269.

Brown, E.H. (2020) 'Archival activism, symbolic annihilation, and the LGBTQ2+ community archive', *Archivaria*, 89, pp. 6–33.

Brügger, N. (2018) 'Web history and social media', in J. Burgess, A. Marwick, and T. Poell (eds) *The SAGE handbook of social media*. London: SAGE Publications Ltd, pp. 196–212.

Brunow, D. (2019) 'Manchester's post-punk heritage: mobilising and contesting transcultural memory in the context of urban regeneration', *Culture Unbound: Journal of Current Cultural Research*, 11(1), pp. 9–29. Available at: https://doi.org/10.3384/cu.2000.1525.19111.

DIY Space for London. (2015) *Build Progress #5: 26th July to 4th August 2015*. 7 August. Available at: https://www.youtube.com/watch?v=ntW4biJCSJQ (Accessed: 8 October 2021).

Bulut, S. (2016) *Viv Albertine Defaces Punk Exhibition for Ignoring Women, Dazed*. Available at: https://www.dazeddigital.com/music/article/32077/1/viv-albertine-defaces-punk-exhibition-for-ignoring-women (Accessed: 9 December 2023).

Burant, J. (1995) 'Ephemera, archives, and another view of history', *Archivaria*, 40, pp. 189–198.

Burnett, R. (1993) 'The popular music industry in transition', *Popular Music and Society*, 17(1), pp. 87–114. Available at: https://doi.org/10.1080/03007769308591507.

Buscatto, M. (2016) 'Practising reflexivity in ethnography', in D. Silverman (ed.) *Qualitative research*. 4th edition. London: SAGE Publications, pp. 153–167. Available at: https://app.kortext.com/borrow/170159 (Accessed: 12 February 2021).

Butz, D. and Besio, K. (2009) 'Autoethnography', *Geography Compass*, 3(5), pp. 1660–1674. Available at: https://doi.org/10.1111/j.1749-8198.2009.00279.x.

Campbell, M.V. (2021) 'Djing archival interruptions: A remix praxis and reflective guide', in E. Navas, O. Gallagher, and xtine burrough (eds) *The Routledge Handbook of Remix Studies and Digital Humanities*. London and New York: Routledge, pp. 488–499.

Campbell, M.V. and Stitski, M. (2018) 'archival activism: deciphering state-sanctioned histories and reporting of Canadian hip hop', *Journal of World Popular Music*, 5(2), pp. 229–249.

Cantillon, Z. and Baker, S. (2018) 'DIY heritage institutions as third places: caring, community and wellbeing among volunteers at the Australian jazz museum', *Leisure Sciences*, 40, pp. 1–19. Available at: https://doi.org/10.1080/01490400.2018.1518173.

Cantillon, Z., Baker, S. and Buttigieg, B. (2017) 'Queering the community music archive', *Australian Feminist Studies*, 32(91–92), pp. 41–57. Available at: https://doi.org/10.1080/08164649.2017.1357004.

Carbajal, I.A. and Caswell, M. (2021) 'Critical digital archives: a review from archival studies', *The American Historical Review*, 126(3), pp. 1102–1120. Available at: https://doi.org/10.1093/ahr/rhab359.

Carlson, S. (2018) 'Bootleg compilations as fan preservation', in S. Carlson and N. Guthrie (eds) *Music preservation and archiving today*. London: Rowman and Littlefield, pp. 157–176.

Carpenter, D. (2018) 'Ethics, reflexivity and virtue', in R. Iphofen and M. Tolich (eds) *The SAGE handbook of qualitative research ethics*. London: SAGE Publications, pp. 1–18.

Carter, E. (2017) '"Setting the record straight": the creation and curation of archives by activist communities. A case study of activist responses to the regeneration of Elephant and Castle, South London', *Archives and Records*, 38(1), pp. 27–44. Available at: https://doi.org/10.1080/23257962.2016.1260532.

Caswell, M. (2014a) *Archiving the unspeakable: silence, memory, and the photographic record in Cambodia*. Madison: University of Wisconsin Press.

Caswell, M. (2014b) 'Seeing yourself in history: community archives and the fight against symbolic annihilation', *The Public Historian*, 36(4), pp. 26–37. Available at: https://doi.org/10.1525/tph.2014.36.4.26.

Caswell, M. (2014c) 'Toward a survivor-centered approach to records documenting human rights abuse: lessons from community archives', *Archival Science*, 14(3–4), pp. 307–322.

Caswell, M. (2016) '"'The archive' is not an archives: on acknowledging the intellectual contributions of archival studies"', *Reconstruction*, 16(1), pp. 1–20.

Caswell, M. *et al.* (2017) '"To be able to imagine otherwise":community archives and the importance of representation', *Archives and Records*, 38(1), pp. 5–26. Available at: https://doi.org/10.1080/23257962.2016.1260445.

Caswell, M. (2019) 'Dusting for fingerprints: introducing feminist standpoint Appraisal', *Journal of Critical Library and Information Studies*, 3(1), pp. 1–36.

Caswell, M. (2020) 'Feeling liberatory memory work: on the archival uses of joy and anger', *Archivaria*, 90(1), pp. 148–164.

Caswell, M. (2021) *Urgent archives: enacting liberatory memory work*. London: Routledge. Available at: https://doi.org/10.4324/9781003001355.

Caswell, M. and Cifor, M. (2016) 'From human rights to feminist ethics: radical empathy in the archives', *Archivaria*, 81(1), pp. 23–43.

Caswell, M. and Cifor, M. (2019) 'Neither a beginning nor an end: applying an ethics of care to digital archival collections', in H. Lewi et al. (eds) *The Routledge International Handbook of New Digital Practices in Galleries, Libraries, Archives, Museums and Heritage Sites*. New York: Routledge, pp. 159–168.

Caswell, M., Cifor, M. and Ramirez, M.H. (2016) '"To suddenly discover yourself existing": uncovering the impact of community archives', *The American Archivist*, 79(1), pp. 56–81. Available at: https://doi.org/10.17723/0360-9081.79.1.56.

Caswell, M. and Mallick, S. (2014) 'Collecting the easily missed stories: digital participatory microhistory and the South Asian American digital archive', *Archives and Manuscripts*, 42(1), pp. 73–86. Available at: https://doi-org.libproxy.ucl.ac.uk/10.1080/01576895.2014.880931.

Caswell, M., Punzalan, R. and Sangwand, T.-K. (2017) 'Critical archival studies: an introduction', *Journal of Critical Library and Information Studies*, 1(2).

Chang, H. (2008) *Autoethnography as method*. Walnut Creek: Left Coast Press (Developing qualitative inquiry).

Charlton, T. (2017) 'The treachery of archives: representation, power, and the urgency for self-reflexivity in archival arrangement and description', *The iJournal: Student Journal of the University of Toronto's Faculty of Information*, 3(1). Available at: https://theijournal.ca/index.php/ijournal/article/view/28894 (Accessed: 31 October 2023).

Chen, C.-I., Dulani, J. and Lakshmi Piepzna-Samarasinha, L. (eds) (2016) *The revolution starts at home: confronting intimate violence within activist communities*. 2nd edition. Chico: AK Press.

Chen, C.W. and Gorski, P.C. (2015) 'Burnout in social justice and human rights activists: symptoms, causes and implications', *Journal of Human Rights Practice*, 7(3), pp. 366–390. Available at: https://doi.org/10.1093/jhuman/huv011.

Chidgey, R. (2006) 'The resisting subject: per-zines as life story data', *University of Sussex Journal of Contemporary History*, 10, pp. 1–13.

Chidgey, R. (2013) 'Reassess your weapons: the making of feminist memory in young women's zines', *Women's History Review*, 22(4), pp. 658–672. Available at: https://doi.org/10.1080/09612025.2012.751773.

Chidgey, R. (2014) 'Hand-made memories: remediating cultural memory in DIY feminist networks', in E. Zobl and R. Drüeke (eds) *Feminist media: participatory spaces, networks and cultural citizenship*. Salzburg: Austrian Science Fund, pp. 87–97.

Chidgey, R. (2020) 'How to curate a "living archive": The restlessness of activist time and labour', in S. Merrill, E. Keightley, and P. Daphi (eds) *Social movements, cultural memory and digital media: mobilising mediated remembrance*. Cham: Springer International Publishing (Palgrave Macmillan Memory Studies), pp. 225–248. Available at: https://doi.org/10.1007/978-3-030-32827-6_9.

Choudry, A. (2015) *Learning activism: the intellectual life of contemporary social movements*. Toronto: University of Toronto Press.

Chrysagis, E. (2014) *Becoming ethical subjects: an ethnography of do-it-yourself music practices in Glasgow*. PhD Thesis. University of Edinburgh. Available at: https://era.ed.ac.uk/handle/1842/9920.

Chrysagis, E. (2019) 'When means and ends coincide: on the value of DiY', *Journal of Cultural Economy*, 13(6), pp. 744–757. Available at: https://doi.org/10.1080/17530350.2019.1646158.

Cifor, M. (2016) 'Affecting relations: introducing affect theory to archival discourse', *Archival Science*, 16(1), pp. 7–31. Available at: https://doi.org/10.1007/s10502-015-9261-5.

Cifor, M. (2017) 'Stains and remains: liveliness, materiality, and the archival lives of queer bodies', *Australian Feminist Studies*, 32(91–92), pp. 5–21. Available at: https://doi.org/10.1080/08164649.2017.1357014.

Cifor, M., Montoya, R.D. and Ramirez, M.H. (2016) 'Developing an undergraduate information studies curriculum in support of social justice', in *IConference 2016 proceedings*. Drexel University, March 20-23. Philadelphia: iSchools. Available at: https://doi.org/10.9776/16133.

Cifor, M. and Wood, S. (2017) 'Critical feminism in the archives', *Journal of Critical Library and Information Studies*, 1(2), pp. 1–27.

CILIP and Archives and Records Association (2015) *A study of the UK information workforce: mapping the library, archives, records, information management and knowledge management and related professions (executive summary)*. London: CILIP and Archives and Records Association.

Clark, J.J. and Walker, R. (2011) 'Research ethics in victimization studies: widening the lens', *Violence Against Women*, 17(12), pp. 1489–1508. Available at: https://doi.org/10.1177/1077801211436167.

Clarke, M. (2015) *Meet the DIY music collectives of Leeds that are killing it in spite of austerity', Vice*. Available at: https://www.vice.com/en/article/rbxwbq/how-leeds-diy-underground-is-fighting-through-austerity-in-unison (Accessed: 13 May 2021).

Clarke, P. and Warren, J. (2009) 'Ephemera: between archival objects and events', *Journal of the Society of Archivists*, 30(1), pp. 45–66. Available at: https://doi.org/10.1080/00379810903264617.

Cogan, B. (2003) 'What do I get? punk rock, authenticity, and cultural capital', *Counterblack: The E-Journal of Culture and Communication*, 2(2). Available at: https://digitalcommons.molloy.edu/com_fac/21.

Cohen, S. (1991) 'Popular music and urban regeneration: the music industries of Merseyside', *Cultural Studies*, 5(3), pp. 332–346. Available at: https://doi.org/10.1080/09502389100490281.

Cohen, S. (2013) 'Musical memory, heritage and local identity: remembering the popular music past in a European capital of culture', *International Journal of Cultural Policy*, 19(5), pp. 576–594. Available at: https://doi.org/10.1080/10286632.2012.676641.

Colette. (2020). Interviewed by Kirsty Fife. 4 March, London.

Collins, J. (2012) *Multiple voices, multiple memories: public history-making and activist archivism in online popular music archives.* University of Birmingham.

Collins, J. (2015) 'Doing-it-together: public history-making and activist archiving in online popular music community archives', in S. Baker (ed.) *Preserving popular music heritage: Do-it-yourself, do-it-together.* New York: Routledge (Routledge Research in Music), pp. 77–90.

Collins, J. and Carter, O. (2015) '"They're not pirates, they're archivists": the role of fans as curators and archivists of popular music heritage', in S. Baker (ed.) *Preserving popular music heritage: Do-it-yourself, do-it-together.* New York: Routledge (Routledge Research in Music), pp. 126–138.

Collins, J. and Long, P. (2015) '"Fillin' in any blanks I can": online archival practice and virtual sites of musical memory', in S. Cohen et al. (eds) *Sites of popular music heritage: memories, histories, places.* London and New York: Routledge (Routledge Studies in Popular Music).

Cook, T. (1997) 'What is past is prologue: A history of archival ideas since 1898, and the future paradigm shift', *Archivaria*, 43, pp. 17–63.

Cook, T. (2011) 'The archive(s) is a foreign country: historians, archivists, and the changing archival landscape', *The American Archivist*, 74(2), pp. 600–632. Available at: https://doi.org/10.1353/can.0.0194.

Cook, T. and Schwartz, J.M. (2002) 'Archives, records, and power: from (postmodern) theory to (archival) performance', *Archival Science*, 2(3–4), pp. 171–185. Available at: https://doi.org/10.1007/BF02435620.

Cooper, C. (2012) 'A queer and trans fat activist timeline: queering fat activist nationality and cultural imperialism', *Fat Studies*, 1(1), pp. 61–74. Available at: https://doi.org/10.1080/21604851.2012.627503.

Cooper, L. (2023) 'In the zine house: the hallway and the balcony', *the polyphony*, 5 January. Available at: https://thepolyphony.org/2023/01/05/in-the-zine-house-the-hallway-and-the-balcony/ (Accessed: 14 December 2023).

Correa, M.B. *et al.* (2019) 'Trans memory archive', *TSQ: Transgender Studies Quarterly*, 6(2), pp. 156–163. Available at: https://doi.org/10.1215/23289252-7348440.

Costantino, T.E. (2008) 'Constructivism', in L. Given (ed.) *The SAGE encyclopedia of qualitative research methods*. Thousand Oaks: SAGE Publications, pp. 116–119. Available at: https://doi.org/10.4135/9781412963909.n64.

Cotera, M. (2015) '"Invisibility Is an unnatural disaster": feminist archival praxis after the digital turn', *South Atlantic Quarterly*, 114(4), pp. 781–801. Available at: https://doi.org/10.1215/00382876-3157133.

Cowan, T.L., McLeod, D. and Rault, J. (2014) 'Speculative praxis towards a queer feminist digital archive: a collaborative research-creation project', *Ada: A Journal of Gender, New Media and Technology*, 5. Available at: https://doi.org/10.7264/N3PZ573Z.

Cowan, T.L. and Rault, J. (2014a) 'The labour of being studied in a free love economy', *Ephemera: Theory and Politics in Organization*, 14(3), pp. 471–488.

Cowan, T.L. and Rault, J. (2014b) 'Trading credit for debt: Queer history-making and debt culture', *Women's Studies Quarterly*, 42(1/2), pp. 294–310.

Cowan, T.L. and Rault, J. (2018) 'Onlining Queer acts: digital research ethics and caring for risky archives', *Women & Performance: a journal of feminist theory*, 28(2), pp. 121–142. Available at: https://doi.org/10.1080/0740770X.2018.1473985.

Cresswell, M. and Spandler, H. (2013) 'The engaged academic: academic Intellectuals and the psychiatric survivor movement', *Social Movement Studies*, 12(2), pp. 138–154. Available at: https://doi.org/10.1080/14742837.2012.696821.

Creswell, J.W. (2014) *Research design: qualitative, quantitative, and mixed methods approaches*. 4th edition. Los Angeles and London: SAGE.

Cross, K. and Peck, J. (2010) 'Editorial: special Issue on photography, archive and memory', *Photographies*, 3(2), pp. 127–138. Available at: https://doi.org/10.1080/17540763.2010.499631.

Crossley, N. (2008) 'Pretty connected: the social network of the early UK punk movement', *Theory, Culture & Society*, 25(6), pp. 89–116. Available at: https://doi.org/10.1177/0263276408095546.

Crossley, N. (2009) 'The man whose web expanded: network dynamics in Manchester's post/punk music scene 1976–1980', *Poetics*, 37(1), pp. 24–49. Available at: https://doi.org/10.1016/j.poetic.2008.10.002.

Crossley, N. (2015) *Networks of sound, style and subversion: the punk and post-punk worlds of Manchester, London, Liverpool and Sheffield, 1975–80, Networks of sound, style and subversion*. Manchester: Manchester University Press.

Cuk, S. (2021) 'Do-it-yourself music archives: a response and alternative to mainstream exclusivity', *The Serials Librarian*, pp. 1–8. Available at: https://doi.org/10.1080/0361526X.2021.1910614.

Cuomo, D. and Massaro, V.A. (2016) 'Boundary-making in feminist research: new methodologies for "intimate insiders"', *Gender, Place & Culture*, 23(1), pp. 94–106. Available at: https://doi.org/10.1080/0966369X.2014.939157.

Cvetkovich, A. (2003a) *An archive of feelings: trauma, sexuality, and lesbian public cultures*. North Carolina: Duke University Press. Available at: https://doi.org/10.1215/9780822384434.

Cvetkovich, A. (2003b) 'Legacies of Trauma, Legacies of Activism: ACT UP's Lesbians', in D.L. Eng and D. Kazanjian (eds) *Loss: The Politics of Mourning*. Berkeley: University of California Press, pp. 427–457.

Dale, J. (2014) 'The story of UK DIY: 131 experimental underground classics from 1977-1985', *FACT*. Available at: https://www.factmag.com/2014/10/01/the-story-of-uk-diy-131-experimental-underground-classics-from-1977-1985/ (Accessed: 9 June 2021).

Dale, P. (2009) 'It was easy, it was cheap, so what?: reconsidering the DIY principle of punk and indie music', *Popular Music History*, 3(2), pp. 171–193. Available at: https://doi.org/10.1558/pomh.v3i2.171.

Dale, P. (2012) *Anyone can do it: empowerment, tradition and the punk underground*. Farnham: Ashgate Publishing (Ashgate Popular and Folk Music Series).

Dampier, H. (2008) 'Re-reading as a methodology: the case of Boer women's Testimonies', *Qualitative Research*, 8(3), pp. 367–377. Available at: https://doi.org/10.1177/1468794106093633.

Davies, J. (1996) 'The future of "no future": punk rock and postmodern theory', *Journal of Popular Culture*, 29(4), pp. 3–25.

Davila, R.C. (2019) 'See no colour, hear no colour, speak no colour: problematizing colourblindness in Los Angeles punk historiography', *Punk & Post Punk*, 8(1), pp. 89–104. Available at: https://doi.org/10.1386/punk.8.1.89_1.

Davyd, M. (2021) '"£2 million for a Beatles museum in Liverpool." This is a great example of the detachment from reality and life experiences of our politicians. On all sides of the debate. Let's start with the easiest bit: It doesn't build a Beatles museum. Thread: https://t.co/s3EFk0TA27', @markdavyd, 28 October. Available at: https://twitter.com/markdavyd/status/1453640817957085185 (Accessed: 28 October 2021).

De Cesari, C. and Dimova, R. (2019) 'Heritage, gentrification, participation: remaking urban landscapes in the name of culture and historic preservation', *International Journal of Heritage Studies*, 25(9), pp. 863–869. Available at: https://doi.org/10.1080/13527258.2018.1512515.

De Kosnik, A. (2016) *Rogue archives: digital cultural memory and media fandom*. Cambridge: MIT Press.

De Kosnik, A. *et al.* (2020) 'Trans memory as transmedia activism', in S. Merrill, E. Keightley, and P. Daphi (eds) *Social movements, cultural memory and digital media: mobilising mediated remembrance*. London: Palgrave Macmillan (Palgrave Macmillan memory studies), pp. 33–57.

Decolonise Fest (2017) *What's it like to be a punk of colour?* London: Decolonise Fest.

Delva, M. and Adams, M. (2016) 'Archival ethics and Indigenous justice: conflict or coexistence?', in F. Foscarini et al. (eds) *Engaging with records and archives: histories and theories*. London: Facet Publishing, pp. 147–172.

Demb, S.R. (2012) 'Records management basics', in C. Brunskill and S.R. Demb (eds) *Records management for museums and galleries*. Hull: Chandos Publishing (Chandos Information Professional Series), pp. 35–46. Available at: https://doi.org/10.1016/B978-1-84334-637-1.50002-8.

Denzin, N.K. and Lincoln, Y.S. (2011) 'Introduction: the discipline and practice of qualitative research', in N.K. Denzin and Y.S. Lincoln (eds) *The SAGE handbook of qualitative research*. Los Angeles: Sage Publications, pp. 29–71.

Detamore, M. (2010) 'Queer(y)ing the ethics of research methods: toward a politics of intimacy in researcher/researched relations', in *Queer Methods and Methodologies*. Routledge.

Dever, M. (2017) 'Archives and new modes of feminist research', *Australian Feminist Studies*, 32(91–92), pp. 1–4. Available at: https://doi.org/10.1080/08164649.2017.1357017.

Deviatnikova, K.G. (2023) 'Permacrisis, metacrisis, polycrisis: determining the nature of the phenomena using semantic analysis', Современное педагогическое образование, (1), pp. 365–370.

DeVille, C. (2019) 'Myspace Confirms Loss Of 50 Million Songs Uploaded Between 2003 And 2015', *Stereogum*. Available at: https://www.stereogum.com/2036026/myspace-50-million-songs-2003-2015-deleted/news/ (Accessed: 19 March 2019).

DiVeglia, A.L. (2012) 'Accessibility, accountability, and activism: models for LGBT archives', in L. Bly and K. Wooten (eds) *Make your own history: Documenting feminist and Queer activism in the 21st century*. Los Angeles: Litwin Books, pp. 23–38.

DIY Space for London (2018) 'Update on our financial situation', *DIY Space for London*, 3 October. Available at: https://diyspaceforlondon.org/update-on-our-financial-situation/ (Accessed: 12 October 2018).

Douglas, J. and Alisauskas, A. (2021) '"It feels like a life's work": recordkeeping as an act of love', *Archivaria*, 91, pp. 6–37.

Douglas, J., Alisauskas, A. and Mordell, D. (2019) '"Treat them with the reverence of archivists": records work, grief work, and relationship work in the archives', *Archivaria*, 88, pp. 84–120.

Downes, J. (2010) *DIY Queer feminist (sub)cultural resistance in the UK*. PhD Thesis. University of Leeds.

Downes, J. (2014) '"We are turning cursive letters into knives": The synthesis of the written word, sound and action in Riot Grrrl cultural resistance', in R. Carroll and A. Hansen (eds) *Litpop: writing and popular music*. Farnham: Ashgate Publishing, pp. 89–105.

Downes, J. (2017) '"It's not the abuse that kills you, it's the silence": the silencing of sexual violence activism in social justice movements in the UK left', *Justice, Power and Resistance*, 1(2), pp. 200–232.

Downes, J., Breeze, M. and Griffin, N. (2013) 'Researching DIY cultures: towards a situated ethical practice for activist-academia.', *Graduate Journal of Social Science*, 10(3), pp. 100–124.

Downes, J., Hanson, K. and Hudson, R. (2016) *Salvage: gendered violence in activist communities*. Salvage Collective.

Drake, P. and Heath, L. (2008) 'Insider research in school and universities: the case of the professional doctorate', in P. Sikes and A. Potts (eds) *Researching education from the inside*. London: Routledge, pp. 127–143.

Duff, W.M. et al. (2013) 'Social justice impact of archives: a preliminary investigation', *Archival Science; Dordrecht* [Preprint]. Available at: http://dx.doi.org.libproxy.ucl.ac.uk/10.1007/s10502-012-9198-x.

Dunbar, A.W. et al. (2022) 'Cultivating collective praxis for scholarly transformation and racial justice: the Critical Race Theory collective's introduction to the special issue', *Education for Information*, 38(4), pp. 275–287. Available at: https://doi.org/10.3233/EFI-220059.

Duncombe, S. (2017) *Notes from underground: zines and the politics of alternative culture*. 3rd edition. Portland: Microcosm Publishing.

Duncombe, S. and Tremblay, M. (eds) (2011) *White riot: punk rock and the politics of race*. Verso Books.

Dwyer, S.C. and Buckle, J.L. (2009) 'The space between: on being an insider-outsider in qualitative research', *International Journal of Qualitative Methods*, 8(1), pp. 54–63. Available at: https://doi.org/10.1177/160940690900800105.

Dyer, S. (2012) 'My life in zines', in L. Bly and K. Wooten (eds) *Make your own history: documenting feminist and Queer activism in the 21st Century*. Los Angeles: Litwin Books, pp. 9–12.

Earhart, A. (2012) 'Recovering the recovered text: diversity, canon building, and digital studies', in. *Digital Humanities Seminar*, University of Kansas. [online video]Available at: https://www.youtube.com/watch?v=7ui9PIjDreo (Accessed: 15 April 2020).

Earhart, A.E. (2015) *Traces of the old, uses of the new: the emergence of digital literary studies*. Ann Arbor, Michigan: University of Michigan Press (Editorial theory and literary criticism).

Eichhorn, K. (2001) 'Sites unseen: ethnographic research in a textual community', *International Journal of Qualitative Studies in Education*, 14(4), pp. 565–578. Available at: https://doi.org/10.1080/09518390110047075.

Eichhorn, K. (2010) 'D.I.Y. collectors, archiving scholars, and activist librarians: legitimizing feminist knowledge and cultural production since 1990', *Women's Studies*, 39(6), pp. 622–646. Available at: https://doi.org/10.1080/00497878.2010.490716.

Eichhorn, K. (2013) *The archival turn in Feminism: outrage in order*. Temple University Press. Available at: https://www.jstor.org/stable/j.ctt14bsx7w (Accessed: 27 May 2020).

Ellis, C. (1999) 'Heartful autoethnography', *Qualitative Health Research*, 9(5), pp. 669–683. Available at: https://doi.org/10.1177/104973299129122153.

Emswiler, A.D. (2020) *'Conditions of possibility' : towards an archival praxis informed by Black feminist anarchism and a critical trans politics*. Masters Thesis. University of Texas. Available at: https://doi.org/10.26153/tsw/14268.

Eng, D.L. and Kazanjian, D. (2003) 'Introduction: mourning remains', in D.L. Eng and D. Kazanjian (eds) *Loss: the politics of mourning*. Berkeley: University of California Press, pp. 1–25.

Erde, J. (2014) 'Constructing archives of the occupy movement', *Archives and Records*, 35(2), pp. 77–92. Available at: https://doi.org/10.1080/23257962.2014.943168.

Espinal, I., Sutherland, T. and Roh, C. (2018) 'A holistic approach for inclusive librarianship: decentering whiteness in our profession', *Library Trends*, 67(1), pp. 147–162. Available at: https://doi.org/10.1353/lib.2018.0030.

Evans, J. *et al.* (2012) 'Bridging communities', *Information, Communication & Society*, 15(7), pp. 1055–1080. Available at: https://doi.org/10.1080/1369118X.2012.704062.

Eveleigh, A. (2014) 'Crowding out the archivist? Locating crowdsourcing within the broader landscape of participatory archives', in M. Ridge (ed.) *Crowdsourcing our cultural heritage*. Farnham: Ashgate Publishing, pp. 211–229.

Fairchild, C. (2021) *Musician in the museum: display and power in neoliberal popular culture*. London and New York: Bloomsbury.

Falconer, E. (2019). Interviewed by Kirsty Fife. 24 October, Margate.

de Farias, M.A.B. (2022) 'A DIY music pedagogy', in. *Keep it simple, make it fast! : an approach to underground music scenes*, Porto, pp. 1–5. Available at: https://ler.letras.up.pt/uploads/ficheiros/19294.pdf (Accessed: 23 May 2023).

Farivar, C. and Solon, O. (2020) ,*FBI arrests of protestors based on social media posts worry legal experts,, NBC News*. Available at: https://www.nbcnews.com/tech/social-media/federal-agents-monitored-facebook-arrest-protesters-inciting-riots-court-records-n1231531 (Accessed: 16 September 2021).

Fatsis, L. (2019) 'Grime: criminal subculture or public counterculture? A critical investigation into the criminalization of Black musical subcultures in the UK', *Crime, Media, Culture*, 15(3), pp. 447–461. Available at: https://doi.org/10.1177/1741659018784111.

Faulkhead, S. and Thorpe, K. (2017) 'Dedication: archives and Indigenous communities. Our knowing Allison Boucher Krebs (September 8, 1951–January 26, 2013)', in A.J. Gilliland, S. McKemmish, and A.J. Lau (eds) *Research in the archival multiverse*. Clayton: Monash University Publishing, pp. 2–15.

Fenster, M. (1993) 'Queer punk fanzines: identity, community, and the articulation of homosexuality and hardcore', *Journal of Communication Inquiry*, 17(1), pp. 73–94. Available at: https://doi.org/10.1177/019685999301700105.

Ferris, S. and Allard, D. (2016) 'Tagging for activist ends and strategic ephemerality: creating the sex work database as an activist digital archive', *Feminist Media Studies*, 16(2), pp. 189–204. Available at: https://doi.org/10.1080/14680777.2015.1118396.

Fife, K. (ed.) (2016) *Move under yr own power: interviews with women and Queers making DIY music #1*. London: Self-published.

Fife, K. (ed.) (2018) *Move under yr own power: Interviews with women and Queers making DIY music #2*. Leeds: Self-published.

Fife, K. (2019a) 'Another one down…', *DIY Archivist*, 20 March. Available at: https://diyarchivist.wordpress.com/2019/03/20/another-one-down/ (Accessed: 28 June 2021).

Fife, K. (2019b) *Archive it ourselves: strategies and tips for documenting and archiving DIY histories*. Self-published.

Fife, K. (2019c) 'Not for you? Ethical implications of archiving zines', *Punk & Post Punk*, 8(2). Available at: https://e-space.mmu.ac.uk/628412/8/art00005.pdf (Accessed: 14 March 2023).

Fife, K. (2021a) *Archive it ourselves: strategies and tips for documenting and archiving DIY histories #2*. Self-published.

Fife, K. (2021b) *From the gut: collected zine writing*. Leeds: Cross Words Zines.

Fife, K. (2022) 'Distant together: creative community in UK DIY music during Covid-19', in S. Bruzzi et al. (eds) *Lockdown cultures: the arts and humanities in the year of the pandemic, 2020-2021*. London: UCL Press, pp. 49–58.

Fife, K. (2024) 'Records, subjects and agents: exploring archives of popular music through critical archival studies', in *Popular music methodologies*. Bristol: Intellect.

Fife, K., Flinn, A. and Nyhan, J. (2023) 'Documenting resistance, conflict and violence: a scoping review of the role of participatory digital platforms in the mobilisation of resistance', *Archival Science* [Preprint]. Available at: https://doi.org/10.1007/s10502-023-09416-8.

Fife, K. and Henthorn, H. (2021) 'Brick walls and tick boxes: experiences of marginalised workers in the U.K. archive workforce', *The International Journal of Information, Diversity, & Inclusion (IJIDI)*, 5(1), pp. 6–32. Available at: https://doi.org/10.33137/ijidi.v5i1.34667.

Findlay, C. (2016) 'Archival activism', *Archives and Manuscripts*, 44(3), pp. 155–159. Available at: https://doi.org/10.1080/01576895.2016.1263964.

First Timers (no date) 'First timers is:', *First Timers*. Available at: http://www.first-timers.org/ (Accessed: 10 April 2019).

Fitzpatrick, S. and Thompson, M. (2015) 'Making space: an exchange about women and the performance of free noise', *Women & Performance: a journal of feminist theory*, 25(2), pp. 237–248. Available at: https://doi.org/10.1080/0740770X.2015.1067070.

Flanagan, A. (2017) 'Dramatic fallout for PWR BTTM after accusations of sexual misconduct,' *NPR*. Available at: https://www.npr.org/sections/therecord/2017/05/15/528456757/dramatic-fallout-for-pwr-bttm-after-accusations-of-sexual-misconduct (Accessed: 11 May 2020).

Flanagan, M. and Carini, P. (2012) 'How games can help us access and understand archival images', *The American Archivist*, 75(2), pp. 514–537.

Flew, T. (2018) 'Social media and the cultural and creative industries', in J. Burgess, A. Marwick, and T. Poell (eds) *The SAGE handbook of social media*. London: SAGE Publications Ltd, pp. 512–525. Available at: https://doi.org/10.4135/9781473984066.

Flinn, A. (2007) 'Community histories, community archives: some opportunities and challenges', *Journal of the Society of Archivists*, 28(2), pp. 151–176. Available at: https://doi.org/10.1080/00379810701611936.

Flinn, A. (2008) 'Other ways of thinking, other ways of being. Documenting the margins and the transitory: what to preserve, how to collect', in L. Craven (ed.) *What are archives?: cultural and theoretical perspectives : a reader*. Farnham: Ashgate Publishing, pp. 109–128.

Flinn, A. (2010) 'Independent community archives and community-generated content: "Writing, saving and sharing our histories"', *Convergence*, 16(1), pp. 39–51. Available at: https://doi.org/10.1177/1354856509347707.

Flinn, A. and Alexander, B. (2015) '"Humanizing an inevitability political craft": introduction to the special issue on archiving activism and activist archiving', *Archival Science*, 15(4), pp. 329–335. Available at: https://doi.org/10.1007/s10502-015-9260-6.

Flinn, A., Stevens, M. and Shepherd, E. (2009) 'Whose memories, whose archives? Independent community archives, autonomy and the mainstream', *Archival Science*, 9(1), pp. 71–86. Available at: https://doi.org/10.1007/s10502-009-9105-2.

Flood, L.E. (2016) *Building and becoming: DIY music technology in New York and Berlin*. PhD Thesis. Columbia University. Available at: https://academiccommons.columbia.edu/doi/10.7916/D8W95918 (Accessed: 7 June 2021).

Forde, E. (2004) 'So, what would the music industry say? Presenting a case for the defence', *Popular Music*, 23(1), pp. 82–86.

Foucault, M. (1972) *The archaeology of knowledge and the discourse on language*. New York: Pantheon Books.

Foucault, M. (1991) *Discipline and punish: the birth of the prison*. London: Penguin Books.

Fraser, N. (1995) 'From redistribution to recognition? Dilemmas of justice in a "post-socialist" age', *New Left Review*, 212(1), pp. 68–93.

Freshwater, D. *et al.* (2010) 'Qualitative research as evidence: criteria for rigour and relevance', *Journal of Research in Nursing*, 15(6), pp. 497–508. Available at: https://doi.org/10.1177/1744987110385278.

Furness, Z.M. (ed.) (2012) *Punkademics: the basement show in the ivory tower.* New York: Autonomedia.

Gabai, S. (2016) 'Teaching authorship, gender and identity through grrrl zines production', *Journal of International Women's Studies*, 18(1), pp. 20–32.

Gaur, R.C. and Tripathi, M. (2012) 'Digital preservation of electronic resources', *DESIDOC Journal of Library & Information Technology*, 32(4), pp. 293–301. Available at: https://doi.org/10.14429/djlit.32.4.2522.

Ghaddar, J.J. and Caswell, M. (2019) '"To go beyond": towards a decolonial archival praxis', *Archival Science*, 19(2), pp. 71–85. Available at: https://doi.org/10.1007/s10502-019-09311-1.

Gibbons, L. (2019) 'Connecting personal and community memory-making: Facebook groups as emergent community archives', *Information Research*, 24(3). Available at: http://informationr.net/ir/24-3/rails/rails1804.html (Accessed: 28 July 2021).

Gilbert, J. (2008) *Anticapitalism and culture: radical theory and popular politics.* Oxford and New York: Berg (Culture machine series).

Gilbertson, S. (2009) *Geocities, identity and the problem with disappearing web services, Wired.* Available at: https://www.wired.com/2009/10/geocities_shutdown_highlights_the_problem_of/ (Accessed: 25 February 2020).

Gillespie, T. (2018) 'Regulation of and by platforms', in J. Burgess, A. Marwick, and T. Poell (eds) *The SAGE handbook of social media.* London: SAGE Publications Ltd, pp. 254–278. Available at: https://doi.org/10.4135/9781473984066.

Gilliland, A. (2011) 'Neutrality, social justice and the obligations of archival education and educators in the twenty-first century', *Archival Science*, 11(3), pp. 193–209. Available at: https://doi.org/10.1007/s10502-011-9147-0.

Gilliland, A. and Flinn, A. (2013) 'Community archives: what are we really talking about?', in. *CIRN Prato Community Informatics Conference.* Monash Centre, 28-30 October. Prato: Monash University.

Gilliland, A.J. (2017) 'Archival and recordkeeping traditions in the multiverse and their importance for researching situations and situating research', in A.J. Gilliland, S. McKemmish, and A.J. Lau (eds) *Research in the archival multiverse.* Clayton: Monash University Publishing, pp. 31–73.

Gilliland, A.J. and McKemmish, S. (2014) 'The role of participatory archives in furthering human rights, reconciliation and recovery', *Atlanti: Review for Modern Archival Theory and Practice*, 24, pp. 78–88.

Gómez, V.R. and Vallès, A.M. (2020) '#Cuéntalo: the path between archival activism and the social archive(s)', *Archives and Manuscripts*, 48(3), pp. 271–290. Available at: https://doi.org/10.1080/01576895.2020.1802306.

Goodley, D. and Moore, M. (2000) 'Doing disability research: activist lives and the academy', *Disability & Society*, 15(6), pp. 861–882. Available at: https://doi.org/10.1080/713662013.

Goold, L. and Graham, P. (2019) 'The uncertain future of the large-format recording studio', in J.O. Gullö (ed.) *Proceedings–Art of record production 2017*. Stockholm: Royal College of Music (KMH) & Art of Record Production, pp. 119–136. Available at: http://urn.kb.se/resolve?urn=urn:nbn:se:kmh:diva-3123 (Accessed: 9 April 2020).

Gordon, B. *et al.* (2016) 'Archives, education, and access: learning at interference archive', *Radical Teacher*, 105, pp. 54–60. Available at: https://doi.org/10.5195/rt.2016.273.

Gorski, P.C. (2019) 'Fighting racism, battling burnout: causes of activist burnout in US racial justice activists', *Ethnic and Racial Studies*, 42(5), pp. 667–687. Available at: https://doi.org/10.1080/01419870.2018.1439981.

Gosselar, A. (2018) '"We out here and we've been here": the role of university archives in student-led campus history initiatives to remember and reassert Black presence in American higher education', *Comma*, 2018(1–2), pp. 87–98. Available at: https://doi.org/10.3828/comma.2018.8.

Graham, B. (2002) 'Heritage as knowledge: capital or culture?', *Urban Studies*, 39(5–6), pp. 1003–1017. Available at: https://doi.org/10.1080/00420980220128426.

Greene, M.A. (2013) 'A critique of social justice as an archival imperative: what is it we're doing that's all that important?', *The American Archivist*, 76(2), pp. 302–334.

Greig, J. (2022)' *How the cost-of-living crisis is reshaping the music industry,*' *Dazed*. Available at: https://www.dazeddigital.com/music/article/57453/1/cost-of-living-crisis-reshaping-music-industry-dance (Accessed: 8 December 2023).

Griffin, N. (2015) *Understanding DIY punk as activism: realising DIY ethics through cultural production, community and everyday negotiations*. PhD Thesis. Northumbria University. Available at: http://nrl.northumbria.ac.uk/30251/ (Accessed: 5 November 2018).

Griffin, N.D.S. and Griffin, N.C. (2019) 'A millennial methodology? Autoethnographic research in do-it-yourself (DIY) punk and activist communities', *Forum: Qualitative Social Research*, 20(3), pp. 1–24. Available at: https://doi.org/10.17169/fqs-20.3.3206.

Griffin, P. (2018) 'Making usable pasts: collaboration, labour and activism in the archive', *Area*, 50(4), pp. 501–508. Available at: https://doi.org/10.1111/area.12384.

Guerra, P. (2020) 'Other scenes, other cities and other sounds in the Global South: DIY music scenes beyond the creative city', *Journal of Cultural Management and Cultural Policy*, 6(1), pp. 55–76. Available at: https://doi.org/10.14361/zkmm-2020-0104.

Guest, G., Bunce, A. and Johnson, L. (2006) 'How many interviews are enough?: an experiment with data saturation and variability', *Field Methods*, 18(1), pp. 59–82. Available at: https://doi.org/10.1177/1525822X05279903.

Guest, G., MacQueen, K. and Namey, E. (2012) *Applied thematic analysis*. Thousand Oaks: SAGE Publications. Available at: https://doi.org/10.4135/9781483384436.

Guthrie, N. and Carlson, S. (2018) 'Pursuing preservation in the do-it-yourself music community', in N. Guthrie and S. Carlson (eds) *Music preservation and archiving today*. London: Rowman and Littlefield, pp. 121–140.

Haenfler, R. (2006) *Straight edge: clean-living youth, hardcore punk, and social change*. Rutgers University Press.

Haimson, O.L. and Hoffmann, A.L. (2016) 'Constructing and enforcing "authentic" identity online: Facebook, real names, and non-normative identities', *First Monday*, 21(6). Available at: https://doi.org/10.5210/fm.v21i6.6791.

Halberstam, J. (2005) *In a Queer time and place: transgender bodies, subcultural lives*. New York: NYU Press.

Halberstam, J. (2008) 'The anti-social turn in Queer studies', *Graduate Journal of Social Science*, 5(2), pp. 140–156.

Hale Wood, K. (2021) 'Listening backward: sonic intimacies and cross-racial, Queer resonance', *Performance Matters*, 6(2), pp. 112–125. Available at: https://doi.org/10.7202/1075804ar.

Hall, S. (1999) 'Whose heritage? Un-settling "the heritage", Re-imagining the post-nation', *Third Text*, 13(49), pp. 3–13. Available at: https://doi.org/10.1080/09528829908576818.

Hall, S. (2001) 'Constituting an archive', *Third Text*, 15(54), pp. 89–92. Available at: https://doi.org/10.1080/09528820108576903.

Hannell, B. (2020) *Fandom and the fourth wave: youth, digital feminisms, and media fandom on Tumblr*. doctoral. University of East Anglia. Available at: https://doi.org/10/1/2020HannellBJPhD.pdf.

Hanson, K. (2017) '"Whitestraightboy" hegemony in punk rock: exploring practices within a purportedly progressive subculture', in M. Dines and L. Way (eds) *Postgraduate voices in punk studies : your wisdom, our youth*. Newcastle-upon-Tyne: Cambridge Scholars Publishing, pp. 117–132.

Harding, T. (1998) 'Viva camcordistas! Video activism and the protest', in G. Mckay (ed.) *DiY culture: party and protest In nineties' Britain*. London and New York: Verso, pp. 79–99.

Harris, V. (2002) 'The archival sliver: power, memory, and archives in South Africa', *Archival Science*, 2(1–2), pp. 63–86.

Hayler, R. (2020). Interviewed by Kirsty Fife. 9 March, Leeds.

Heathcott, J. (2007) 'Reading the accidental archive: architecture, ephemera, and landscape as evidence of an urban public culture', *Winterthur Portfolio*, 41(4), pp. 239–268. Available at: https://doi.org/10.1086/523019.

Hebdige, D. (2013) *Subculture*. London and New York: Routledge.

Hedstrom, M. (2002) 'Archives, memory, and interfaces with the past', *Archival Science*, 2(1–2), pp. 21–43. Available at: https://doi.org/10.1007/BF02435629.

Henig, D. and Knight, D.M. (2023) 'Polycrisis: prompts for an emerging worldview', *Anthropology Today*, 39(2), pp. 3–6. Available at: https://doi.org/10.1111/1467-8322.12793.

Henningham, N., Evans, J. and Morgan, H. (2017) 'The Australian women's archives project: creating and co-curating community Feminist archives in a post-custodial age', *Australian Feminist Studies*, 32(91–92), pp. 91–107. Available at: https://doi.org/10.1080/08164649.2017.1357015.

Henthorn, H. and Fife, K. (2018) 'Decentring qualification: a radical examination of archival employment possibility', in *Radical collections: re-examining the roots of collections, practices and information professions*. London: University of London Senate House Library, pp. 51–64.

Hernández, R. (2015) 'Drawn from the scraps: The finding AIDS of Mundo Meza', *Radical History Review*, 2015(122), pp. 70–88. Available at: https://doi.org/10.1215/01636545-2849540.

Hess, A. (2007) 'In digital remembrance: vernacular memory and the rhetorical construction of web memorials', *Media, Culture & Society*, 29(5), pp. 812–830. Available at: https://doi.org/10.1177/0163443707080539.

Hicks, M. (2013) 'De-brogramming the history of computing', *IEEE annals of the history of computing*, 35, pp. 85–87.

Hill, A. (2019) 'UK's renting millennials face homelessness crisis when they retire', *The Guardian*, 17 July. Available at: https://www.theguardian.com/society/2019/jul/17/renting-millennials-homelessness-crisis-retire (Accessed: 2 September 2020).

Hitchcock, T. (2013) 'Confronting the digital', *Cultural and Social History*, 10(1), pp. 9–23. Available at: https://doi.org/10.2752/147800413X13515292098070.

Holman Jones, S., Adams, T. and Ellis, C. (2013) 'Introduction', in *Handbook of autoethnography*. London and New York: Routledge Handbooks Online. Available at: https://doi.org/10.4324/9781315427812.intro.

Holman Jones, S., Adams, T.E. and Ellis, C. (eds) (2016) *Handbook of autoethnography*. London and New York: Routledge.

Holmes, K. (2015) 'What's the tea: gossip and the production of Black gay social history', *Radical History Review*, 2015(122), pp. 55–69. Available at: https://doi.org/10.1215/01636545-2849531.

Honma, T. (2016) 'From archives to action: zines, participatory culture, and community engagement in Asian America', *Radical Teacher*, 105, pp. 33–43. Available at: https://doi.org/10.5195/rt.2016.277.

hooks, bell (1989) 'Choosing the margin as a space of radical openness', *Framework: The Journal of Cinema and Media*, 36, pp. 15–23.

Hoskins, K. (2015) 'Researching female professors: the difficulties of representation, positionality and power in feminist research', *Gender and Education*, 27(4), pp. 393–411. Available at: https://doi.org/10.1080/09540253.2015.1021301.

Hoyer, J. and Almeida, N. (2021) *The Social movement archive*. Sacramento: Litwin Books.

Humphreys, L. (2018) *The qualified self: social media and the accounting of everyday life*. MIT Press.

Hunt, E. (2017) 'LGBT community anger over YouTube restrictions which make their videos invisible,' *The Guardian*. Available at: https://www.theguardian.com/technology/2017/mar/20/lgbt-community-anger-over-youtube-restrictions-which-make-their-videos-invisible (Accessed: 21 November 2019).

Iphofen, R. and Tolich, M. (2018) 'Foundational Issues in Qualitative Research Ethics', in R. Iphofen and M. Tolich (eds) *The SAGE handbook of qualitative research ethics*. London: SAGE Publications, pp. 1–18. Available at: https://doi.org/10.4135/9781526435446.

Ishmael, H.J.M. (2018) 'Reclaiming history: Arthur Schomburg', *Archives and Manuscripts*, 46(3), pp. 269–288. Available at: https://doi.org/10.1080/01576895.2018.1559741.

Ishmael, H.J.M. et al. (2020) 'Locating the Black archive', in S. Popple, A. Prescott, and D. Mutibwa (eds) *Communities, archives and new collaborative practices*. Bristol and Chicago: Policy Press (Connected Communities), pp. 207–218.

Ishmael, H.J.M. (2020) *The development of Black-led archives in London*. PhD Thesis. UCL.

Istvandity, L. (2020) 'How does music heritage get lost? Examining cultural heritage loss in community and authorised music archives', *International Journal of Heritage Studies*, 27(4), pp. 331–343. Available at: https://doi.org/10.1080/13527258.2020.1795904.

Jamal, N. (2019). Interviewed by Kirsty Fife. 3 September, London.

Janik, J. and Vella, D. (2022) 'Editorial: games in a time of crisis?', *Przegląd Kulturoznawczy*, 4(54), pp. 521–526. Available at: https://doi.org/10.4467/20843860PK.22.035.17089.

Jones, A. (1997) '"Presence" in absentia', *Art Journal*, 56(4), pp. 11–18. Available at: https://doi.org/10.1080/00043249.1997.10791844.

Jones, E. (2018) *Platform DIY: examining the impact of social media on cultural resistance in contemporary DIY music*. PhD Thesis. University of Leeds.

Jones, E. (2021) *DIY music and the politics of social media*. London: Bloomsbury.

Joseph, E. (2018) *Living the archive: race, music and place at the Africa centre (1960-2000)*. PhD Thesis. University of Sussex.

Joseph, E. and Bell, C. (2020) 'Everything is everything: embodiment, affect, and the Black Atlantic archive', *Transactions of the Institute of British Geographers*, 45(3), pp. 520–524. Available at: https://doi.org/10.1111/tran.12380.

Jules, B., Summers, E. and Mitchell, Jr., V. (2018) *Documenting the now white paper: ethical considerations for archiving social media content generated by contemporary social movements: challenges, opportunities, and recommendations. Documenting the Now.*

Karabinos, M.J. (2015) *The shadow continuum: testing the records continuum model through the Djogdja documenten and the migrated archives*. PhD Thesis. Leiden University. Available at: https://hdl.handle.net/1887/33293 (Accessed: 28 July 2021).

Keenan, E.K. and Darms, L. (2013) 'Safe space: The Riot Grrrl collection', *Archivaria*, 76, pp. 55–74.

Keidl, P.D. (2021) 'The labor of curating: fandom, museums, and the value of fan heritage', *The Journal of Popular Culture*, 54(2), pp. 407–431. Available at: https://doi.org/10.1111/jpcu.13014.

Kelleher, C. (2017) 'Archives without archives: (re)locating and (re)defining the archive through post-custodial praxis', *Journal of Critical Library and Information Studies*, 1(2). Available at: https://doi.org/10.24242/jclis.v1i2.29.

Kendall Adams, G. (2020) 'Dowden letter on contested heritage stokes fears of government interference,' *Museums Association*. Available at: https://www.museumsassociation.org/museums-journal/news/2020/10/dowden-letter-on-contested-heritage-stokes-fears-of-government-interference/ (Accessed: 28 October 2021).

Kenny, S. (2019) 'A "radical project": youth culture, leisure, and politics in 1980s Sheffield', *Twentieth Century British History*, 30(4), pp. 557–584. Available at: https://doi.org/10.1093/tcbh/hwz006.

Ketelaar, E. (2017) 'Archival turns and returns: studies of the archive', in A.J. Gilliland, S. McKemmish, and A.J. Lau (eds) *Research in the archival multiverse*. Clayton: Monash University Publishing, pp. 228–268.

Khabra, G. (2014) 'Music in the margins? Popular music heritage and British Bhangra music', *International Journal of Heritage Studies*, 20(3), pp. 343–355. Available at: https://doi.org/10.1080/13527258.2012.758652.

Khlystova, O., Kalyuzhnova, Y. and Belitski, M. (2022) 'The impact of the COVID-19 pandemic on the creative industries: A literature review and future research agenda', *Journal of Business Research*, 139, pp. 1192–1210. Available at: https://doi.org/10.1016/j.jbusres.2021.09.062.

Kinpaisby, M. (2008) 'Taking stock of participatory geographies: envisioning the communiversity', *Transactions of the Institute of British Geographers*, 33(3), pp. 292–299. Available at: https://doi.org/10.1111/j.1475-5661.2008.00313.x.

Kitch, C. (2018) '"A living archive of modern protest": Memory-making in the Women's March', *Popular Communication*, 16(2), pp. 119–127. Available at: https://doi.org/10.1080/15405702.2017.1388383.

Knifton, R. (2018) 'Local and global intersections of popular music and heritage', in S. Baker et al. (eds) *The Routledge companion to popular music history and heritage*. London and New York: Routledge, pp. 144–152.

Knobel, M. and Lankshear, C. (2010) 'DIY media: A contextual background and some contemporary themes', in M. Knobel and C. Lankshear (eds) *DIY media: creating, sharing and learning with new technologies*. New York: Peter Lang Publishing.

Kølvraa, C. and Stage, C. (2016) 'Street protests and affects on YouTube investigating DIY videos of violent street protests as an archive of affect and event desire', *Culture Unbound: Journal of Current Cultural Research*, 8(2), pp. 122–143. Available at: https://doi.org/10.3384/cu.2000.1525.1608122.

Kotrady, P.A. (2016) *Consuming authenticity: deconstructing "do-it-yourself" punk rock ethics in Philadelphia*. Masters Thesis. Dickinson College.

Kruse, H. (2010) 'Local Identity and Independent Music Scenes, Online and Off', *Popular Music and Society*, 33(5), pp. 625–639. Available at: https://doi.org/10.1080/03007760903302145.

Kuhn, A. (2002) *Family secrets: acts of memory and imagination*. Second edition. London and New York: Verso.

Kuhn, A. (2010) 'Memory texts and memory work: performances of memory in and with visual media', *Memory Studies*, 3(4), pp. 298–313. Available at: https://doi.org/10.1177/1750698010370034.

Kumbier, A. (2012) 'Inventing history: The watermelon woman and archival activism', in L. Bly and K. Wooten (eds) *Make your own history: documenting feminist and Queer activism in the 21st century*. Los Angeles: Litwin Books, pp. 90–107.

Kwame Harrison, A. (2006) '"Cheaper than a CD, plus we really mean it": Bay Area underground hip hop tapes as subcultural artefacts', *Popular Music*, 25(2), pp. 283–301.

Laberge, D. (1987) 'Information, knowledge, and rights: the preservation of archives as a political and social issue', *Archivaria*, 25, pp. 44–50.

LaDIYfest Sheffield (2014) *The deletion of the LaDIYfest Facebook account*, LaDIYfest Sheffield. Available at: https://ladiyfestsheffield.wordpress.com/2014/11/18/the-deletion-of-the-ladiyfest-facebook-account/ (Accessed: 29 October 2018).

Lashua, B. (2015) 'Mapping the politics of "race": place and memory in Liverpool's popular music heritage', in S. Cohen et al. (eds) *Sites of popular music heritage: memories, histories, places*. London and New York: Routledge (Routledge Studies in Popular Music), pp. 45–61.

Lashua, B.D. (2011) 'An atlas of musical memories: popular music, leisure and urban change in Liverpool', *Leisure*, 35(2), pp. 133–152. Available at: https://doi.org/10.1080/14927713.2011.567063.

Laurent, N. and Hart, M. (2018) 'Emotional labour and archival practice–reflection', *Journal for the Society of North Carolina Archivists*, 15, pp. 13–22.

Lee, A.Y.L. and Ting, K.W. (2017) 'Media and information praxis of young activists in the Umbrella Movement', *Chinese Journal of Communication*, 8(4), pp. 376–392. Available at: https://doi.org/10.1080/17544750.2015.1086399.

Lee, J.A. (2015) *A Queer/ed archival methodology: theorising practice through radical interrogations of the archival body*. PhD Thesis. University of Arizona.

Lee, J.A. (2017) 'Beyond pillars of evidence: exploring the shaky ground of Queer/ed archives and their methodologies', in A.J. Gilliland, S. McKemmish, and A.J. Lau (eds) *Research in the archival multiverse*. Clayton: Monash University Publishing, pp. 324–351.

Lee, J.A. (2020) *Producing the archival body*. London: Routledge. Available at: https://doi.org/10.4324/9780429060168.

Leeds DIY (no date) *Leeds DIY (@leedsdiy)*. Available at: https://www.instagram.com/leedsdiy/ (Accessed: 10 February 2020).

Leigh. (2020). Interviewed by Kirsty Fife. 4 February, Sheffield.

Leonard, M. (1997) '"Rebel girl, you are the queen of my world": feminism, "subculture" and Grrrl Power', in S. Whiteley (ed.) *Sexing the groove: popular music and gender*. London and New York: Routledge, pp. 230–255.

Leonard, M. (1998) 'Paper planes: travelling the New Grrrl geographies', in T. Skelton and G. Valentine (eds) *Cool places: geographies of youth cultures*. Florence: Routledge, pp. 102–121. Available at: https://doi.org/10.4324/9780203975596.

Leonard, M. (2010) 'Exhibiting popular music: museum audiences, inclusion and social history', *Journal of New Music Research*, 39(2), pp. 171–181. Available at: https://doi.org/10.1080/09298215.2010.494199.

Leonard, M. (2015) 'The shaping of heritage: collaborations between independent popular music heritage practitioners and the museum sector', in S. Baker (ed.) *Preserving popular music heritage: do-it-yourself, do-it-together*. New York: Routledge (Routledge Research in Music), pp. 19–30.

Levers, M.-J.D. (2013) 'Philosophical paradigms, grounded theory, and perspectives on emergence', *SAGE Open*, 3(4), p. 2158244013517243. Available at: https://doi.org/10.1177/2158244013517243.

Lewis, A. (2018) 'Omelettes in the stack: archival fragility and the aforeafter', *Archivaria*, 86, pp. 44–67.

Licona, A.C. (2005) '(B)orderlands' rhetorics and representations: the transformative potential of feminist third-space scholarship and zines', *NWSA Journal*, 17(2), pp. 104–129.

Licona, A.C. (2013) *Zines in third space: radical cooperation and borderlands rhetoric*. State University of New York Press.

Linchuan Qiu, J. (2018) 'Labor and social media: the exploitation and emancipation of (almost) everyone online', in J. Burgess, A. Marwick, and T. Poell (eds) *The SAGE handbook of social media*. London: SAGE Publications Ltd, pp. 297–313. Available at: https://doi.org/10.4135/9781473984066.

Lingel, J. *et al.* (2012) 'Practices of information and secrecy in a punk rock subculture', in *Proceedings of the ACM 2012 conference on computer supported cooperative work–CSCW '12. The ACM 2012 conference*, Seattle: ACM Press, pp. 157–166. Available at: https://doi.org/10.1145/2145204.2145230.

Lohman, K. (2020). Interviewed by Kirsty Fife. 3 April, online.

Lohman, K. (2015) *Punk lives: contesting boundaries in the Dutch punk scene*. PhD Thesis. University of Warwick (United Kingdom).

Long, P. (2015) '"Really saying something?" What do we talk about when we talk about popular music heritage, memory, archives and the digital?', in S. Baker (ed.) *Preserving popular music heritage: do-it-yourself, do-it-together*. London and New York: Routledge (Routledge Research in Music), pp. 62–76.

Long, P. *et al.* (2017) 'A labour of love: the affective archives of popular music culture', *Archives & Records*, 38(1), pp. 61–79. Available at: https://doi.org/10.1080/23257962.2017.1282347.

Long, P. *et al.* (2020) 'Popular music, community archives and public history online: cultural justice and the DIY approach to heritage', in J.A. Bastian and A. Flinn (eds) *Community archives, community spaces: heritage, memory and identity*. London: Facet Publishing, pp. 97–112.

Lothian, A. (2013) 'Archival anarchies: online fandom, subcultural conservation, and the transformative work of digital ephemera', *International Journal of Cultural Studies*, 16(6), pp. 541–556. Available at: https://doi.org/10.1177/1367877912459132.

Lott-Lavigna, R. (2019) *The great millennial housing divide: the renters vs the owners*, Vice. Available at: https://www.vice.com/en_uk/embed/article/pa7gb9/co-living-collective-canary-wharf-rent-crisis?utm_source=stylizedembed_vice.com&utm_campaign=8xw8gk&site=vice (Accessed: 22 October 2021).

Lymn, J.A. (2014) *Queering archives: the practices of zines*. PhD Thesis. University of Technology. Available at: https://opus.lib.uts.edu.au/handle/10453/29211 (Accessed: 17 December 2019).

Maalsen, S. and McLean, J. (2018) 'Record collections as musical archives: gender, record collecting, and whose music is heard', *Journal of Material Culture*, 23(1), pp. 39–57. Available at: https://doi.org/10.1177/1359183517725101.

Mann, Z. (2018) 'Wire playlist: Stephanie Phillips–The Wire', *The Wire*. Available at: https://www.thewire.co.uk/audio/tracks/wire-playlist-by-stephanie-phillips (Accessed: 15 October 2021).

Manning, J. (2017) 'In vivo coding', in J. Matthes (ed.) *The international encyclopedia of communication research methods*. New York: Wiley-Blackwell, pp. 1–2. Available at: https://doi.org/10.1002/9781118901731.iecrm0270.

Martin-Iverson, S. (2012) 'Autonomous youth? Independence and precariousness in the Indonesian underground music scene', *The Asia Pacific Journal of Anthropology*, 13(4), pp. 382–397. Available at: https://doi.org/10.1080/14442213.2011.636062.

Mbembe, A. (2002) 'The power of the archive and its limits', in C. Hamilton et al. (eds) *Refiguring the archive*. 2002 edition. Dordrecht and Boston: Springer, pp. 19–28.

McKay, G. (1998) 'DiY culture: notes towards an intro', in G. Mckay (ed.) *DiY Culture: Party And Protest In Nineties' Britain*. London and New York: Verso, pp. 1–53.

McKemmish, S. (1996) 'Evidence of me…. [personal recordkeeping.]', *Archives and Manuscripts*, 24(1), pp. 28–45.

McKemmish, S. (2005) 'Traces: document, record, archive, archives', in S. McKemmish et al. (eds) *Archives: Recordkeeping in Society*. Wagga Wagga: Centre for Information Studies, Charles Stuart University (Topics in Australasian Library and Information Studies, 24), pp. 1–21.

McKinney, C. (2015) 'Newsletter networks in the feminist history and archives movement', *Feminist Theory*, 16(3), pp. 309–328. Available at: https://doi.org/10.1177/1464700115604135.

McKinney, C. (2020) *Information activism: a Queer history of lesbian media technologies*. Durham: Duke University Press Books.

McKinney, C. and Mitchell, A. (2019) 'Lesbian rule: welcome to the Hell House', in C. McKinney and A. Mitchell (eds) *Inside Killjoy's Kastle: dykey Ghosts, feminist monsters, and other lesbian hauntings*. Vancouver: UBC Press, pp. 3–20.

McNeil, L. and McCain, G. (2016) *Please kill me: the uncensored oral history of punk*. New York: Grove Press.

Mercer, J. (2007) 'The challenges of insider research in educational institutions: wielding a double-edged sword and resolving delicate dilemmas', *Oxford Review of Education*, 33(1), pp. 1–17. Available at: https://doi.org/10.1080/03054980601094651.

Merriam, S.B. et al. (2001) 'Power and positionality: negotiating insider/outsider status within and across cultures', *International Journal of Lifelong Education*, 20(5), pp. 405–416. Available at: https://doi.org/10.1080/02601370120490.

Merrill, S., Keightley, E. and Daphi, P. (2020a) 'Introduction: the digital memory work practices of social movements', in S. Merrill, E. Keightley, and P. Daphi (eds) *Social movements, cultural memory and digital media: mobilising mediated remembrance*. London: Palgrave Macmillan (Palgrave Macmillan Memory Studies), pp. 1–30.

Merrill, S., Keightley, E. and Daphi, P. (eds) (2020b) *Social movements, cultural memory and digital media: mobilising mediated remembrance*. London: Palgrave Macmillan (Palgrave Macmillan memory studies). Available at: http://search.ebscohost.com/login.aspx?direct=true&AuthType=ip,shib&db=nlebk&AN=2380167&site=ehost-live&scope=site (Accessed: 18 August 2021).

Merton, R.K. (1972) 'Insiders and outsiders: a chapter in the sociology of knowledge', *American Journal of Sociology*, 78(1), pp. 9–47. Available at: https://doi.org/10.1086/225294.

Messick, K.J. (2021) 'The impact of a novel coronavirus on touring metal bands, promoters, and venues.', in V. Bozkurt et al. (eds) *The societal impacts of Covid-19: a transnational perspective*. Istanbul: Istanbul University Press, pp. 83–98. Available at: https://doi.org/10.26650/B/SS49.2021.006.

Milligan, I. (2019) *History in the age of abundance?: How the Web Is Transforming Historical Research*. Montreal: McGill-Queen's University Press.

Mitchell, A. and McKinney (eds) (2019) *Inside Killjoy's Kastle: dykey Ghosts, feminist monsters, and other lesbian hauntings*. Vancouver: UBC Press.

Moloney, I. (2019) *Community spirit: how DIY culture is transforming Leeds' music scene, Mixmag*. Available at: https://mixmag.net/feature/leeds-diy-wharf-chambers-chunk-scene-report (Accessed: 14 September 2020).

Montgomery, R. (1985) 'Interpreting gentrification case studies: a perspective', *Washington University Journal of Urban and Contemporary Law*, 28, pp. 241–250.

Moore, N. (2017) 'Weaving archival imaginaries: researching community archives', in N. Moore et al. (eds) *The archive project: archival research in the social sciences*. Abingdon: Routledge, pp. 129–152. Available at: https://doi.org/10.4324/9781315612577 (Accessed: 28 January 2021).

Moore, N. (2020) '"Wibbly-wobbly timey-wimey" LGBT histories: community archives as boundary objects', in S. Popple, A. Prescott, and D.H. Mutibwa (eds) *Communities, archives and new collaborative practices*. Bristol: Bristol University Press, pp. 195–206. Available at: https://doi.org/10.2307/j.ctvx1hvvd.20.

Mōri, Y. (2009) 'J-Pop: from the ideology of creativity to DiY music culture', *Inter-Asia Cultural Studies*, 10(4), pp. 474–488. Available at: https://doi.org/10.1080/14649370903166093.

Morin, E. and Kern, A.B. (1999) *Homeland earth: a manifesto for the new millennium*. New York: Hampton Press.

Morris, A. (2015) *A practical introduction to In-depth interviewing*. Thousand Oaks: SAGE Publications Ltd. Available at: https://doi.org/10.4135/9781473921344.

Muñoz, J.E. (1996) 'Ephemera as evidence: introductory notes to Queer acts', *Women & Performance*, 8(2), pp. 5–16. Available at: https://doi.org/10.1080/07407709608571228.

Mussell, J. (2012) 'The passing of print', *Media History*, 18(1), pp. 77–92. Available at: https://doi.org/10.1080/13688804.2011.637666.

Mutibwa, D.H. (2016) 'Memory, storytelling and the digital archive: revitalizing community and regional identities in the virtual age', *International Journal of Media & Cultural Politics*, 12(1), pp. 7–26. Available at: https://doi.org/10.1386/macp.12.1.7_1.

Naicker, R. (2022) 'Critically appraising for antiracism', *Education for Information*, 38(4), pp. 291–308. Available at: https://doi.org/10.3233/EFI-220052.

Nathan, L. (2012) 'Ecovillages: information tools and deeply sustainable living', in P.H. Kahn (Jr.) and P.H. Hasbach (eds) *Ecopsychology: science, totems, and the technological species.* Boston, MA: MIT Press, pp. 173–194.

Newman, J. (2012) 'Sustaining community archives', *Australasian Public Libraries and Information Services*, 25(1), pp. 37–45. Available at: https://doi.org/10.3316/ielapa.073403515991060.

Nguyen, H.-A. (2022) 'The 3%: positive action for positive change', *Education for Information*, 38(4), pp. 309–314. Available at: https://doi.org/10.3233/EFI-220053.

Nguyen, M.T. (2012a) 'Making waves: other punk feminisms', *Women & Performance*, 22(2–3), pp. 355–359. Available at: https://doi.org/10.1080/0740770X.2012.720895.

Nguyen, M.T. (2012b) 'Riot Grrrl, race, and revival', *Women & Performance*, 22(2–3), pp. 173–196. Available at: https://doi.org/10.1080/0740770X.2012.721082.

Nguyen, M.T. (2015) 'Minor threats', *Radical History Review*, 2015(122), pp. 11–24. Available at: https://doi.org/10.1215/01636545-2849495.

Noble, S.U. (2018) *Algorithms of oppression: how search engines reinforce racism.* New York: NYU Press.

Nogic, A. and Riley, A. (2007) '"So what is the normal amount of bumps allowed in a pit?": Some empirical notes on the (re)construction of a youth music subculture/scene', *Journal of Youth Studies*, 10(3), pp. 317–329. Available at: https://doi.org/10.1080/13676260701262558.

Not Right (2012) 'Intersectionality Song', 13 May. Available at: https://notright-punk.com/lyrics/intersectionality-song/ (Accessed: 14 October 2021).

Nyong'o, T. (2008) 'Do you want queer theory (or do you want the truth)? Intersections of punk and Queer in the 1970s', *Radical History Review*, (100), pp. 103–119.

O'Connor, R. (2018) 'Hookworms split as frontman denies sexual abuse allegations', *The Independent*. Available at: https://www.independent.co.uk/arts-entertainment/music/news/hookworms-split-matthew-mj-johnson-allegations-sexual-abuse-statement-latest-a8611926.html (Accessed: 11 May 2020).

O'Driscoll, G. and Bawden, D. (2022) 'Health information equity: rebalancing healthcare collections for racial diversity in UK public service contexts', *Education for Information*, 38(4), pp. 315–336. Available at: https://doi.org/10.3233/EFI-220051.

Odumosu, T. (2020) 'The crying child: on colonial archives, digitization, and ethics of care in the ultural commons', *Current Anthropology*, 61(S22), pp. S289–S302. Available at: https://doi.org/10.1086/710062.

O'Meara, E. (2013) 'Perfecting thenew wave of collecting: documenting feminist activism in the digital age', in L. Bly and K. Wooten (eds) *Make your own history: documenting feminist and Queer activism in the 21st century.* Los Angeles: Litwin Books, pp. 108–121.

O'Shea, S. (2014) *The art worlds of punk-inspired feminist networks–a social network analysis of the Ladyfest feminist music and cultural movement in the UK*. PhD Thesis. The University of Manchester (United Kingdom). Available at: https://www.proquest.com/docview/1780282051/abstract/77149C8B-818C4C33PQ/1 (Accessed: 16 August 2021).

O'Sullivan, C. (2022) 'Déan é tú féin–DIY music and music culture in Ireland: introduction', *Irish Communication Review*, 18(1), pp. 2–8.

Palmer-Mehta, V. (2018) 'The subversive power of survivor rhetoric: an innovative archive of survivor discourse in New York Magazine', *Women's Studies in Communication*, 41(2), pp. 159–182. Available at: https://doi.org/10.1080/07491409.2018.1471764.

Participant C. (2019). Interviewed in focus group by Kirsty Fife. 25 May, London.

Past Tense (2017) 'Today in London's radical History: Eileen House, Elephant & Castle, squatted as anti-gentrification centre, 2013.', *past tense*, 19 February. Available at: https://pasttenseblog.wordpress.com/2017/02/19/today-in-londons-radical-history-eileen-house-elephant-castle-squatted-as-anti-gentrification-centre-2013/ (Accessed: 9 July 2020).

Peake, B. (2015) 'WP:THREATENING2MEN: Misogynist [nfopolitics and the hegemony of the asshole consensus on English Wikipedia', *Ada New Media* [Preprint], (7). Available at: https://adanewmedia.org/2015/04/issue7-peake/ (Accessed: 10 December 2021).

Pearce, R. (2020) 'A methodology for the marginalised: surviving oppression and traumatic fieldwork in the neoliberal academy', *Sociology*, 54(4), pp. 806–824. Available at: https://doi.org/10.1177/0038038520904918.

Pearce, R. (2019). Interviewed by Kirsty Fife. 28 October, Leeds.

Pearce, R. and Lohman, K. (2019) 'De/constructing DIY identities in a trans music scene', *Sexualities*, 22(1–2), pp. 97–113. Available at: https://doi.org/10.1177/1363460717740276.

Pearson, J. (2019) '*MySpace lost 12 years of music in 'server migration'*', *Motherboard*. Available at: https://motherboard.vice.com/en_us/article/nexyn8/myspace-lost-12-years-of-music-in-server-migration (Accessed: 19 March 2019).

Pelly, L. (2018) 'The Antisocial Network', *Logic Magazine*. Available at: https://logicmag.io/06-the-antisocial-network/ (Accessed: 10 January 2019).

Perkins, B. (2019). Interviewed by Kirsty Fife. 5 July, London.

Petro, A.M. (2015) 'Beyond accountability: the Queer archive of Catholic sexual abuse', *Radical History Review*, 2015(122), pp. 160–176. Available at: https://doi.org/10.1215/01636545-2849594.

Phillips, S. (2019). Interviewed by Kirsty Fife. 12 September, online.

Phillips, S. and Mokoena, T. (2018) *All the places musicians move to when London gets too expensive*, *noisey*. Available at: https://noisey.vice.com/en_uk/article/evqzb4/london-expensive-city-musicians-arrows-love-petrol-girls (Accessed: 30 October 2018).

Pickard, A.J. (2017) *Research methods in information*. 2nd edn. London: Facet Publishing.

Pidd, H. (2017) *Digging the Reno: Moss Side's legendary club unearthed—30 years on, the Guardian*. Available at: http://www.theguardian.com/uk-news/2017/oct/27/digging-the-reno-moss-sides-legendary-club-unearthed-30-years-on (Accessed: 24 June 2021).

Piggott, M. (2012) '12–Two cheers for the records continuum', in M. Piggott (ed.) *Archives and societal provenance*. Chandos Publishing (Chandos Information Professional Series), pp. 175–195. Available at: https://doi.org/10.1016/B978-1-84334-712-5.50012-0.

Poell, T. and van Dijck, J. (2018) 'Social media and new protest movements', in J. Burgess, A. Marwick, and T. Poell (eds) *The SAGE handbook of social media*. London: SAGE Publications, pp. 546–561. Available at: https://doi.org/10.4135/9781473984066.

Popple, S., Prescott, A. and Mutibwa, D. (eds) (2020a) *Communities, archives and new collaborative practices*. Bristol, England ; Chicago, Illinois: Policy Press (Connected communities (Bristol, England)).

Popple, S., Prescott, A. and Mutibwa, D. (2020b) 'Community archives and the creation of living knowledge', in S. Popple, A. Prescott, and D. Mutibwa (eds) *Communities, archives and new collaborative practices*. Bristol and Chicago: Policy Press (Connected Communities), pp. 1–18.

Poutch, S. (2016) 'Building an archivist: exploring career paths in our profession since 2008 (an Irish perspective)', *Archives and Records*, 37(2), pp. 157–169. Available at: https://doi.org/10.1080/23257962.2016.1191453.

Pratt, L. (2018) 'The (fat) body and the archive: toward the creation of a fat community archive', *Fat Studies*, 7(2), pp. 227–239. Available at: https://doi.org/10.1080/21604851.2017.1374128.

Prescott, A. (2020) 'Community archives and the health of the internet', in S. Popple, A. Prescott, and D. Mutibuwa (eds) *Communities, archives and new collaborative practices*. Bristol: Bristol University Press (Connected Communities), pp. 251–268.

Press Association (2016) 'Punk funeral: Joe Corré Burns £5m of memorabilia on Thames', *The Guardian*. Available at: https://www.theguardian.com/music/2016/nov/26/punx-not-dead-joe-corre-burns-memorabilia-worth-5m-on-thames (Accessed: 18 December 2018).

Prey, R., Esteve Del Valle, M. and Zwerwer, L. (2022) 'Platform pop: disentangling Spotify's intermediary role in the music industry', *Information, Communication & Society*, 25(1), pp. 74–92. Available at: https://doi.org/10.1080/1369118X.2020.1761859.

Ptolomey, A.M. and Nelson, E.L. (2022) 'A creative conversation for re-imagining creative visual methods with children and young people in pandemic times and beyond', *Sociological Research Online*, 27(3), pp. 684–689. Available at: https://doi.org/10.1177/13607804221089681.

Putnam, M. and Schicker, J. (2014) 'Straight outta Marzahn: (re)constructing communicative memory in East Germany through hip hop', *Popular Music and Society*, 37(1), pp. 85–100. Available at: https://doi.org/10.1080/03007766.2012.726040.

Quinn, K. and Papacharissi, Z. (2018) 'Our networked selves: personal connection and relational maintenance in social media use', in J. Burgess, A. Marwick, and T. Poell (eds) *The SAGE Handbook of Social Media*. London: SAGE Publications, pp. 353–371. Available at: https://doi.org/10.4135/9781473984066.

Ramdarshan Bold, M. (2017) 'Why diverse zines matter: a case study of the people of color zines project', *Publishing Research Quarterly*, 33(3), pp. 215–228. Available at: https://doi.org/10.1007/s12109-017-9533-4.

Ramírez, C.D. (2019) 'Abuela, si estas aquí: writing our histories as liberatory praxis', in J. Enoch and J. Jack (eds) *Retellings: opportunities for feminist research in Rhetoric and Composition Studies*. Anderson: Parlor Press LLC.

Ramirez, H.N.R. (2005) 'A living archive of desire: Teresita La Campesina and the embodiment of Queer Latino community histories', in A.M. Burton (ed.) *Archive Stories: Facts, Fictions, and the Writing of History*. Durham: Duke University Press, pp. 111–135.

Ramirez, M.H. (2015) 'Being assumed not to be: a critique of Whiteness as an archival imperative', *The American Archivist*, 78(2), pp. 339–356. Available at: https://doi.org/10.17723/0360-9081.78.2.339.

Reading, A. (2014) 'Seeing red: a political economy of digital memory', *Media, Culture & Society*, 36(6), pp. 748–760. Available at: https://doi.org/10.1177/0163443714532980.

Reading, A. (2020) 'Afterword/afterweb: the antisocial memory assemblage', in S. Merrill, E. Keightley, and P. Daphi (eds) *Social movements, cultural memory and digital media: mobilising mediated remembrance*. London: Palgrave Macmillan (Palgrave Macmillan Memory Studies), pp. 275–288.

Reagle, J. and Rhue, L. (2011) 'Gender bias in Wikipedia and Britannica', *International Journal of Communication*, 5, pp. 1138–1158.

Reichard, D.A. (2012) 'Animating ephemera through oral history: interpreting visual traces of California gay college student organizing from the 1970s', *Oral History Review*, 39(1), pp. 37–60. Available at: https://doi.org/10.1093/ohr/ohs042.

Reitsamer, R. (2015) 'Alternative histories and counter-memories: Feminist music archives in Europe', in S. Baker (ed.) *Preserving popular music heritage: do-it-yourself, do-it-together*. London and New York: Routledge, pp. 91–103.

Reitsamer, R. (2018) 'Gendered narratives of popular music history and heritage', in S. Baker et al. (eds) *The Routledge companion to popular music history and heritage*. London and New York: Routledge, pp. 26–35.

Reitsamer, R. and Prokop, R. (2018) 'Keepin' it real in central Europe: The DIY rap music careers of male hip hop artists in Austria', *Cultural Sociology*, 12(2), pp. 193–207. Available at: https://doi.org/10.1177/1749975517694299.

Rex, B. (2020) 'Which museums to fund? Examining local government decision-making in austerity', *Local Government Studies*, 46(2), pp. 186–205. Available at: https://doi.org/10.1080/03003930.2019.1619554.

Reynolds, S. (2012) *Retromania: pop culture's addiction to its own past*. London: Faber & Faber.

Richards, J. (2016) 'Shifting gender in electronic music: DIY and maker communities', *Contemporary Music Review*, 35(1), pp. 40–52. Available at: https://doi.org/10.1080/07494467.2016.1176771.

Richardson, L. and Adams St. Pierre, E. (2018) 'Writing: a method of inquiry', in N.K. Denzin and Y.S. Lincoln (eds) *The SAGE handbook of qualitative research*. Fifth edition. Thousand Oaks, California: SAGE, pp. 1410–1444. Available at: https://app.kortext.com/borrow/253527 (Accessed: 12 February 2021).

Risam, R. (2018) *New digital worlds: postcolonial digital humanities in theory, praxis, and pedagogy*. Chicago: Northwestern University Press.

Robb, J. and Craske, O. (2006) *Punk rock: an oral history*. London: Ebury Press.

Roberts, L. (2014) 'Talkin bout my generation: popular music and the culture of heritage', *International Journal of Heritage Studies*, 20(3), pp. 262–280. Available at: https://doi.org/10.1080/13527258.2012.740497.

Roberts, L. and Cohen, S. (2014) 'Unauthorising popular music heritage: outline of a critical framework', *International Journal of Heritage Studies*, 20(3), pp. 241–261. Available at: https://doi.org/10.1080/13527258.2012.750619.

Robinson, L. (2018) 'Exhibition review punk's 40th anniversary—an itchy sort of heritage', *Twentieth Century British History*, 29(2), pp. 309–317. Available at: https://doi.org/10.1093/tcbh/hwx047.

Romano, A. (2018) *Tumblr's adult content ban hurts all of internet culture*, Vox. Available at: https://www.vox.com/2018/12/4/18124120/tumblr-porn-adult-content-ban-user-backlash (Accessed: 22 November 2019).

Rosen, S.S. (2021) 'Caring Work: reflections on care and librarianship', in *LIS Interrupted: Intersections of Mental Illness and Library Work*. Sacramento: Library Juice Press, pp. 203–217.

Ross, S.G. (2017) 'Development versus preservation interests in the making of a music city: a case study of select iconic Toronto music venues and the treatment of their intangible cultural heritage value', *International Journal of Cultural Property*, 24(1), pp. 31–56.

Roy, M. *et al.* (2022) 'CRT in praxis: library and archival collections at San Jose State University', *Education for Information*, 38(4), pp. 347–366. Available at: https://doi.org/10.3233/EFI-220054.

Ruberg, B. (2019) *Video games have always been queer*. New York: NYU Press.

Saber, D. and Long, P. (2017) '"I will not leave, my freedom is more precious than my blood". From ato precarity: crowd-sourced citizen archives as memories of the Syrian war', *Archives and Records*, 38(1), pp. 80–99. Available at: https://doi.org/10.1080/23257962.2016.1274256.

Sabiescu, A.G. (2020) 'Living archives and the social transmission of memory', *Curator: The Museum Journal*, 63(4), pp. 497–510. Available at: https://doi.org/10.1111/cura.12384.

Savage, B. (2019). Interviewed by Kirsty Fife. 19 November, London.

Savage, M. (2018) *Millennial housing crisis engulfs Britain*, The Guardian. Available at: https://www.theguardian.com/society/2018/apr/28/proportion-home-owners-halves-millennials (Accessed: 1 September 2020).

Sawicki, J. (1991) *Disciplining Foucault: feminism, power, and the body*. London and New York: Routledge (Thinking Gender).

Scattergood, K. (2020). Interviewed by Kirsty Fife. 20 January, Leeds.

Schellenberg, T.R. (1956) *Modern archives: principles and techniques*. Chicago: University of Chicago Press.

Schlesselman-Tarango, G. (2016) 'The legacy of Lady Bountiful: white women in the Library', *Library Trends*, 64(4), pp. 667–686. Available at: https://doi.org/10.1353/lib.2016.0015.

Schneider, R. (2001) 'Performance remains', *Performance Research*, 6(2), pp. 100–108. Available at: https://doi.org/10.1080/13528165.2001.10871792.

Schuchter, V. (2019) 'Toward a feminist archival ethics of accountability: researching with the Aritha van Herk Fonds', *Studies in Canadian Literature*, 44(2), pp. 332–351.

Schwartz, J.M. and Cook, T. (2002) 'Archives, records, and power: the making of modern memory', *Archival Science*, 2(1–2), pp. 1–19. Available at: https://doi.org/10.1007/BF02435628.

Sellie, A. et al. (2015) 'Interference archive: a free space for social movement culture', *Archival Science*, 15(4), pp. 453–472. Available at: https://doi.org/10.1007/s10502-015-9245-5.

Sexton, A. (2020) 'Mainstream institutional collecting of anti-institutional archives: opportunities and challenges', in S. Popple, A. Prescott, and D. Mutibuwa (eds) *Communities, archives and new collaborative practices*. Bristol: Bristol University Press (Connected Communities), pp. 167–180.

Sexton, A. and Sen, D. (2018) 'More voice, less ventriloquism– exploring the relational dynamics in a participatory archive of mental health recovery', *International Journal of Heritage Studies*, 24(8), pp. 874–888. Available at: https://doi.org/10.1080/13527258.2017.1339109.

Sexton, A.K. (2016) *Archival activism and mental health: being participatory, sharing control and building legitimacy*. PhD Thesis. UCL. Available at: http://discovery.ucl.ac.uk/1474368/ (Accessed: 1 November 2018).

Sharp, D. (2006) 'Participatory cultural production and the DIY internet: from theory to practice and back again', *Media International Australia Incorporating Culture and Policy*, 118(1), pp. 16–24. Available at: https://doi.org/10.1177/1329878X0611800104.

Sheffield, R. (2018) 'Facebook Live as a recordmaking technology', *Archivaria*, 85, pp. 96–121.

Sheffield, R.T. (2016) 'More than acid-free folders: extending the concept of preservation to include the stewardship of unexplored histories', *Library Trends*, 64(3), pp. 572–584.

Shuker, R. (2016) *Understanding Popular Music Culture*. London and New York: Routledge.

Sicca, L.M., Auriemma, M. and Napolitano, D. (2022) 'Organizing resistance: DiY as ethical and political praxis', in G. Faldetta, E. Mollona, and M.M. Pellegrini (eds) *Philosophy and business ethics: organizations, CSR and moral practice*. Cham: Springer International Publishing, pp. 455–486. Available at: https://doi.org/10.1007/978-3-030-97106-9_18.

Sinha, S. and Back, L. (2014) 'Making methods sociable: dialogue, ethics and authorship in qualitative research', *Qualitative Research*, 14(4), pp. 473–487. Available at: https://doi.org/10.1177/1468794113490717.

Sinor, J. (2003) 'Another form of crying: girl zines as life writing', *Prose Studies*, 26(1–2), pp. 240–264. Available at: https://doi.org/10.1080/0144035032000235909.

Smit, R. (2020) 'Connective memory work on justice for Mike Brown', in S. Merrill, E. Keightley, and P. Daphi (eds) *Social movements, cultural memory and digital media: mobilising mediated remembrance*. London: Palgrave Macmillan (Palgrave Macmillan Memory Studies), pp. 85–108.

Smit, R., Heinrich, A. and Broersma, M. (2018) 'Activating the past in the Ferguson protests: memory work, digital activism and the politics of platforms', *New Media and Society*, 20(9), pp. 3119–3139. Available at: https://doi.org/10.1177/1461444817741849.

Smith, K.G. (2016) 'Negotiating community literacy practice: public memory work and the Boston Marathon Bombing digital archive', *Computers and Composition*, 40, pp. 115–130. Available at: https://doi.org/10.1016/j.compcom.2016.03.003.

Smith, L. (2006) *The uses of heritage*, uses of heritage. London and New York: Routledge, pp. 15–22. Available at: https://doi.org/10.4324/9780203602263-9.

Solis, G.D. (2018) 'Documenting state violence: (symbolic) annihilation & archives of survival', *KULA: Knowledge Creation, Dissemination, and Preservation Studies*, 2(1), pp. 1–11. Available at: https://doi.org/10.5334/kula.28.

Sowards, S.K. and Renegar, V.R. (2006) 'Reconceptualizing rhetorical activism in contemporary feminist contexts', *Howard Journal of Communications*, 17(1), pp. 57–74. Available at: https://doi.org/10.1080/10646170500487996.

Spencer, A. (2008) *DIY: the rise of lo-fi culture*. London: Marion Boyars.

Spracklen, K., Henderson, S. and Procter, D. (2016) 'Imagining the scene and the memory of the F-Club: talking about lost punk and postpunk spaces in Leeds', *Punk & Post Punk*, 5(2), pp. 147–162. Available at: https://doi.org/10.1386/punk.5.2.147_1.

Stead, L. (2016) 'Letter writing, cinemagoing and archive ephemera', in C. Smith (ed.) *The boundaries of the literary archive: reclamation and representation*. London and New York: Routledge, pp. 139–157.

Stephens Griffin, N. (2014) 'Doing critical animal studies differently: reflexivity and intersectionality in practice', in N. Taylor and R. Twine (eds) *The rise of critical animal studies: from the margins to the centre*. Routledge, pp. 111–135.

Stephens-Griffin, N. (2015) *Queering veganism: a biographical, visual and autoethnographic study of animal advocacy*. PhD Thesis. University of Durham.

Stevens, M., Flinn, A. and Shepherd, E. (2010) 'New frameworks for community engagement in the archive sector: from handing over to handing on', *International Journal of Heritage Studies*, 16(1–2), pp. 59–76. Available at: https://doi.org/10.1080/13527250903441770.

Stewart, F. (2019) '"No more heroes anymore": marginalized identities in punk memorialization and curation', *Punk & Post Punk*, 8(2), pp. 209–226. Available at: https://doi.org/10.1386/punk.8.2.209_1.

Stinson, E. (2012) 'Writing zines, playing music, and being a Black punk feminist: an interview with Osa Atoe', *Women & Performance*, 22(2–3), pp. 261–274. Available at: https://doi.org/10.1080/0740770X.2012.721084.

Stoler, A.L. (2002) 'Colonial archives and the arts of governance', *Archival Science*, 2(1–2), pp. 87–109. Available at: https://doi.org/10.1007/BF02435632.

Stoler, A.L. (2010) *Along the archival grain: Epistemic anxieties and the colonial common sense*. Princeton: Princeton University Press. Available at: https://press.princeton.edu/books/paperback/9780691146362/along-the-archival-grain (Accessed: 25 August 2021).

Stosuy, B. (2017) *On taking the riskier path*, The Creative Independent. Available at: https://thecreativeindependent.com/people/hanif-abdurraqib-on-the-writer-as-archivist/ (Accessed: 11 December 2023).

Straw, W. (1997) 'Sizing up record collections: gender and connoisseurship in rock music Culture', in S. Whiteley (ed.) *Sexing the groove: popular music and gender*. London ; New York: Routledge, pp. 3–16.

Strohmayer, A. and Meissner, J. (2020) 'The partnership quilt: an interactive living archive of sex worker voices', *Curator: The Museum Journal*, 63(2), pp. 275–279. Available at: https://doi.org/10.1111/cura.12360.

Stromblad, C. and Baker, A. (2023) 'Music-making beyond the pub: the importance of community music and DIY enterprise in maintaining regional music scenes (Gippsland case study)', *Popular Music and Society*, pp. 1–23. Available at: https://doi.org/10.1080/03007766.2022.2161240.

Strong, C. (2011) 'Grunge, Riot Grrrl and the forgetting of women in popular culture', *The Journal of Popular Culture*, 44(2), pp. 398–416. Available at: https://doi.org/10.1111/j.1540-5931.2011.00839.x.

Strong, C. (2018) 'Burning punk and bulldozing clubs: the role of destruction and loss in popular music heritage', in S. Baker et al. (eds) *The Routledge Companion to Popular Music History and Heritage*. London and New York: Routledge, pp. 180–188.

Strong, C. and Rush, E. (2018) 'Musical genius and/or nasty piece of work? Dealing with violence and sexual assault in accounts of popular music's past', *Continuum: Journal of Media and Cultural Studies*, 32(5), pp. 569–580. Available at: https://doi.org/10.1080/10304312.2018.1483009.

Strong, C. and Whiting, S. (2018) '"We love the bands and we want to keep them on the walls": gig posters as heritage-as-praxis in music venues', *Continuum*, 32(2), pp. 151–161. Available at: https://doi.org/10.1080/10304312.2 017.1370538.

Sturken, M. (2008) 'Memory, consumerism and media: reflections on the emergence of the field', *Memory Studies*, 1(1), pp. 73–78. Available at: https://doi.org/10.1177/1750698007083890.

Sutherland, T. (2017) 'Archival amnesty: In search of Black American transitional and restorative justice', *Critical Archival Studies*, 1(2), pp. 1–23.

Sutherland, T. (2019) 'Reading gesture: Katherine Dunham, the Dunham Technique, and the vocabulary of dance as decolonizing archival praxis', *Archival Science*, 19(2), pp. 167–183. Available at: https://doi.org/10.1007/s10502-019-09308-w.

Swilling, M. (2013) 'Economic crisis, long waves and the sustainability transition: an African perspective', *Environmental Innovation and Societal Transitions*, 6, pp. 96–115. Available at: https://doi.org/10.1016/j.eist.2012.11.001.

Szkudlarek, T. (2017) 'Punk theory: the future of thinking in the time of no future', *Research in Education*, 97(1), pp. 49–55. Available at: https://doi.org/10.1177/0034523717714070.

Tailor, N. (2019) *Unearthing The Reno, Manchester's lost mixed-race clubbing haven, gal-dem*. Available at: https://gal-dem.com/the-reno-whitworth-gallery-manchesters-lost-mixed-race-clubbing-haven/ (Accessed: 19 February 2021).

Taves Sheffield, R. (2020) 'Archival optimism, or, how to sustain a community archives', in J.A. Bastian and A. Flinn (eds) *Community archives, community spaces: heritage, memory and Identity*. London: Facet Publishing, pp. 3–20. Available at: https://doi.org/10.29085/9781783303526 (Accessed: 10 March 2020).

Taylor, J. (2011) 'The intimate insider: negotiating the ethics of friendship when doing insider research', *Qualitative Research*, 11(1), pp. 3–22. Available at: https://doi.org/10.1177/1468794110384447.

Taylor, S. (2023) 'Methodological challenges of researching an emerging scene: experimental electronic music in contemporary Manchester', *DIY, Alternative Cultures & Society*, pp. 1–13. Available at: https://doi.org/10.1177/27538702231172365.

Taylor, T. (2021) *Rishi Sunak has announced new Beatles museum for Liverpool, Far Out*. Available at: https://faroutmagazine.co.uk/rishi-sunak-has-announced-a-new-beatles-museum-for-liverpool-in-the-uk-budget/ (Accessed: 28 October 2021).

Terras, M. (2015) 'Opening access to collections: the making and using of open digitised cultural content', *Online Information Review*, 39(5), pp. 733–752.

Thalmann, F., Wilmering, T. and Sandler, M.B. (2018) 'Cultural heritage documentation and exploration of live music events with linked data', in *Proceedings of the 1st International Workshop on Semantic Applications for Audio and Music*. Asilomar Conference Grounds, 9 October. Monterey: Association for Computing Machinery.

The Kitchen Sisters (no date) 'Archiving the underground: the hiphop archive at Harvard'. Available at: http://www.kitchensisters.org/present/archiving-the-underground-the-hiphop-archive-at-harvard/ (Accessed: 19 February 2021).

The Watermelon Woman [DVD] (1997). Directed by Cheryl Dunye. USA: First Run Features.

Thornton, S. (1995) *Club cultures: music, media and subcultural capital*. Cambridge: Polity.

Thrasher, S.W. (2018) What Tumblr's porn ban really means, *The Atlantic*. Available at: https://www.theatlantic.com/technology/archive/2018/12/tumblr-adult-content-porn/577471/ (Accessed: 22 November 2019).

Tolich, M. (2004) 'Internal confidentiality: when confidentiality assurances fail relational informants', *Qualitative Sociology*, 27(1), pp. 101–106. Available at: https://doi.org/10.1023/B:QUAS.0000015546.20441.4a.

Toy-Cronin, B. (2018) 'Ethical issues in insider-outsider research', in R. Iphofen and M. Tolich (eds) *The SAGE handbook of qualitative research ethics*. Thousand Oaks: SAGE Publications Ltd, pp. 455–468. Available at: https://doi.org/10.4135/9781526435446.

Tracy, S.J. (2013) *Qualitative research methods: collecting evidence, crafting analysis, communicating impact*. Malden: Wiley-Blackwell.

Trade Union Congress (2014) *SERTUC Supports PCS reps at the Victoria and Albert museum, TUC*. Available at: https://www.tuc.org.uk/research-analysis/reports/sertuc-supports-pcs-reps-victoria-and-albert-museum (Accessed: 4 January 2021).

Trapp, A. (2020). Interviewed by Kirsty Fife. 12 May, online.

Tsioulakis, I. (2020) *Musicians in crisis: working and playing in the Greek popular music industry*. London and New York: Routledge.

Turnbull, N. (2022) *Permacrisis: what it means and why it's word of the year for 2022, The Conversation*. Available at: http://theconversation.com/permacrisis-what-it-means-and-why-its-word-of-the-year-for-2022-194306 (Accessed: 15 May 2023).

Turrini, J.M. (2013) '"Well I don't care about history": oral history and the making of collective memory in punk rock', *Notes*, 70(1), pp. 59–77.

Twyman, M., Keegan, B.C. and Shaw, A. (2017) 'Black Lives Matter in Wikipedia: collective memory and collaboration around online social movements', in *Proceedings of the 2017 ACM conference on computer supported cooperative work and social computing*. 25 February-1 March: Association for Computing Machinery. Portland: Association for Computing Machinery.

Upward, F. (1996) 'Structuring the records continuum (series of two parts) part 1: post custodial principles and properties', *Archives and Manuscripts*, 24(2), p. 268.

Upward, F. (1997) 'Structuring the records continuum (series of two parts) part 2: structuration theory and recordkeeping', *Archives and Manuscripts*, 25(1), p. 10.

Valeonti, F., Terras, M. and Hudson-Smith, A. (2020) 'How open is OpenGLAM? Identifying barriers to commercial and non-commercial reuse of digitised art images', *Journal of Documentation*, 76(1), pp. 1–26.

Vanhercke, B., Sabato, S. and Spasova, S. (2023) *Social policy in the European Union: state of play 2022. Policymaking in a permacrisis*. Brussels: ETUI and OSE. Available at: https://www.etui.org/sites/default/files/2023-01/Social%20policy%20in%20the%20European%20Union-state%20of%20play%202022-Policy%20making%20in%20a%20permacrisis-2023.pdf (Accessed: 15 May 2023).

Vaughan, L. (2015) 'Performance, practice and presence: design parameters for the living archive', in *Performing Digital*. Routledge, London and New York.

Verbuč, D. (2023) '"A whole society, with its own economic system": the reciprocal and capitalist configurations of American DIY music scenes', in *Ethnomusicology Forum*. Taylor & Francis, pp. 1–23.

Vogel, S. (2006) 'Closing time: Langston Hughes and the Queer poetics of Harlem nightlife', *Criticism*, 48(3), pp. 397–425.

Waite, S. (2015) 'Cultivating the scavenger: A Queerer feminist future for composition and rhetoric', *Peitho Journal*, 18(1), pp. 51–71.

Warfield, L., Crasshole, W. and Leyser, Y. (2021) *Queercore: how to punk a revolution: an oral history*. Oakland: PM Press.

Waterson, J. (2018) *Tumblr to ban all adult content, Guardian*. Available at: https://www.theguardian.com/technology/2018/dec/03/tumblr-to-ban-all-adult-content (Accessed: 12 March 2019).

Waterton, E. and Smith, L. (2010) 'The recognition and misrecognition of community heritage', *International Journal of Heritage Studies*, 16(1–2), pp. 4–15. Available at: https://doi.org/10.1080/13527250903441671.

Watson, J.B. (2020) *The persistence of punk rock: a statistical network analysis of underground punk worlds in Manchester and Liverpool 2013-2015*. PhD Thesis. The University of Manchester. Available at: https://www.proquest.com/docview/2429556227/abstract/C3DACF7F52C143ADPQ/1 (Accessed: 16 August 2021).

Watson, M. and Shove, E. (2008) 'Product, competence, project and practice: DIY and the dynamics of craft consumption', *Journal of Consumer Culture*, 8(1), pp. 69–89. Available at: https://doi.org/10.1177/1469540507085726.

Wehr, K. (2012) *DIY: the search for control and self-reliance in the 21st Century*. London and New York: Routledge (Framing 21st Century Social Issues).

Welsh, A.C. (2015) *How DIY culture Is thriving in the U.K.*, *The Fader*. Available at: https://www.thefader.com/2015/12/23/how-diy-culture-is-thriving-in-the-uk (Accessed: 30 October 2018).

Wharf Chambers Coop and Club Collective (2018) *Accountability & abuse—Wharf Chambers*, *Wharf Chambers*. Available at: https://www.wharfchambers.org/accountability/ (Accessed: 26 February 2019).

Williams, C. (2013) 'Records and archives: concepts, roles and definitions', in C. Brown (ed.) *Archives and Recordkeeping: theory into practice*. London: Facet Publishing, pp. 1–30.

Williams, J.P. and Jauhari bin Zaini, M.K. (2016) 'Rude boy subculture, critical pedagogy, and the collaborative construction of an analytic and evocative autoethnography', *Journal of Contemporary Ethnography*, 45(1), pp. 34–59. Available at: https://doi.org/10.1177/0891241614549835.

Williams, R. (2006) 'The analysis of culture', in J. Storey (ed.) *Cultural theory and popular culture: a reader*. London: Pearson Education, pp. 32–41.

WIlliams, S.M. and Drake, J. (2017) 'Power to the people: documenting police violence in Cleveland', *Journal of Critical Library and Information Studies*, 1(2), pp. 1–27.

Withers, D. (2017) 'Ephemeral feminist histories and the politics of transmission within digital culture', *Women's History Review*, 26(5), pp. 678–691. Available at: https://doi.org/10.1080/09612025.2016.1166887.

Withers, D.M. (2014) 'Re-enacting process: temporality, historicity and the Women's liberation music Archive', *International Journal of Heritage Studies*, 20(7–8), pp. 688–701. Available at: https://doi.org/10.1080/13527258.2013.794745.

Withers, D.M. (2015) 'Intangible cultural heritage and the Women's liberation music archive', in L. Roberts et al. (eds) *Sites of Popular Music Heritage: Memories, Histories, Places*. London and New York: Routledge (Routledge Studies in Popular Music), pp. 125–142.

Woods, P.J. (2020) 'The aesthetic pedagogies of DIY music', *Review of Education, Pedagogy, and Cultural Studies*, pp. 1–20. Available at: https://doi.org/10.1080/10714413.2020.1830663.

Wright Edelman, M. (2015) 'It's hard to be what you can't see', *Children's Defense Fund*. Available at: https://www.childrensdefense.org/child-watch-columns/health/2015/its-hard-to-be-what-you-cant-see/ (Accessed: 1 June 2020).

Wright, K. (2019) 'Archival interventions and the language we use', *Archival Science*, 19(4), pp. 331–348. Available at: https://doi.org/10.1007/s10502-019-09306-y.

X, A., Campbell, T. and Stevens, M. (2009) 'Love and lubrication in the archives, or rukus!: A Black Queer archive for the United Kingdom', *Archivaria*, 68, pp. 271–294.

Yaqub, N. (2016) 'Working with grassroots digital humanities projects: the case of the Tall al-Za-'tar Facebook groups', in E. Muhanna (ed.) *The digital humanities and Islamic & Middle East Studies*. Berlin: Walter de Gruyter GmbH & Co KG, pp. 103–116.

Yeo, G. (2018) *Records, information and data: exploring the role of record keeping in an information culture*. London: Facet Publishing (Principles and Practice in Records Management and Archives).

Zavala, J. *et al.* (2017) '"A process where we're all at the table": Community archives challenging dominant modes of Archival Practice', *Archives and Manuscripts*, 45(3), pp. 202–215. Available at: https://doi.org/10.1080/01576895.2017.1377088.

Zinn, H. (1977) 'Secrecy, archives and the public interest', *The Midwestern Archivist*, 2(2), pp. 14–26.

Ziyad, H. (2017) *Saying "representation matters" is not enough. All representation is not created equally*, *Afropunk*. Available at: https://afropunk.com/2017/08/saying-representation-matters-not-enough-representation-not-created-equally/ (Accessed: 3 June 2020).

Zuberi, N. (2018) 'Racialising music's past and the media archive', in S. Baker et al. (eds) *The Routledge companion to popular music history and heritage*. London and New York: Routledge, pp. 36–45.

Zuboff, S. (2019) *The age of surveillance capitalism: the fight for a human future at the new frontier of power*. Main edition. London: Profile Books.

Zuleeg, F., Emmanouilidis, J.A. and Borges de Castro, R. (2021) *Europe in the age of permacrisis*, *European Policy Centre*. Available at: https://epc.eu/en/Publications/Europe-in-the-age-of-permacrisis~3c8a0c (Accessed: 15 May 2023).

Index

activist archivist research. *See* research, activist archivist
activist research. *See* research, activist
archival accountability, 66, 93-99
archival formation, 130-134
archival multiplicity, 93-99
archival praxis. *See* praxis, archival
archival studies, 17, 55
archival theory, critical, 15-17
archival traces, 139-144
archival turns, 214, 224-229
archives, 6, 16, 17, 21, 27-28, 68, 123-129, 249
archives, living, 18-20, 68
archiving, 6, 16, 17, 21, 66, 68-73, 99-100, 239-243
archivist research. *See* research, archivist
autoethnography, 32, 33-35
autonomous music spaces, 2, 3, 177-181, 186-192, 207-208
authorised music heritage. *See* music heritage, authorised

blogging platforms, 167

canonisation, 21, 66, 68-82
canons, 21, 66, 68-73
CHUNK, 2
citational practices, 79-80, 139-140
citational praxis. *See* praxis, citational
communicative memory, 158-159
community-led music heritage projects. *See* music heritage projects, community-led
creative practice, 205-206
critical archival theory. *See* archival theory, critical
cultural activism, 151-155
cultural injustice, 84-85
cultural legacy, 139-144
cultural memory, 68
cultural networks. *See* networks, cultural
cultural production, 56, 74-75, 139-140
cultural tourism, 8-9

data analysis, inductive, 39-41
digital information, 52, 149, 164, 167

digital marketing, 195
digital memory, 151-155
digital preservation, 123-129, 148-149
digital recovery project, 162-164
DIY. *See* do it yourself
DIY cultural ideals. *See* do it yourself cultural ideals
DIY cultural research. *See* do it yourself cultural research
DIY historical narratives. *See* do it yourself historical narratives
DIY music. *See* music, do it yourself
DIY music communities. *See* do it yourself music communities
DIY music heritage. *See* music heritage, do it yourself
DIY Space for London, 2, 180-181, 203-204
do it yourself, 2, 23
do it yourself cultural ideals, 2-3, 23-26
do it yourself cultural research
  distance within, 49-52
  position and power within, 41-48
  voice within, 54-60
  wellbeing in relation to, 60-63
do it yourself historical narratives, 82-87
do it yourself music communities
  complexity of historicizing and archiving, 5, 14, 21, 65-68, 90-92, 249, 251-252
  examples of collaborations with archival organizations, 214-215, 235-246
  history of, 2
  importance of networks in, 185-186
  in the United Kingdom, 5-6
  issues of precarity in relation to, 3-4, 12, 21-22, 177-181, 186-192, 199-202, 207-208, 253-255
  politics of, 6
  production of cultural heritage about, 17, 193-199, 214-224, 249, 251-255
  relationship with digital platforms, 21, 66, 147-149, 155-162, 175-176
  relationship with heritage organizations, 22, 65-66
  relationship with social media platforms, 3-4, 21, 147-149, 155-162, 175-176

representation in archival collections, 4, 5, 65-66, 193-199
representations in museum collections, 4, 5, 65-66, 193-199

ephemera, 3, 10, 116, 194-199

Facebook, 3-4, 127, 131-132, 144, 155-158, 165-167
feminism, 80, 85, 162, 224-225, 238
feminist networks. See networks, feminist
for(a)ging, 21, 101-102
foraging, 21, 101-102, 112-115
forging, 21, 101-102, 116-122
frozen memory, 80

GeoCities, 174
Glasgow Autonomous Space, 2

heritage, 68-73
heritage praxis. See praxis, heritage
historical networks. See networks, historical
historicisation, 6, 21, 66, 99

inductive data analysis. See data analysis, inductive
information activism, 17
information lives, 17-20
information praxis. See praxis, information
information sharing, 135-139
information use, 139-144
Instagram, 127, 155-158, 165-167
institutional music heritage projects. See music heritage projects, institutional
international networks. See networks, international
interviewing, 32, 35-38

knowledge production, 56
knowledge sharing, 243-246

LaDIYfest Sheffield, 3-4, 173
living archives. See archives, living
local networks. See networks, local
London and Glasgow Women's Library, 227-228

memory sharing, 135-139
memory traces, 10
memory work, 51, 139-144, 155-162
Move Under Yr Own Power, 1, 4
music, do it yourself, 215-224

music heritage, authorised, 85, 103-111, 256-257
music heritage, do it yourself, 10-11, 73-82
music heritage, popular, 6-11, 14, 51, 256-257
music heritage, self-authorised, 9, 103-111
music heritage, unauthorised, 9, 102-111, 256-257
music heritage projects, community-led, 9-10, 85-87
music heritage projects, institutional, 9-10
MySpace, 124, 127, 168
MySpace Music, 4, 147, 175-176, 198

national networks. See networks, national
networks, 181
networks, cultural, 181-186
networks, feminist, 182-183
networks, historical, 184-185
networks, international, 182, 183
networks, local, 182
networks, national182, 183
networks, social, 2, 183
networks, translocal, 182

Partisan, 2
permacrisis, 6-7, 11-14
polycrisis, 11-14
popular music heritage. See music heritage, popular
positionality, 20-21, 44, 50, 257
praxis, 107-109
praxis, archival, 21, 106-107
praxis, citational, 141-144
praxis, heritage, 105
praxis, information, 102-111

records, 16, 17, 27-28, 123-129
recordkeeping, 16, 17, 27-28
recordkeeping theory, 108
relationality, 50
representational belonging, 66, 87-92
research, activist, 20-21
research, activist archivist, 20-21, 59
research, archivist, 20-21
role conflict, 54

self-authorised music heritage. See music heritage, self-authorised
skill sharing, 243-246
social movements, 86
social networks. See networks, social
subcultural capital, 26

subcultures, 5, 12, 24

third space, 22, 55, 214, 229-235
translocal networks. *See* networks, translocal
translocality, 5
Twitter, 131, 151, 170, 172

unauthorised music heritage. *See* music heritage, unauthorised

YouTube, 151, 197-198

websites, 81, 121-122
Wikipedia, 159-160

Women's Library in London, 226-227
Wordpress, 167
workshops, 32, 38-39

zines
  archiving of, 10
  creation of, 4-5, 56-57, 78-80, 104-105, 140, 142-144
  definition of, 1, 23
  ephemeral nature of, 169-175
  examples of, 1, 4, 104-105, 140, 142-144
  relationship to do it yourself music communities, 2, 4-5, 78-80, 118-121, 142-144

www.ingramcontent.com/pod-product-compliance
Lightning Source LLC
Chambersburg PA
CBHW070810300426
44111CB00014B/2464